WORD BY WORD

Second Edition

ENGLISH/ BRAZILIAN PORTUGUESE

DICIONÁRIO ILUSTRADO DE INGLÊS

Steven J. Molinsky • Bill Bliss

Isabella Laterman, Translator

Illustrated by
Richard E. Hill

PEARSON
Longman

Word by Word Picture Dictionary,
English/Brazilian Portuguese second edition

Pearson Education, 10 Bank Street, White Plains, NY 10606

Editorial director: Pam Fishman
Vice president, director of design and
production: Rhea Banker
Director of electronic production: Aliza Greenblatt
Director of manufacturing: Patrice Fraccio
Senior manufacturing manager: Edith Pullman
Marketing manager: Oliva Fernandez
Associate development editor: Mary Perrotta Rich
Assistant editor: Katherine Keyes

Senior digital layout specialist: Wendy Wolf
Text design: Wendy Wolf
Cover design: Tracey Munz Cataldo
Realia creation: Warren Fischbach, Paula Williams
Illustrations: Richard E. Hill
Contributing artists: Steven Young, Charles Cawley,
Willard Gage, Marlon Violette
Reviewer: Patricia Sobral, Ph.D., Brown University
Project management by TransPac Education Services,
Victoria, BC, Canada with assistance from Robert Zacharias

ISBN-10 0-13-191633-5   ISBN-13 9780131916333
Longman on the Web
Longman.com offers online resources for teachers and
students. Access our Companion Websites, our online
catalog, and our local offices around the world.

Visit us at www.pearsonlongman.com.

Printed in the United States of America
8 9 10 11 12 V0YM 16 15 14 13 12

CONTENTS
CONTEÚDO

Unit / Theme	Communication Skills	Writing & Discussion
1 **Personal Information and Family**	• Asking for & giving personal information • Identifying information on a form • Spelling name aloud • Identifying family members • Introducing others	• Telling about yourself • Telling about family members • Drawing a family tree
2 **Common Everyday Activities and Language**	• Identifying classroom objects & locations • Identifying classroom actions • Giving & following simple classroom commands • Identifying everyday & leisure activities • Inquiring by phone about a person's activities • Asking about a person's plan for future activities • Social communication: Greeting people, Leave taking, Introducing yourself & others, Getting someone's attention, Expressing gratitude, Saying you don't understand, Calling someone on the telephone • Describing the weather • Interpreting temperatures on a thermometer (Fahrenheit & Centigrade) • Describing the weather forecast for tomorrow	• Describing a classroom • Making a list of daily activities • Describing daily routine • Making a list of planned activities • Describing favorite leisure activities • Describing the weather
3 **Numbers/ Time/ Money/ Calendar**	• Using cardinal & ordinal numbers • Giving information about age, number of family members, residence • Telling time • Indicating time of events • Asking for information about arrival & departure times • Identifying coins & currency – names & values • Making & asking for change • Identifying days of the week • Identifying months of the year • Asking about the year, month, day, date • Asking about the date of a birthday, anniversary, appointment • Giving date of birth	• Describing numbers of students in a class • Identifying a country's population • Describing daily schedule with times • Telling about time management • Telling about the use of time in different cultures or countries • Describing the cost of purchases • Describing coins & currency of other countries • Describing weekday & weekend activities • Telling about favorite day of the week & month of the year
4 **Home**	• Identifying types of housing & communities • Requesting a taxi • Calling 911 for an ambulance • Identifying rooms of a home • Identifying furniture • Complimenting • Asking for information in a store • Locating items in a store • Asking about items on sale • Asking the location of items at home • Telling about past weekend activities • Identifying locations in an apartment building • Identifying ways to look for housing: classified ads, listings, vacancy signs • Renting an apartment • Describing household problems • Securing home repair services • Making a suggestion • Identifying household cleaning items, home supplies, & tools • Asking to borrow an item • Describing current home activities & plans for future activities	• Describing types of housing where people live • Describing rooms & furniture in a residence • Telling about baby products & early child-rearing practices in different countries • Telling about personal experiences with repairing things • Describing an apartment building • Describing household cleaning chores
5 **Community**	• Identifying places in the community • Exchanging greetings • Asking & giving the location of places in the community • Identifying government buildings, services, & other places in a city/town center • Identifying modes of transportation in a city/town center	• Describing places in a neighborhood • Making a list of places, people, & actions observed at an intersection

Unit / Theme	Communication Skills	Writing & Discussion
6 **Describing**	• Describing people by age • Describing people by physical characteristics • Describing a suspect or missing person to a police officer • Describing people & things using adjectives • Describing physical states & emotions • Expressing concern about another person's physical state or emotion	• Describing physical characteristics of yourself & family members • Describing physical characteristics of a favorite actor or actress or other famous person • Describing things at home & in the community • Telling about personal experiences with different emotions
7 **Food**	• Identifying food items (fruits, vegetables, meat, poultry, seafood, dairy products, juices, beverages, deli, frozen foods, snack foods, groceries) • Identifying non-food items purchased in a supermarket (e.g., household supplies, baby products, pet food) • Determining food needs to make a shopping list • Asking the location of items in a supermarket • Identifying supermarket sections • Requesting items at a service counter in a supermarket • Identifying supermarket checkout area personnel & items • Identifying food containers & quantities • Identifying units of measure • Asking for & giving recipe instructions • Complimenting someone on a recipe • Offering to help with food preparation • Identifying food preparation actions • Identifying kitchen utensils & cookware • Asking to borrow an item • Comprehending product advertising • Ordering fast food items, coffee shop items, & sandwiches • Indicating a shortage of supplies to a co-worker or supervisor • Taking customers' orders at a food service counter • Identifying restaurant objects, personnel, & actions • Making & following requests at work • Identifying & correctly positioning silverware & plates in a table setting • Inquiring in person about restaurant job openings • Ordering from a restaurant menu • Taking customers' orders as a waiter or waitress in a restaurant	• Describing favorite & least favorite foods • Describing foods in different countries • Making a shopping list • Describing places to shop for food • Telling about differences between supermarkets & food stores in different countries • Making a list of items in kitchen cabinets & the refrigerator • Describing recycling practices • Describing a favorite recipe using units of measure • Telling about use of kitchen utensils & cookware • Telling about experience with different types of restaurants • Describing restaurants and menus in different countries • Describing favorite foods ordered in restaurants
8 **Colors and Clothing**	• Identifying colors • Complimenting someone on clothing • Identifying clothing items, including outerwear, sleepwear, underwear, exercise clothing, footwear, jewelry, & accessories • Talking about appropriate clothing for different weather conditions • Expressing clothing needs to a store salesperson • Locating clothing items • Inquiring about ownership of found clothing items • Indicating loss of a clothing item • Asking about sale prices in a clothing store • Reporting theft of a clothing item to the police • Stating preferences during clothing shopping • Expressing problems with clothing & the need for alterations • Identifying laundry objects & activities • Locating laundry products in a store	• Describing the flags of different countries • Telling about emotions associated with different colors • Telling about clothing & colors you like to wear • Describing clothing worn at different occasions (e.g., going to schools, parties, weddings) • Telling about clothing worn in different weather conditions • Telling about clothing worn during exercise activities • Telling about footwear worn during different activities • Describing the color, material, size, & pattern of favorite clothing items • Comparing clothing fashions now & a long time ago • Telling about who does laundry at home

Unit / Theme	Communication Skills	Writing & Discussion
9 **Shopping**	• Identifying departments & services in a department store • Asking the location of items in a department store • Asking to buy, return, exchange, try on, & pay for department store items • Asking about regular & sales prices, discounts, & sales tax • Interpreting a sales receipt • Offering assistance to customers as a salesperson • Expressing needs to a salesperson in a store • Identifying electronics products, including video & audio equipment, telephones, cameras, & computers • Identifying components of a computer & common computer software • Complimenting someone about an item & inquiring where it was purchased • Asking a salesperson for advice about different brands of a product • Identifying common toys & other items in a toy store • Asking for advice about an appropriate gift for a child	• Describing a department store • Telling about stores that have sales • Telling about an item purchased on sale • Comparing different types & brands of video & audio equipment • Describing telephones & cameras • Describing personal use of a computer • Sharing opinions about how computers have changed the world • Telling about popular toys in different countries • Telling about favorite childhood toys
10 **Community Services**	• Requesting bank services & transactions (e.g., deposit, withdrawal, cashing a check, obtaining traveler's checks, opening an account, applying for a loan, exchanging currency) • Identifying bank personnel • Identifying bank forms • Asking about acceptable forms of payment (cash, check, credit card, money order, traveler's check) • Identifying household bills (rent, utilities, etc.) • Identifying family finance documents & actions • Following instructions to use an ATM machine • Requesting post office services & transactions • Identifying types of mail & mail services • Identifying different ways to buy stamps • Requesting non-mail services available at the post office (money order, selective service registration, passport application) • Identifying & locating library sections, services, & personnel • Asking how to find a book in the library • Identifying community institutions, services, and personnel (police, fire, city government, public works, recreation, sanitation, religious institutions) • Identifying types of emergency vehicles • Reporting a crime • Identifying community mishaps (gas leak, water main break, etc.) • Expressing concern about community problems	• Describing use of bank services • Telling about household bills & amounts paid • Telling about the person responsible for household finances • Describing use of ATM machines • Describing use of postal services • Comparing postal systems in different countries • Telling about experience using a library • Telling about the location of community institutions • Describing experiences using community institutions • Telling about crime in the community • Describing experience with a crime or emergency
11 **Health**	• Identifying parts of the body & key internal organs • Describing ailments, symptoms, & injuries • Asking about the health of another person • Identifying items in a first-aid kit • Describing medical emergencies • Identifying emergency medical procedures (CPR, rescue breathing, Heimlich maneuver) • Calling 911 to report a medical emergency • Identifying major illnesses • Talking with a friend or co-worker about illness in one's family • Following instructions during a medical examination • Identifying medical personnel, equipment, & supplies in medical & dental offices • Understanding medical & dental personnel's description of procedures during treatment • Understanding a doctor's medical advice and instructions • Identifying over-the-counter medications • Understanding dosage instructions on medicine labels • Identifying medical specialists • Indicating the date & time of a medical appointment • Identifying hospital departments & personnel • Identifying equipment in a hospital room • Identifying actions & items related to personal hygiene • Locating personal care products in a store • Identifying actions & items related to baby care	• Describing self • Telling about a personal experience with an illness or injury • Describing remedies or treatments for common problems (cold, stomachache, insect bite, hiccups) • Describing experience with a medical emergency • Describing a medical examination • Describing experience with a medical or dental procedure • Telling about medical advice received • Telling about over-the-counter medications used • Comparing use of medications in different countries • Describing experience with a medical specialist • Describing a hospital stay • Making a list of personal care items needed for a trip • Comparing baby products in different countries

Unit / Theme	Communication Skills	Writing & Discussion

12 School, Subjects, and Activities	• Identifying types of educational institutions
	• Giving information about previous education during a job interview
	• Identifying school locations & personnel
	• Identifying school subjects
	• Identifying extracurricular activities
	• Sharing after-school plans
	• MATH:
	  • Asking & answering basic questions during a math class
	  • Using fractions to indicate sale prices
	  • Using percents to indicate test scores & probability in weather forecasts
	  • Identifying high school math subjects
	  • Using measurement terms to indicate height, width, depth, length, distance
	  • Interpreting metric measurements
	  • Identifying types of lines, geometric shapes, & solid figures
	• ENGLISH LANGUAGE ARTS:
	  • Identifying types of sentences
	  • Identifying parts of speech
	  • Identifying punctuation marks
	  • Providing feedback during peer-editing
	  • Identifying steps of the writing process
	  • Identifying types of literature
	  • Identifying forms of writing
	• GEOGRAPHY:
	  • Identifying geographical features & bodies of water
	  • Identifying natural environments (desert, jungle, rainforest, etc.)
	• SCIENCE:
	  • Identifying science classroom/laboratory equipment
	  • Asking about equipment needed to do a science procedure
	  • Identifying steps of the scientific method
	  • Identifying key terms to describe the universe, solar system, & space exploration
		• Telling about different types of schools in the community
		• Telling about schools attended, where, when, & subjects studied
		• Describing a school
		• Comparing schools in different countries
		• Telling about favorite school subject
		• Telling about extracurricular activities
		• Comparing extracurricular activities in different countries
		• Describing math education
		• Telling about something bought on sale
		• Researching & sharing information about population statistics using percents
		• Describing favorite books & authors
		• Describing newspapers & magazines read
		• Telling about use of different types of written communication
		• Describing the geography of your country
		• Describing geographical features experienced
		• Describing experience with scientific equipment
		• Describing science education
		• Brainstorming a science experiment & describing each step of the scientific method
		• Drawing & naming a constellation
		• Expressing an opinion about the importance of space exploration

13 Work	• Identifying occupations • Stating work experience (including length of time in an occupation) during a job interview • Talking about occupation during social conversation • Expressing job aspirations • Identifying job skills & work activities • Indicating job skills during an interview (including length of time) • Identifying types of job advertisements (help wanted signs, job notices, classified ads) • Interpreting abbreviations in job advertisements • Identifying each step in a job-search process • Identifying workplace locations, furniture, equipment, & personnel • Identifying common office tasks • Asking the location of a co-worker • Engaging in small-talk with co-workers • Identifying common office supplies • Making requests at work • Repeating to confirm understanding of a request or instruction • Identifying factory locations, equipment, & personnel • Asking the location of workplace departments & personnel to orient oneself as a new employee • Asking about the location & activities of a co-worker • Identifying construction site machinery, equipment, and building materials • Asking a co-worker for a workplace item • Warning a co-worker of a safety hazard • Asking whether there is a sufficient supply of workplace materials • Identifying job safety equipment • Interpreting warning signs at work • Reminding someone to use safety equipment • Asking the location of emergency equipment at work	• Career exploration: sharing ideas about occupations that are interesting, difficult • Describing occupation & occupations of family members • Describing job skills • Describing a familiar job (skill requirements, qualifications, hours, salary) • Telling about how people found their jobs • Telling about experience with a job search or job interview • Describing a familiar workplace • Telling about office & school supplies used • Describing a nearby factory & working conditions there • Comparing products produced by factories in different countries • Describing building materials used in ones dwelling • Describing a nearby construction site • Telling about experience with safety equipment • Describing the use of safety equipment in the community

Unit / Theme	Communication Skills	Writing & Discussion
14 **Transportation and Travel**	• Identifying modes of local & inter-city public transportation • Expressing intended mode of travel • Asking about a location to obtain transportation (bus stop, bus station, train station, subway station) • Locating ticket counters, information booths, fare card machines, & information signage in transportation stations • Identifying types of vehicles • Indicating to a car salesperson need for a type of vehicle • Describing a car accident • Identifying parts of a car & maintenance items • Indicating a problem with a car • Requesting service or assistance at a service station • Identifying types of highway lanes & markings, road structures (tunnels, bridges, etc.), traffic signage, & local intersection road markings • Reporting the location of an accident • Giving & following driving directions (using prepositions of motion) • Interpreting traffic signs • Warning a driver about an upcoming sign • Interpreting compass directions • Asking for driving directions • Following instructions during a driver's test • Repeating to confirm instructions • Identifying airport locations & personnel (check-in, security, gate, baggage claim, Customs & Immigration) • Asking for location of places & personnel at an airport • Indicating loss of travel documents or other items • Identifying airplane sections, seating areas, emergency equipment, & flight personnel • Identifying steps in the process of airplane travel (actions in the security area, at the gate, boarding, & being seated) • Following instructions of airport security personnel, gate attendants, & flight crew • Identifying sections of a hotel & personnel • Asking for location of places & personnel in a hotel	• Describing mode of travel to different places in the community • Describing local public transportation • Comparing transportation in different countries • Telling about common types of vehicles in different countries • Expressing opinion about favorite type of vehicle & manufacturer • Expressing opinion about most important features to look for when making a car purchase • Describing experience with car repairs • Describing a local highway • Describing a local intersection • Telling about dangerous traffic areas where many accidents occur • Describing your route from home to school • Describing how to get to different places from home and school • Describing local traffic signs • Comparing traffic signs in different countries • Describing a familiar airport • Telling about an experience with Customs & Immigration • Describing an air travel experience • Using imagination: being an airport security officer giving passengers instructions; being a flight attendant giving passengers instructions before take-off • Describing a familiar hotel • Expressing opinion about hotel jobs that are most interesting, most difficult
15 **Recreation and Entertainment**	• Identifying common hobbies, crafts, & games & related materials/equipment • Describing favorite leisure activities • Purchasing craft supplies, equipment, & other products in a store • Asking for & offering a suggestion for a leisure activity • Identifying places to go for outdoor recreation, entertainment, culture, etc. • Describing past weekend activities • Describing activities planned for a future day off or weekend • Identifying features & equipment in a park & playground • Asking the location of a park feature or equipment • Warning a child to be careful on playground equipment • Identifying features of a beach, common beach items, & personnel • Identifying indoor & outdoor recreation activities & sports, & related equipment & supplies • Asking if someone remembered an item when preparing for an activity • Identifying team sports & terms for players, playing fields, & equipment • Commenting on a player's performance during a game • Indicating that you can't find an item • Asking the location of sports equipment in a store • Reminding someone of items needed for a sports activity • Identifying types of winter/water sports, recreation, & equipment • Engaging in small talk about favorite sports & recreation activities • Using the telephone to inquire whether a store sells a product • Making & responding to an invitation • Following a teacher or coach's instructions during sports practice, P.E. class, & an exercise class • Identifying types of entertainment & cultural events, & the performers • Commenting on a performance • Identifying genres of music, plays, movies, & TV programs • Expressing likes about types of entertainment • Identifying musical instruments • Complimenting someone on musical ability	• Describing a favorite hobby, craft, or game • Comparing popular games in different countries, and how to play them • Describing favorite places to go & activities there • Describing a local park & playground • Describing a favorite beach & items used there • Describing an outdoor recreation experience • Describing favorite individual sports & recreation activities • Describing favorite team sports & famous players • Comparing popular sports in different countries • Describing experience with winter or water sports & recreation • Expressing opinions about Winter Olympics sports (most exciting, most dangerous) • Describing exercise habits & routines • Using imagination: being an exercise instructor leading a class • Telling about favorite types of entertainment • Comparing types of entertainment popular in different countries • Telling about favorite performers • Telling about favorite types of music, movies, & TV programs • Describing experience with a musical instrument • Comparing typical musical instruments in different countries

Unit / Theme	Communication Skills	Writing & Discussion
16 **Nature**	• Identifying places & people on a farm • Identifying farm animals & crops • Identifying animals & pets • Identifying birds & insects • Identifying fish, sea animals, amphibians, & reptiles • Asking about the presence of wildlife in an area • Identifying trees, plants, & flowers • Identifying key parts of a tree and flower • Asking for information about trees & flowers • Warning someone about poisonous vegetation in an area • Identifying sources of energy • Describing the kind of energy used to heat homes & for cooking • Expressing an opinion about good future sources of energy • Identifying behaviors that promote conservation (recycling, conserving energy, conserving water, carpooling) • Expressing concern about environmental problems • Identifying different kinds of natural disasters	• Comparing farms in different countries • Telling about local animals, animals in a zoo, & common local birds & insects • Comparing common pets in different countries • Using imagination: what animal you would like to be, & why • Telling a popular folk tale or children's story about animals, birds, or insects • Describing fish, sea animals, & reptiles in different countries • Identifying endangered species • Expressing opinions about wildlife – most interesting, beautiful, dangerous • Describing local trees & flowers, & favorites • Comparing different cultures' use of flowers at weddings, funerals, holidays, & hospitals • Expressing an opinion about an environmental problem • Telling about how people prepare for natural disasters
17 **U.S. Civics**	• Producing correct form of identification when requested (driver's license, social security card, student I.D. card, employee I.D. badge, permanent resident card, passport, visa, work permit, birth certificate, proof of residence) • Identifying the three branches of U.S. government (legislative, executive, judicial) & their functions • Identifying senators, representatives, the president, vice-president, cabinet, Supreme Court justices, & the chief justice, & the branches of government in which they work • Identifying the key buildings in each branch of government (Capitol Building, White House, Supreme Court Building) • Identifying the Constitution as "the supreme law of the land" • Identifying the Bill of Rights • Naming freedoms guaranteed by the 1st Amendment • Identifying key amendments to the Constitution • Identifying key events in United States history • Answering history questions about events and the dates they occurred • Identifying key holidays & dates they occur • Identifying legal system & court procedures (arrest, booking, obtaining legal representation, appearing in court, standing trial, acquittal, conviction, sentencing, prison, release) • Identifying people in the criminal justice system • Engaging in small talk about a TV crime show's characters & plot • Identifying rights & responsibilities of U.S. citizens • Identifying steps in applying for citizenship	• Telling about forms of identification & when needed • Describing how people in a community "exercise their 1st Amendment rights" • Brainstorming ideas for a new amendment to the Constitution • Expressing an opinion about the most important event in United States history • Telling about important events in the history of different countries • Describing U.S. holidays you celebrate • Describing holidays celebrated in different countries • Describing the legal system in different countries • Telling about an episode of a TV crime show • Expressing an opinion about the most important rights & responsibilities of people in their communities • Expressing an opinion about the rights of citizens vs. non-citizens

Welcome to the second edition of the WORD BY WORD Picture Dictionary! This text presents more than 4,000 vocabulary words through vibrant illustrations and simple accessible lesson pages that are designed for clarity and ease-of-use with learners at all levels. Our goal is to prepare students for success using English in everyday life, in the community, in school, and at work.

WORD BY WORD organizes the vocabulary into 17 thematic units, providing a careful research-based sequence of lessons that integrates students' development of grammar and vocabulary skills through topics that begin with the immediate world of the student and progress to the world at large. Early lessons on the family, the home, and daily activities lead to lessons on the community, school, workplace, shopping, recreation, and other topics. The text offers extensive coverage of important lifeskill competencies and the vocabulary of school subjects and extracurricular activities, and it is designed to meet the objectives of current national, state, and local standards-based curricula you can find in the Scope & Sequence on the previous pages.

Since each lesson in *Word by Word* is self-contained, it can be used either sequentially or in any desired order. For users' convenience, the lessons are listed in two ways: sequentially in the Table of Contents, and alphabetically in the Thematic Index. These resources, combined with the Glossary in the appendix, allow students and teachers to quickly and easily locate all words and topics in the Picture Dictionary.

The *Word by Word* Picture Dictionary is the centerpiece of the complete *Word by Word* Vocabulary Development Program, which offers a wide selection of print and media support materials for instruction at all levels.

A unique choice of workbooks at Beginning and Intermediate levels offers flexible options to meet students' needs. Vocabulary Workbooks feature motivating vocabulary, grammar, and listening practice, and standards-based Lifeskills Workbooks provide competency-based activities and reading tied to national, state, and local curriculum frameworks. A Literacy Workbook is also available.

The Teacher's Guide and Lesson Planner with CD-ROM includes lesson-planning suggestions, community tasks, Internet weblinks, and reproducible masters to save teachers hours of lesson preparation time. An Activity Handbook with step-by-step teaching strategies for key vocabulary development activities is included in the Teacher's Guide.

The Audio Program includes all words and conversations for interactive practice and —as bonus material—an expanded selection of WordSongs for entertaining musical practice with the vocabulary.

Additional ancillary materials include Color Transparencies, Vocabulary Game Cards, and a Testing Program. Bilingual Editions are also available.

Teaching Strategies

Word by Word presents vocabulary words in context. Model conversations depict situations in which people use the words in meaningful communication. These models become the basis for students to engage in dynamic, interactive practice. In addition, writing and discussion questions in each lesson encourage students to relate the vocabulary and themes to their own lives as they share experiences, thoughts, opinions, and information about themselves, their cultures, and their countries. In this way, students get to know each other "word by word."

In using *Word by Word*, we encourage you to develop approaches and strategies that are compatible with your own teaching style and the needs and abilities of your students. You may find it helpful to incorporate some of the following techniques for presenting and practicing the vocabulary in each lesson.

1. **Preview the Vocabulary:** Activate students' prior knowledge of the vocabulary by brainstorming with students the words in the lesson they already know and writing them on the board, or by having students look at the transparency or the illustration in *Word by Word* and identify the words they are familiar with.

2. **Present the Vocabulary:** Using the transparency or the illustration in the Picture Dictionary, point to the picture of each word, say the word, and have the class repeat it chorally and individually. (You can also play the word list on the Audio Program.) Check students' understanding and pronunciation of the vocabulary.

3. **Vocabulary Practice:** Have students practice the vocabulary as a class, in pairs, or in small groups. Say or write a word, and have students point to the item or tell the number. Or, point to an item or give the number, and have students say the word.

4. **Model Conversation Practice:** Some lessons have model conversations that use the first word in the vocabulary list. Other models are in the form of skeletal dialogs, in which vocabulary words can be inserted. (In many skeletal dialogs, bracketed numbers indicate which words can be used for practicing the conversation. If no bracketed numbers appear, all the words in the lesson can be used.)

The following steps are recommended for Model Conversation Practice:

   a. Preview: Have students look at the model illustration and discuss who they think the speakers are and where the conversation takes place.

   b. The teacher presents the model or plays the audio one or more times and checks students' understanding of the situation and the vocabulary.

   c. Students repeat each line of the conversation chorally and individually.

   d. Students practice the model in pairs.

   e. A pair of students presents a conversation based on the model, but using a different word from the vocabulary list.

   f. In pairs, students practice several conversations based on the model, using different words on the page.

   g. Pairs present their conversations to the class.

5. **Additional Conversation Practice:** Many lessons provide two additional skeletal dialogs for further conversation practice with the vocabulary. (These can be found in the yellow-shaded area at the bottom of the page.) Have students practice and present these conversations using any words they wish. Before they practice the additional conversations, you may want to have students listen to the sample additional conversations on the Audio Program.

6. **Spelling Practice:** Have students practice spelling the words as a class, in pairs, or in small groups. Say a word, and have students spell it aloud or write it. Or, using the transparency, point to an item and have students write the word.

7. **Themes for Discussion, Composition, Journals, and Portfolios:** Each lesson of *Word by Word* provides one or more questions for discussion and composition. (These can be found in a blue-shaded area at the bottom of the page.) Have students respond to the questions as a class, in pairs, or in small groups. Or, have students write their responses at home, share their written work with other students, and discuss as a class, in pairs, or in small groups.

Students may enjoy keeping a journal of their written work. If time permits, you may want to write a response in each student's journal, sharing your own opinions and experiences as well as reacting to what the student has written. If you are keeping portfolios of students' work, these compositions serve as excellent examples of students' progress in learning English.

8. **Communication Activities:** The *Word by Word* Teacher's Guide and Lesson Planner with CD-ROM provides a wealth of games, tasks, brainstorming, discussion, movement, drawing, miming, role-playing, and other activities designed to take advantage of students' different learning styles and particular abilities and strengths. For each lesson, choose one or more of these activities to reinforce students' vocabulary learning in a way that is stimulating, creative, and enjoyable.

WORD BY WORD aims to offer students a communicative, meaningful, and lively way of practicing English vocabulary. In conveying to you the substance of our program, we hope that we have also conveyed the spirit: that learning vocabulary can be genuinely interactive . . . relevant to our students' lives . . . responsive to students' differing strengths and learning styles . . . and fun!

Steven J. Molinsky

Bill Bliss

INFORMAÇÕES PESSOAIS

Registration Form

Name	Gloria	P.	Sánchez	
	First	Middle Initial	Last	
Address	95	Garden Street		3G
	Number	Street		Apartment Number
	Los Angeles		CA	90036
	City		State	Zip Code

Telephone 323-524-3278   Cell Phone 323-695-1864

E-Mail Address gloria97@ail.com   SSN 227-93-6185   Sex M__ F X

Date of Birth 5/12/88   Place of Birth Centerville, Texas

nome	**1** name	código de endereçamento postal	**11** zip code
nome/prenome	**2** first name	código de área	**12** area code
inicial do segundo nome	**3** middle initial	número de telefone	**13** telephone number/ phone number
sobrenome	**4** last name/family name/ surname	número do telefone celular	**14** cell phone number
endereço	**5** address	endereço de e-mail	**15** e-mail address
número	**6** street number	número de seguridade social	**16** social security number
rua	**7** street	sexo	**17** sex
número do apartamento	**8** apartment number	data de nascimento	**18** date of birth
cidade	**9** city	local de nascimento	**19** place of birth
estado	**10** state		

A. What's your **name**?
B. Gloria P. Sánchez.

A. What's your _____?
B. ....
A. Did you say ....?
B. Yes. That's right.

A. What's your last name?
B. ....
A. How do you spell that?
B. ....

Tell about yourself:
My name is ....
My address is ....
My telephone number is ....

Now interview a friend.

marido/esposo	**1**	**husband**	**filhos**	**children**	**avós**	**grandparents**	
mulher/esposa	**2**	**wife**	filha	**5**	**daughter**	avó	**10**	**grandmother**
			filho	**6**	**son**	avô	**11**	**grandfather**
pais		**parents**	bebê/nenê	**7**	**baby**			
pai	**3**	**father**				**netos**	**grandchildren**	
mãe	**4**	**mother**	**irmãos**	**siblings**	neta	**12**	**granddaughter**
			irmã	**8**	**sister**	neto	**13**	**grandson**
			irmão	**9**	**brother**			

A. Who is he?
B. He's my **husband**.
A. What's his name?
B. His name is *Jack*.

A. Who is she?
B. She's my **wife**.
A. What's her name?
B. Her name is *Nancy*.

A. I'd like to introduce my _____ .
B. Nice to meet you.
C. Nice to meet you, too.

A. What's your _____ 's name?
B. His/Her name is ....

Who are the people in your family?
What are their names?

Tell about photos of family members.

tio	**1**	uncle	sogro	**7**	father-in-law
tia	**2**	aunt	genro	**8**	son-in-law
sobrinha	**3**	niece	nora	**9**	daughter-in-law
sobrinho	**4**	nephew	cunhado	**10**	brother-in-law
primo	**5**	cousin	cunhada	**11**	sister-in-law
sogra	**6**	mother-in-law			

1. Jack is Alan's _____.
2. Nancy is Alan's _____.
3. Jennifer is Frank and Linda's _____.
4. Timmy is Frank and Linda's _____.
5. Alan is Jennifer and Timmy's _____.

6. Helen is Jack's _____.
7. Walter is Jack's _____.
8. Jack is Helen and Walter's _____.
9. Linda is Helen and Walter's _____.
10. Frank is Jack's _____.
11. Linda is Jack's _____.

A. Who is he/she?
B. He's/She's my _____.
A. What's his/her name?
B. His/Her name is _____.

A. Let me introduce my _____.
B. I'm glad to meet you.
C. Nice meeting you, too.

Tell about your relatives:
  What are their names?
  Where do they live?

Draw your family tree and tell about it.

THE CLASSROOM

A SALA DE AULA

professora	1	teacher	retroprojetor	8	overhead projector	lousa branca/	15	whiteboard/
assistente de	2	teacher's aide	tela	9	screen	lousa		board
professor			quadro negro/lousa	10	chalkboard/board	globo	16	globe
estudante/aluno	3	student	relógio	11	clock	estante de livros/	17	bookcase/
carteira	4	desk	mapa	12	map	estante		bookshelf
assento/cadeira	5	seat/chair	quadro de avisos	13	bulletin board	mesa da professora	18	teacher's desk
mesa	6	table	alto-falante	14	P.A. system/	cesta de papéis	19	wastebasket
computador	7	computer			loudspeaker			

caneta	**20**	**pen**	fichário/caderno	**27**	**binder/notebook**
lápis	**21**	**pencil**	papel para fichário	**28**	**notebook paper**
borracha	**22**	**eraser**	papel milimetrado	**29**	**graph paper**
apontador de lápis	**23**	**pencil sharpener**	régua	**30**	**ruler**
livro/livro didático	**24**	**book/textbook**	calculadora	**31**	**calculator**
livro de exercícios	**25**	**workbook**	giz	**32**	**chalk**
caderno espiral	**26**	**spiral notebook**	apagador	**33**	**eraser**

caneta hidrográfica	**34**	**marker**
tachinha/percevejo	**35**	**thumbtack**
teclado	**36**	**keyboard**
monitor	**37**	**monitor**
mouse	**38**	**mouse**
impressora	**39**	**printer**

A. Where's the **teacher**?
B. The **teacher** is *next to* the **board**.

A. Where's the **globe**?
B. The **globe** is *on* the **bookcase**.

A. Is there a/an _____ in your classroom?*
B. Yes. There's a/an _____
   next to/on the _____.

A. Is there a/an _____ in your classroom?*
B. No, there isn't.

Describe your classroom.
(There's a/an ....)

* With 28, 29, 32, use: Is there _____ in your classroom?

AÇÕES EM SALA DE AULA

Diga o seu nome.	**1** Say your name.	Levante a sua mão.	**16** Raise your hand.
Repita o seu nome.	**2** Repeat your name.	Faça uma pergunta.	**17** Ask a question.
Soletre o seu nome.	**3** Spell your name.	Ouça a pergunta.	**18** Listen to the question.
Escreva o seu nome com letras de forma.	**4** Print your name.	Responda à pergunta.	**19** Answer the question.
		Ouça a resposta.	**20** Listen to the answer.
Assine o seu nome.	**5** Sign your name.	Faça a lição de casa.	**21** Do your homework.
Levante-se.	**6** Stand up.	Traga a lição de casa.	**22** Bring in your homework.
Vá até a lousa.	**7** Go to the board.	Confira as respostas.	**23** Go over the answers.
Escreva na lousa.	**8** Write on the board.	Corrija os seus erros.	**24** Correct your mistakes.
Apague a lousa.	**9** Erase the board.	Entregue a sua lição de casa.	**25** Hand in your homework.
Sente-se.	**10** Sit down./Take your seat.		
Abra o seu livro.	**11** Open your book.	Divida um livro.	**26** Share a book.
Leia a página dez.	**12** Read page ten.	Discuta sobre a questão.	**27** Discuss the question.
Estude a página dez.	**13** Study page ten.	Ajudem-se um ao outro.	**28** Help each other.
Feche o seu livro.	**14** Close your book.	Trabalhem juntos.	**29** Work together.
Guarde o seu livro.	**15** Put away your book.	Mostre para a classe.	**30** Share with the class.

Consulte o dicionário.	31	Look in the dictionary.	Pegue uma folha de papel.	46	Take out a piece of paper.

Consulte o dicionário. **31** Look in the dictionary.
Procure uma palavra. **32** Look up a word.
Pronuncie a palavra. **33** Pronounce the word.
Leia a definição. **34** Read the definition.
Copie a palavra. **35** Copy the word.
Trabalhe sozinho./ **36** Work alone./
Faça o seu próprio   Do your own work.
trabalho.
Trabalhe com **37** Work with a partner.
um colega.
Dividam-se em **38** Break up into small
grupos pequenos.   groups.
Trabalhe em grupo. **39** Work in a group.
Trabalhe junto com **40** Work as a class.
a classe toda.
Abaixe as persianas. **41** Lower the shades.
Desligue as luzes. **42** Turn off the lights.
Olhe para a tela. **43** Look at the screen.
Faça anotações. **44** Take notes.
Ligue as luzes. **45** Turn on the lights.

Pegue uma folha **46** Take out a piece of paper.
de papel.
Distribua os testes. **47** Pass out the tests.
Responda à pergunta. **48** Answer the questions.
Confira as suas respostas. **49** Check your answers.
Recolha os testes. **50** Collect the tests.
Escolha a resposta correta. **51** Choose the correct answer.
Faça um círculo na **52** Circle the correct answer.
resposta correta.
Preencha o espaço em branco. **53** Fill in the blank.
Marque a folha de resposta./ **54** Mark the answer sheet./
Escureça o círculo da resposta.   Bubble the answer.
Ligue as palavras. **55** Match the words.
Sublinhe a palavra. **56** Underline the word.
Risque a palavra. **57** Cross out the word.
Decifre a palavra. **58** Unscramble the word.
Coloque as palavras em ordem. **59** Put the words in order.
Escreva em uma folha **60** Write on a separate
de papel separada.   sheet of paper.

You're the teacher! Give instructions to your students!

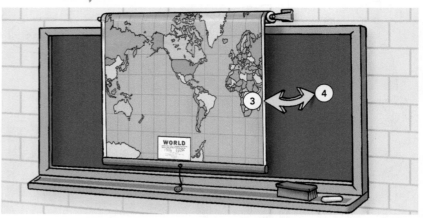

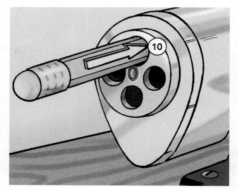

acima	1	above
abaixo	2	below
na frente de/ diante de	3	in front of

atrás	4	behind
ao lado	5	next to
sobre/em	6	on
sob	7	under
à esquerda de	8	to the left of

à direita de	9	to the right of
dentro	10	in
entre	11	between

[1–10]
A. Where's the *clock*?
B. The *clock* is **above** the *bulletin board*.

[11]
A. Where's the *dictionary*?
B. The *dictionary* is **between** the *globe* and the *pencil sharpener*.

Tell about the classroom on page 4. Use the prepositions in this lesson.

Tell about your classroom.

ATIVIDADES COTIDIANAS I

levantar-se	**1**	get up	tirar a roupa	**11**	get undressed
tomar banho de chuveiro	**2**	take a shower	tomar banho de banheira	**12**	take a bath
escovar *meus* dentes	**3**	brush *my** teeth	ir para a cama	**13**	go to bed
barbear-se	**4**	shave	dormir	**14**	sleep
vestir-se	**5**	get dressed	preparar o café da manhã	**15**	make breakfast
lavar *meu* rosto	**6**	wash *my** face	preparar o almoço	**16**	make lunch
colocar a maquiagem	**7**	put on makeup	preparar o jantar/fazer o jantar	**17**	cook / make dinner
escovar *meus* cabelos	**8**	brush *my** hair	tomar o café da manhã	**18**	eat / have breakfast
pentear *meus* cabelos	**9**	comb *my** hair	almoçar	**19**	eat / have lunch
fazer a cama	**10**	make the bed	jantar	**20**	eat / have dinner

* my, his, her, our, your, their

A. What do you do every day?
B. I **get up**, I **take a shower**, and I **brush my teeth**.

A. What does he do every day?
B. He _____s, he _____s, and he _____s.

A. What does she do every day?
B. She _____s, she _____s, and she_____s.

What do you do every day? Make a list.

Interview some friends and tell about their everyday activities.

ATIVIDADES COTIDIANAS II

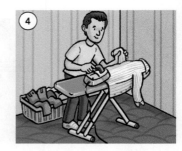

limpar o apartamento/ limpar a casa	**1**	clean the apartment/ clean the house
lavar a louça	**2**	wash the dishes
lavar a roupa	**3**	do the laundry
passar a ferro	**4**	iron
alimentar o bebê	**5**	feed the baby
alimentar o gato	**6**	feed the cat
levar o cachorro para passear	**7**	walk the dog
estudar	**8**	study

ir para o trabalho	**9**	go to work
ir para a escola	**10**	go to school
ir de carro até o trabalho/ guiar até o trabalho	**11**	drive to work
tomar o ônibus para a escola	**12**	take the bus to school
trabalhar	**13**	work
sair do trabalho	**14**	leave work
ir ao supermercado/ir à loja	**15**	go to the store
voltar para casa/ chegar em casa	**16**	come home/get home

A. Hello. What are you doing?
B. I'm **clean**ing the **apartment**.

A. Hello, ... This is ....
    What are you doing?
B. I'm _____ing. How about you?
A. I'm _____ing.

A. Are you going to _____ soon?
B. Yes. I'm going to _____ in a little while.

What are you going to do tomorrow? Make a list of everything you are going to do.

LEISURE ACTIVITIES
ATIVIDADES DE LAZER

assistir TV	1	watch TV
ouvir o rádio	2	listen to the radio
ouvir música	3	listen to music
ler um livro	4	read a book
ler o jornal	5	read the newspaper
brincar	6	play
jogar cartas/jogar baralho	7	play cards
jogar basquetebol/jogar basquete	8	play basketball
tocar violão	9	play the guitar
exercitar-se ao piano	10	practice the piano
fazer exercício/exercitar-se	11	exercise
nadar	12	swim
plantar flores	13	plant flowers
usar o computador	14	use the computer
escrever uma carta	15	write a letter
relaxar/descansar	16	relax

A. Hi. What are you doing?
B. I'm **watch**ing **TV**.

A. Hi, ... Are you _____ing?
B. No, I'm not. I'm _____ing.

A. What's your (husband/wife/son/daughter/...) doing?
B. He's/She's _____ing.

What leisure activities do you like to do?

What do your family members and friends like to do?

EVERYDAY CONVERSATION
CONVERSAÇÕES COTIDIANAS

Greeting People   *Cumprimentar pessoas*

Leave Taking   *Despedidas*

Olá./Oi.	**1** Hello./Hi.	Quais são as novidades?/	**7** What's new?/
Bom dia.	**2** Good morning.	O que há de novo?	What's new with you?
Boa tarde.	**3** Good afternoon.	Tudo na mesma./	**8** Not much./
Boa noite.	**4** Good evening.	O mesmo de sempre.	Not too much.
Como vai?/	**5** How are you?/	Até logo./Tchau.	**9** Good-bye./Bye.
Como vai você?	How are you doing?	Boa noite.	**10** Good night.
Bem./Bem, obrigado./	**6** Fine./Fine, thanks./	Até mais tarde./	**11** See you later./
Ok.	Okay.	Até breve.	See you soon.

Introducing Yourself and Others   Apresentar-se a si mesmo e outras pessoas

Getting Someone's Attention
Chamar atenção de alguém

Expressing Gratitude
Expressar gratidão

Saying You Don't Understand
Dizer que não entende

Calling Someone on the Telephone
Telefonar para alguém

Olá. Meu nome é .... / Oi. Sou	12	Hello. My name is .... / Hi. I'm ....
Muito prazer em conhecê-lo.	13	Nice to meet you.
Muito prazer em conhecê-lo também.	14	Nice to meet you, too.
Gostaria de lhe apresentar .... / Esta é	15	I'd like to introduce .... / This is ....
Com licença.	16	Excuse me.
Posso fazer uma pergunta?	17	May I ask a question?
Obrigada.	18	Thank you. / Thanks.
De nada.	19	You're welcome.
Não estou entendendo. / Desculpe. Não estou entendendo.	20	I don't understand. / Sorry. I don't understand.
Você pode repetir, por favor? / Você poderia repetir novamente, por favor?	21	Can you please repeat that? / Can you please say that again?
Olá. Aqui é .... Gostaria de falar com ....?	22	Hello. This is .... May I please speak to ....?
Sim. Aguarde um instante.	23	Yes. Hold on a moment.
Sinto muito. ....não está aqui no momento.	24	I'm sorry. .... isn't here right now.

Practice conversations with other students. Use all the expressions on pages 12 and 13.

O TEMPO

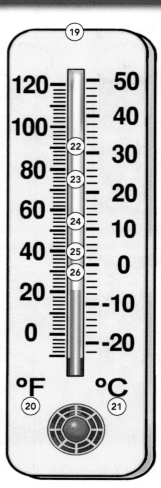

Tempo/clima		Weather
ensolarado	**1**	sunny
nublado	**2**	cloudy
límpido/céu azul	**3**	clear
nevoeiro	**4**	hazy
cerração/neblina	**5**	foggy
smog	**6**	smoggy
ventoso	**7**	windy
úmido/abafado	**8**	humid/muggy
chovendo	**9**	raining
garoando	**10**	drizzling
nevando	**11**	snowing
caindo granizo	**12**	hailing
geando	**13**	sleeting

relampejando	**14**	lightning
tempestade com trovoadas	**15**	thunderstorm
tempestade de neve	**16**	snowstorm
tempestade de poeira	**17**	dust storm
frente quente	**18**	heat wave

Temperatura		Temperature
termômetro	**19**	thermometer
Fahrenheit	**20**	Fahrenheit
Centígrado/Celsius	**21**	Centigrade/Celsius
quente	**22**	hot
quente/morno	**23**	warm
fresco	**24**	cool
gelado/frio	**25**	cold
congelando	**26**	freezing

[1–13]
A. What's the weather like?
B. It's _____.

[14–18]
A. What's the weather forecast?
B. There's going to be ___[14]___ /
   a ___[15–18]___ .

[20–26]
A. How's the weather?
B. It's ___[22–26]___ .
A. What's the temperature?
B. It's . . . degrees ___[20–21]___ .

What's the weather like today? What's the temperature?   What's the weather forecast for tomorrow?

NÚMEROS

Cardinal Numbers   Números cardinais

0 zero	**11** eleven	**21** twenty-one	**101** one hundred (and) one
1 one	**12** twelve	**22** twenty-two	**102** one hundred (and) two
2 two	**13** thirteen	**30** thirty	**1,000** one thousand
3 three	**14** fourteen	**40** forty	**10,000** ten thousand
4 four	**15** fifteen	**50** fifty	**100,000** one hundred thousand
5 five	**16** sixteen	**60** sixty	**1,000,000** one million
6 six	**17** seventeen	**70** seventy	**1,000,000,000** one billion
7 seven	**18** eighteen	**80** eighty	
8 eight	**19** nineteen	**90** ninety	
9 nine	**20** twenty	**100** one hundred	
10 ten			

A. How old are you?
B. I'm _____ years old.

A. How many people are there in your family?
B. _____.

Ordinal Numbers   Números ordinais

1st first	**11th** eleventh	**21st** twenty-first	**101st** one hundred (and) first
2nd second	**12th** twelfth	**22nd** twenty-second	**102nd** one hundred (and) second
3rd third	**13th** thirteenth	**30th** thirtieth	**1,000th** one thousandth
4th fourth	**14th** fourteenth	**40th** fortieth	**10,000th** ten thousandth
5th fifth	**15th** fifteenth	**50th** fiftieth	**100,000th** one hundred thousandth
6th sixth	**16th** sixteenth	**60th** sixtieth	**1,000,000th** one millionth
7th seventh	**17th** seventeenth	**70th** seventieth	**1,000,000,000th** one billionth
8th eighth	**18th** eighteenth	**80th** eightieth	
9th ninth	**19th** nineteenth	**90th** ninetieth	
10th tenth	**20th** twentieth	**100th** one hundredth	

A. What floor do you live on?
B. I live on the _____ floor.

A. Is this your first trip to our country?
B. No. It's my _____ trip.

How many students are there in your class?

How many people are there in your country?

What were the names of your teachers in elementary school? (My *first*-grade teacher was Ms./Mrs./Mr. . . .)

TIME

HORAS

two o'clock

two fifteen /
a quarter after *two*

two thirty /
half past *two*

two forty-five
a quarter to *three*

two oh five

two twenty /
twenty after *two*

two forty /
twenty to *three*

two fifty-five
five to *three*

A. What time is it?
B. It's _____.

A. What time does the movie
   begin?
B. At _____.

two A.M.

two P.M.

noon /
twelve noon

midnight /
twelve midnight

A. When does the train leave?
B. At _____.

A. What time will we arrive?
B. At _____.

Tell about your daily schedule:
   What do you do? When?
   (I get up at _____. I ....)

Do you usually have enough time to do
things, or do you "run out of time"?
Tell about it.

Tell about the use of time in different cultures or countries you know:
   Do people arrive on time for work? appointments? parties?
   Do trains and buses operate exactly on schedule?
   Do movies and sports events begin on time?
   Do workplaces use time clocks or timesheets to record employees' work hours?

Coins Moedas

Name	Value	Written as:	
1 penny	one cent	1¢	$ .01
2 nickel	five cents	5¢	$ .05
3 dime	ten cents	10¢	$ .10
4 quarter	twenty-five cents	25¢	$ .25
5 half dollar	fifty cents	50¢	$ .50
6 silver dollar	one dollar		$1.00

A. How much is a **penny** worth?
B. A **penny** is worth **one cent**.

A. *Soda* costs *ninety-five cents.* Do you have enough change?
B. Yes. I have a/two/three _____(s) and . . . .

Currency Dinheiro

Name	We sometimes say:	Value	Written as:
7 (one-) dollar bill	a one	one dollar	$ 1.00
8 five-dollar bill	a five	five dollars	$ 5.00
9 ten-dollar bill	a ten	ten dollars	$ 10.00
10 twenty-dollar bill	a twenty	twenty dollars	$ 20.00
11 fifty-dollar bill	a fifty	fifty dollars	$ 50.00
12 (one-) hundred dollar bill	a hundred	one hundred dollars	$100.00

A. I'm going to the supermarket. Do you have any cash?
B. I have a **twenty-dollar bill**.
A. **Twenty dollars** is enough. Thanks.

A. Can you change a **five-dollar bill/a five**?
B. Yes. I have *five one-dollar bills/five ones.*

Written as:	We say:
$1.30	a dollar and thirty cents / a dollar thirty
$2.50	two dollars and fifty cents / two fifty
$56.49	fifty-six dollars and forty-nine cents / fifty-six forty-nine

Tell about some things you usually buy. What do they cost?

Name and describe the coins and currency in your country. What are they worth in U.S. dollars?

		Meses do ano	**Months of the Year**	3 de janeiro de 2012	**25**	**January 3, 2012**
ano	**1** year	janeiro	**13** January	três de janeiro de		January third,
mês	**2** month	fevereiro	**14** February	dois mil e doze		two thousand
semana	**3** week	março	**15** March			twelve
dia	**4** day	abril	**16** April	aniversário	**26**	birthday
fim de semana	**5** weekend	maio	**17** May	aniversário	**27**	anniversary
		junho	**18** June	(de casamento/		
Dias da semana	**Days of the Week**	julho	**19** July	de acontecimentos		
domingo	**6** Sunday	agosto	**20** August	especiais)		
segunda-feira	**7** Monday	setembro	**21** September	hora marcada	**28**	appointment
terça-feira	**8** Tuesday	outubro	**22** October			
quarta-feira	**9** Wednesday	novembro	**23** November			
quinta-feira	**10** Thursday	dezembro	**24** December			
sexta-feira	**11** Friday					
sábado	**12** Saturday					

A. What year is it?
B. It's _____.

[13–24]
A. What month is it?
B. It's _____.

[6–12]
A. What day is it?
B. It's _____.

A. What's today's date?
B. It's _____.

[26–28]
A. When is your _____?
B. It's on _____.

Which days of the week do you go to work/school?
(I go to work/school on _____.)

What do you do on the weekend?

What is your date of birth?
(I was born on ..... *month, day, year* .....)

What's your favorite day of the week? Why?

What's your favorite month of the year? Why?

EXPRESSÕES TEMPORAIS E ESTAÇÕES

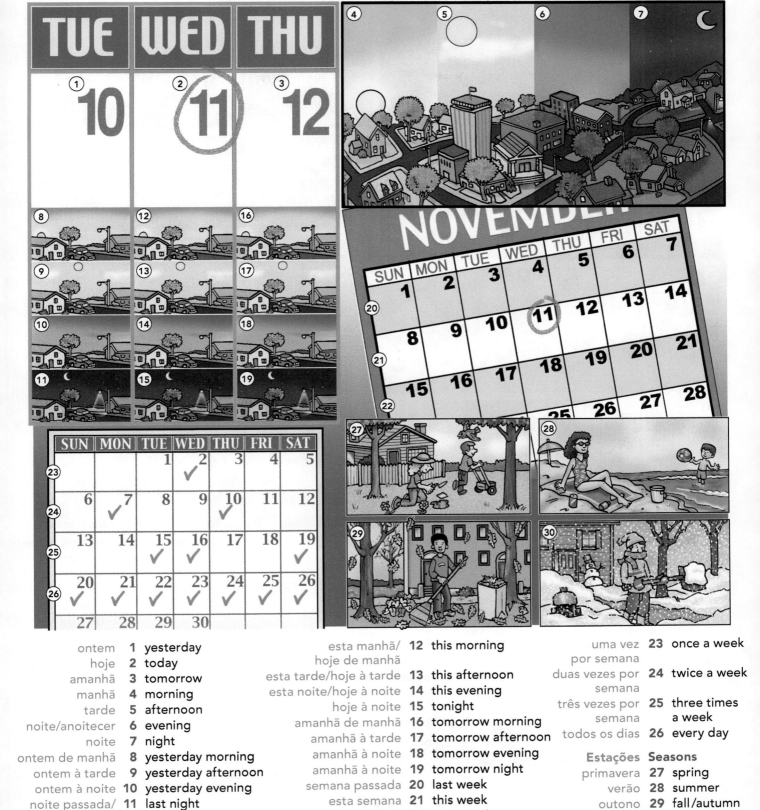

ontem	**1**	yesterday
hoje	**2**	today
amanhã	**3**	tomorrow
manhã	**4**	morning
tarde	**5**	afternoon
noite/anoitecer	**6**	evening
noite	**7**	night
ontem de manhã	**8**	yesterday morning
ontem à tarde	**9**	yesterday afternoon
ontem à noite	**10**	yesterday evening
noite passada/ ontem à noite	**11**	last night

esta manhã/ hoje de manhã	**12**	this morning
esta tarde/hoje à tarde	**13**	this afternoon
esta noite/hoje à noite	**14**	this evening
hoje à noite	**15**	tonight
amanhã de manhã	**16**	tomorrow morning
amanhã à tarde	**17**	tomorrow afternoon
amanhã à noite	**18**	tomorrow evening
amanhã à noite	**19**	tomorrow night
semana passada	**20**	last week
esta semana	**21**	this week
semana que vem	**22**	next week

uma vez por semana	**23**	once a week
duas vezes por semana	**24**	twice a week
três vezes por semana	**25**	three times a week
todos os dias	**26**	every day

Estações		**Seasons**
primavera	**27**	spring
verão	**28**	summer
outono	**29**	fall/autumn
inverno	**30**	winter

What did you do yesterday morning/afternoon/ evening? What did you do last night?

What are you going to do tomorrow morning/ afternoon/evening/night?

What did you do last week?

What are your plans for next week?

How many times a week do you have English class?/go to the supermarket?/exercise?

What's your favorite season? Why?

TIPOS DE HABITAÇÕES E COMUNIDADES

prédio de apartamentos	**1 apartment building**	casa de saúde	**8 nursing home**
casa	**2 house**	abrigo	**9 shelter**
casa geminada/	**3 duplex/**	fazenda	**10 farm**
casa de moradia de duas famílias	**two-family house**	fazenda de criação de gado	**11 ranch**
casa geminada em condomínio	**4 townhouse/townhome**	casa flutuante	**12 houseboat**
condomínio	**5 condominium/condo**	cidade (a)	**13 the city**
alojamento universitário/	**6 dormitory/**	cidades vizinhas com bairros residenciais	**14 the suburbs**
alojamento estudantil	**dorm**	interior/campo (o)	**15 the country**
casa pré-fabricada do tipo trailer	**7 mobile home**	cidade menor/vila	**16 a town/village**

A. Where do you live?

B. I live
- in a/an _____ [1–9].
- on a _____ [10–12].
- in _____ [13–16].

[1–12]

A. Town Taxi Company.

B. Hello. Please send a taxi to
.....(address).....

A. Is that a house or an apartment building?

B. It's a/an _____.

A. All right. We'll be there right away.

[1–12]

A. This is the Emergency Operator.

B. Please send an ambulance to
.....(address).....

A. Is that a private home?

B. It's a/an _____.

A. What's your name and telephone number?

B. ....

Tell about people you know and where they live.

Discuss:
Who lives in dormitories?
Who lives in nursing homes?
Who lives in shelters?
Why?

A SALA DE ESTAR

estante de livros	**1**	bookcase	parede	**10**	wall	sofá	**20** sofa / couch
foto / fotografia	**2**	picture / photograph	teto	**11**	ceiling	planta	**21** plant
pintura / quadro	**3**	painting	cortinas	**12**	drapes	mesinha de centro	**22** coffee table
console de lareira	**4**	mantel	janela	**13**	window	tapete	**23** rug
lareira	**5**	fireplace	sofá de dois	**14**	loveseat	pé do abajur	**24** lamp
tela de lareira	**6**	fireplace screen	lugares			abajur	**25** lampshade
aparelho de DVD	**7**	DVD player	estante	**15**	wall unit	mesinha	**26** end table
televisão / TV	**8**	television / TV	alto-falante	**16**	speaker	assoalho	**27** floor
videocassete /	**9**	VCR / video cassette	sistema estéreo	**17**	stereo system	luminária de chão	**28** floor lamp
gravador de vídeo		recorder	porta-revistas	**18**	magazine holder	poltrona	**29** armchair
			almofada	**19**	(throw) pillow		

A. Where are you?
B. I'm in the living room.
A. What are you doing?
B. I'm dusting* the **bookcase**.

*dusting / cleaning

A. You have a very nice living room!
B. Thank you.
A. Your _____ is / are beautiful!
B. Thank you for saying so.

A. Uh-oh! I just spilled coffee on your _____!
B. That's okay. Don't worry about it.

Tell about your living room.
(In my living room there's ....)

mesa de jantar	1	(dining room) table
cadeira para mesa de jantar	2	(dining room) chair
aparador	3	buffet
bandeja	4	tray
bule de chá	5	teapot
cafeteira/ bule de café	6	coffee pot
açucareiro	7	sugar bowl
cremeira	8	creamer
jarro	9	pitcher
lustre	10	chandelier
armário de louça	11	china cabinet
louça	12	china
saladeira	13	salad bowl
tigela	14	serving bowl
prato de servir	15	serving dish
vaso	16	vase
vela	17	candle
castiçal	18	candlestick
travessa	19	platter
manteigueira	20	butter dish
saleiro	21	salt shaker
pimenteiro	22	pepper shaker
toalha de mesa	23	tablecloth
guardanapo	24	napkin
garfo	25	fork
prato	26	plate
faca	27	knife
colher	28	spoon
prato fundo	29	bowl
caneca	30	mug
copo	31	glass
xícara	32	cup
pires	33	saucer

A. This **dining room table** is very nice.
B. Thank you. It was a gift from my *grandmother*.*

*grandmother/grandfather/aunt/uncle/. . .

[In a store]
A. May I help you?
B. Yes, please. Do you have _____s?*
A. Yes. _____s* are right over there.
B. Thank you.

*With 12, use the singular.

[At home]
A. Look at this old _____ I just bought!
B. Where did you buy it?
A. At a yard sale. How do you like it?
B. It's VERY unusual!

Tell about your dining room.
(In my dining room there's
..............)

cama	**1**	bed	colcha	**10**	bedspread	mesa de cabeceira/	**19**	night table/
cabeceira	**2**	headboard	acolchoado/	**11**	comforter/	criado-mudo		nightstand
travesseiro	**3**	pillow	edredon		quilt	espelho	**20**	mirror
fronha	**4**	pillowcase	carpete	**12**	carpet	porta-jóias	**21**	jewelry box
lençol de baixo/	**5**	fitted sheet	cômoda	**13**	chest (of drawers)	toucador/cômoda	**22**	dresser/bureau
com elástico			persiana	**14**	blinds	colchão	**23**	mattress
lençol	**6**	(flat) sheet	cortinas	**15**	curtains	box	**24**	box spring
cobertor	**7**	blanket	abajur	**16**	lamp	estrado	**25**	bed frame
cobertor elétrico	**8**	electric blanket	despertador	**17**	alarm clock			
saia para cama	**9**	dust ruffle	rádio relógio	**18**	clock radio			

A. Ooh! Look at that big bug!
B. Where?
A. It's on the **bed**!
B. I'LL get it.

[In a store]

A. Excuse me. I'm looking for a/an _____.*

B. We have some very nice _____s, and they're all on sale this week!

A. Oh, good!

* With 14 & 15, use: Excuse me. I'm looking for _____

[In a bedroom]

A. Oh, no! I just lost my contact lens!

B. Where?

A. I think it's on the _____.

B. I'll help you look.

Tell about your bedroom.
(In my bedroom there's ....)

geladeira/ refrigerador	**1**	**refrigerator**	torneira	**11**	**faucet**	chaleira	**23**	**tea kettle**
congelador	**2**	**freezer**	pia da cozinha	**12**	**(kitchen) sink**	fogão	**24**	**stove/range**
lata de lixo	**3**	**garbage pail**	máquina de lavar louça	**13**	**dishwasher**	queimador	**25**	**burner**
batedeira (elétrica)	**4**	**(electric) mixer**	trituradora de lixo para pia	**14**	**(garbage) disposal**	forno	**26**	**oven**
armário	**5**	**cabinet**	toalha de prato	**15**	**dish towel**	torradeira	**27**	**toaster**
porta-toalha de papel	**6**	**paper towel holder**	escorredor/ escorredor	**16**	**dish rack/ dish drainer**	cafeteira elétrica	**28**	**coffeemaker**
potes	**7**	**canister**	de pratos			compactador de lixo	**29**	**trash compactor**
bancada da cozinha	**8**	**(kitchen) counter**	porta-condimentos	**17**	**spice rack**	tábua de cortar	**30**	**cutting board**
detergente para máquina de lavar louça	**9**	**dishwasher detergent**	abridor de latas (elétrico)	**18**	**(electric) can opener**	livro de receitas	**31**	**cookbook**
			liquidificador	**19**	**blender**	processador de alimentos	**32**	**food processor**
detergente líquido	**10**	**dishwashing liquid**	miniforno elétrico	**20**	**toaster oven**	cadeira de cozinha	**33**	**kitchen chair**
			microondas	**21**	**microwave (oven)**	mesa de cozinha	**34**	**kitchen table**
			pegador	**22**	**potholder**	jogo americano	**35**	**placemat**

A. I think we need a new **refrigerator**.
B. I think you're right.

[In a store]

A. Excuse me. Are your _____s
   still on sale?
B. Yes, they are. They're twenty percent off.

[In a kitchen]

A. When did you get this/these
   new _____(s)?
B. I got it/them last week.

Tell about your kitchen.
(In my kitchen there's ....)

ursinho de pelúcia	**1**	teddy bear	chocalho	**17**	rattle
babá eletrônica	**2**	baby monitor/intercom	andador	**18**	walker
cômoda	**3**	chest (of drawers)	berço	**19**	cradle
berço	**4**	crib	carrinho de passeio	**20**	stroller
protetor de berço	**5**	crib bumper/bumper pad	carrinho de bebê	**21**	baby carriage
móbile	**6**	mobile	cadeira para automóvel/	**22**	car seat/
trocador	**7**	changing table	assento infantil para automóvel		safety seat
macacão	**8**	stretch suit	bebê conforto para automóvel	**23**	baby carrier
colchonete de trocador	**9**	changing pad	prato térmico	**24**	food warmer
lixeira de fraldas	**10**	diaper pail	assento para cadeira/	**25**	booster seat
iluminador fotoelétrico/	**11**	night light	assento de segurança		
abajur de parede			bebê conforto	**26**	baby seat
baú de brinquedos	**12**	toy chest	cadeirão	**27**	high chair
bichinho de pelúcia	**13**	stuffed animal	berço portátil	**28**	portable crib
boneca	**14**	doll	penico	**29**	potty
balanço	**15**	swing	canguru	**30**	baby frontpack
cercadinho	**16**	playpen	mochila para carregar bebê	**31**	baby backpack

A. Thank you for the **teddy bear**. It's a very nice gift.
B. You're welcome. Tell me, when are you due?
A. In a few more weeks.

A. That's a very nice _____.
   Where did you get it?
B. It was a gift from ....

A. Do you have everything you need
   before the baby comes?
B. Almost everything. We're still
   looking for a/an _____ and a/an
   _____.

Tell about your country:
   What things do people buy for a new baby?
   Does a new baby sleep in a separate room,
   as in the United States?

O BANHEIRO

cesto de lixo de banheiro	**1**	wastebasket	escova de dente elétrica	**13**	electric toothbrush	vaso sanitário/ privada	**26** toilet
bancada da pia	**2**	vanity	secador de cabelo	**14**	hair dryer	assento de vaso sanitário	**27** toilet seat
sabonete	**3**	soap	prateleira	**15**	shelf	chuveiro	**28** shower
saboneteira	**4**	soap dish	cesto de roupa suja	**16**	hamper	chuveiro	**29** shower head
porta-sabonete líquido	**5**	soap dispenser	exaustor	**17**	fan	cortina de chuveiro	**30** shower curtain
pia do banheiro	**6**	(bathroom) sink	toalha de banho	**18**	bath towel	banheira	**31** bathtub/tub
torneira	**7**	faucet	toalha de mão	**19**	hand towel	tapete de borracha	**32** rubber mat
armário de banheiro	**8**	medicine cabinet	toalha de rosto	**20**	washcloth/ facecloth	ralo	**33** drain
espelho	**9**	mirror	porta-toalha	**21**	towel rack	esponja	**34** sponge
copo	**10**	cup	desentupidor	**22**	plunger	tapete de banheiro	**35** bath mat
escova de dente	**11**	toothbrush	escova para vaso sanitário/ escova sanitária	**23**	toilet brush	balança	**36** scale
porta-escova de dente	**12**	toothbrush holder	papel higiênico	**24**	toilet paper		
			aromatizador de ambiente	**25**	air freshener		

A. Where's the **hair dryer**?
B. It's *on* the **vanity**.

A. Where's the **soap**?
B. It's *in* the **soap dish**.

A. Where's the **plunger**?
B. It's *next to* the **toilet brush**.

A. [Knock. Knock.] Did I leave my glasses in there?
B. Yes. They're on/in/next to the _____.

A. *Bobby*? You didn't clean up the bathroom! There's toothpaste on the _____, and there's powder all over the _____!
B. Sorry. I'll clean it up right away.

Tell about your bathroom. (In my bathroom there's ....)

FORA DE CASA

Jardim da frente	Front Yard		Quintal	Backyard
poste de iluminação	**1** lamppost		cadeira de jardim	**17** lawn chair
caixa de correio	**2** mailbox		cortador de grama	**18** lawnmower
caminho da entrada da casa	**3** front walk		oficina	**19** tool shed
degraus da frente	**4** front steps		porta tela	**20** screen door
varanda	**5** (front) porch		porta dos fundos	**21** back door
porta de proteção	**6** storm door		maçaneta	**22** door knob
porta de entrada da frente	**7** front door		deque	**23** deck
campainha	**8** doorbell		churrasqueira	**24** barbecue/(outdoor) grill
luminária externa	**9** (front) light		pátio	**25** patio
janela	**10** window		calha	**26** gutter
tela	**11** (window) screen		cano de escoamento/	**27** drainpipe
persiana externa/contravento	**12** shutter		cano condutor	
telhado	**13** roof		antena de satélite	**28** satellite dish
garagem	**14** garage		antena de TV	**29** TV antenna
portão da garagem	**15** garage door		chaminé	**30** chimney
entrada para carros	**16** driveway		porta lateral	**31** side door
			cerca	**32** fence

A. When are you going to repair the **lamppost**?
B. I'm going to repair it next Saturday.

[On the telephone]
A. Harry's Home Repairs.
B. Hello. Do you fix _____ s?
A. No, we don't.
B. Oh, okay. Thank you.

[At work on Monday morning]
A. What did you do this weekend?
B. Nothing much. I repaired my _____ and my _____.

Do you like to repair things?
What things can you repair yourself?
What things can't you repair? Who repairs them?

O PRÉDIO DE APARTAMENTOS

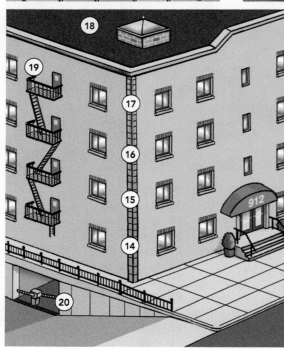

À procura de um apartamento	**Looking for an Apartment**
anúncios imobiliários/ anúncio classificado	**1** apartment ads/ classified ads
listas de apartamentos	**2** apartment listings
placa de aluguel	**3** vacancy sign

Assinatura do contrato	**Signing a Lease**
inquilino/locatário	**4** tenant
proprietário/locador	**5** landlord
contrato de aluguel	**6** lease
depósito-caução	**7** security deposit

La mudanza	**Moving In**
caminhão de mudança/ caminhonete de mudança	**8** moving truck/ moving van
vizinha	**9** neighbor
zelador	**10** building manager
porteiro	**11** doorman
chave	**12** key
fechadura	**13** lock
primeiro andar (térreo)	**14** first floor
segundo andar	**15** second floor
terceiro andar	**16** third floor
quarto andar	**17** fourth floor
telhado	**18** roof

saída de incêndio	**19** fire escape
garagem	**20** parking garage
varanda	**21** balcony
pátio	**22** courtyard
estacionamento	**23** parking lot
vaga	**24** parking space
piscina	**25** swimming pool
hidromassagem	**26** whirlpool
lixeira	**27** trash bin
ar condicionado	**28** air conditioner

Sagüão		Lobby
interfone/ alto-falante	29	intercom/ speaker
campainha	30	buzzer
caixa de correio	31	mailbox
elevador	32	elevator
escadas	33	stairway

Entrada		Doorway
olho mágico	34	peephole
corrente de segurança	35	(door) chain
trinco de segurança	36	dead-bolt lock
detector de fumaça	37	smoke detector

Corredor		Hallway
saída de emergência/ escada de incêndio	38	fire exit/ emergency stairway
alarme de incêndio	39	fire alarm
sprinkler/chuveiro automático para extinção de incêndio	40	sprinkler system
zelador	41	superintendent
duto da lixeira/ duto de lixo	42	garbage chute/ trash chute

Subsolo		Basement
depósito	43	storage room
armário do depósito	44	storage locker
lavanderia	45	laundry room
portão de segurança	46	security gate

[19–46]
A. Is there a **fire escape**?
B. Yes, there is. Do you want to see the apartment?
A. Yes, I do.

[19–46]
[Renting an apartment]
A. Let me show you around.
B. Okay.
A. This is the _____, and here's the _____.
B. I see.

[19–46]
[On the telephone]
A. Mom and Dad? I found an apartment.
B. Good. Tell us about it.
A. It has a/an _____ and a/an _____.
B. That's nice. Does it have a/an _____?
A. Yes, it does.

Do you or someone you know live in an apartment building? Tell about it.

PROBLEMAS E CONSERTOS DOMÉSTICOS

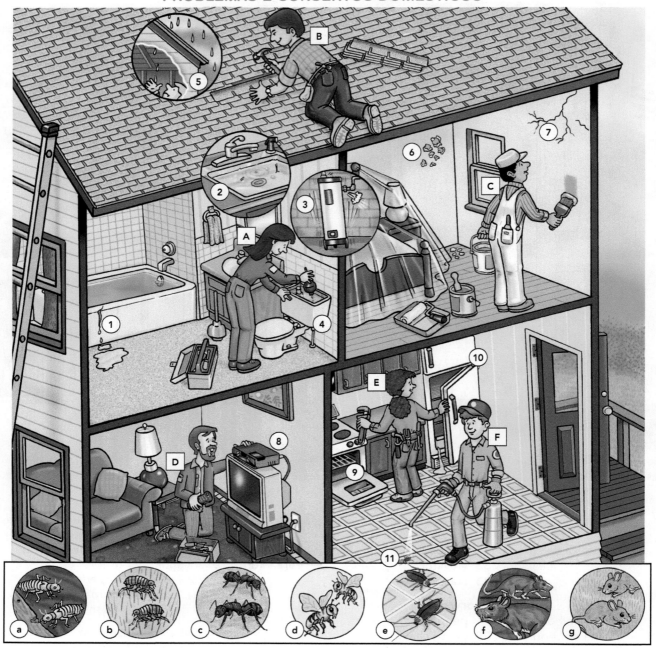

encanador/	**A plumber**	**técnico de**	**E appliance repairperson**
bombeiro hidráulico		**eletrodomésticos**	
A banheira está vazando.	**1** The bathtub is leaking.	O fogão não	**9** The stove isn't working.
A pia está entupida.	**2** The sink is clogged.	está funcionando.	
O aquecedor de água	**3** The hot water heater	A geladeira está quebrada.	**10** The refrigerator is broken.
não está funcionando.	isn't working.		
A privada está quebrada.	**4** The toilet is broken.	**dedetizador**	**F exterminator/**
			pest control specialist
telhador	**B roofer**	Tem ___ na cozinha.	**11** There are ___ in the
O telhado tem goteira.	**5** The roof is leaking.		kitchen.
		cupins	**a** termites
pintor	**C (house) painter**	pulgas	**b** fleas
A pintura está descascando.	**6** The paint is peeling.	formigas	**c** ants
A parede está rachada.	**7** The wall is cracked.	abelhas	**d** bees
		baratas	**e** cockroaches
empresa de TV a cabo	**D cable TV company**	ratos	**f** rats
A TV a cabo não	**8** The cable TV isn't working.	camundongos	**g** mice
está funcionando.			

Chaveiro	**G locksmith**	**Técnico de reparos e manutenção/faz-tudo**	**J home repairperson/ "handyman"**
A fechadura está quebrada.	**12** The lock is broken.	Os azulejos do banheiro estão soltos.	**17** The tiles in the bathroom are loose.
Eletricista	**H electrician**	**Carpinteiro**	**K carpenter**
A luz da frente não acende.	**13** The front light doesn't go on.	Os degraus estão quebrados.	**18** The steps are broken.
A campainha não toca.	**14** The doorbell doesn't ring.	A porta não abre.	**19** The door doesn't open.
A sala está sem eletricidade.	**15** The power is out in the living room.	**Serviço de aquecimento e ar condicionado**	**L heating and air conditioning service**
Limpador de chaminés	**I chimneysweep**	O sistema de aquecimento está quebrado.	**20** The heating system is broken.
A chaminé está suja.	**16** The chimney is dirty.	O ar condicionado não está funcionando.	**21** The air conditioning isn't working.

A. What's the matter?
B. _____[1–21]_____.
A. I think we should call a/an _____[A–L]_____.

[1–21]

A. I'm having a problem in my apartment/house.

B. What's the problem?

A. _____.

[A–L]

A. Can you recommend a good _____?

B. Yes. You should call ....

What do you do when there are problems in your home? Do you fix things yourself, or do you call someone?

LIMPEZA DA CASA

varrer o chão	**A**	sweep the floor	esfregão de assoalho/mop seco	**9** (dust) mop/(dry) mop
passar aspirador	**B**	vacuum	rodo de esponja/	**10** (sponge) mop
passar o esfregão no chão	**C**	mop the floor	rodo absorvente	
lavar as janelas	**D**	wash the windows	mop úmido/esfregão	**11** (wet) mop
tirar o pó	**E**	dust	toalhas de papel	**12** paper towels
encerar o chão	**F**	wax the floor	limpa-vidro	**13** window cleaner
polir os móveis	**G**	polish the furniture	amônia	**14** ammonia
limpar o banheiro	**H**	clean the bathroom	pano de pó	**15** dust cloth
levar o lixo para fora	**I**	take out the garbage	espanador	**16** feather duster
			cera de assoalho	**17** floor wax
vassoura	**1**	broom	lustra-móveis	**18** furniture polish
pá de lixo	**2**	dustpan	saponáceo em pó	**19** cleanser
espanadeira	**3**	whisk broom	escova de limpeza	**20** scrub brush
vassoura mágica	**4**	carpet sweeper	esponja	**21** sponge
aspirador de pó	**5**	vacuum (cleaner)	balde	**22** bucket/pail
acessórios do aspirador	**6**	vacuum cleaner attachments	lixeira/lata de lixo	**23** trash can/garbage can
saco do aspirador	**7**	vacuum cleaner bag	caixa de material reciclável	**24** recycling bin
aspirador portátil	**8**	hand vacuum		

[A–I]
A. What are you doing?
B. I'm **sweep**ing **the floor**.

[1–24]
A. I can't find the **broom**.
B. Look over there!

[1–12, 15, 16, 20–24]
A. Excuse me. Do you sell _____(s)?
B. Yes. They're at the back of the store.
A. Thanks.

[13, 14, 17–19]
A. Excuse me. Do you sell _____?
B. Yes. It's at the back of the store.
A. Thanks.

What household cleaning chores do people do in your home? What things do they use?

MATERIAIS PARA CONSERTOS E REPAROS DOMÉSTICO

régua do comprimento de uma jarda	**1** yardstick	fita isolante	**10** electrical tape	mata-barata	**19** roach killer
mata-moscas	**2** fly swatter	fita silver-tape	**11** duct tape	lixa de papel	**20** sandpaper
desentupidor	**3** plunger	pilhas	**12** batteries	tinta	**21** paint
lanterna	**4** flashlight	lâmpadas	**13** lightbulbs/bulbs	solvente	**22** paint thinner
extensão elétrica	**5** extension cord	fusíveis	**14** fuses	pincel	**23** paintbrush/brush
fita métrica	**6** tape measure	óleo	**15** oil		
escada de abrir	**7** step ladder	cola	**16** glue	bandeja para pintura	**24** paint pan
ratoeira	**8** mousetrap	luvas de trabalho	**17** work gloves	rolo de pintura	**25** paint roller
fita crepe	**9** masking tape	mata-insetos/ inseticida	**18** bug spray/ insect spray	pistola de pintura	**26** spray gun

A. I can't find the **yardstick**!
B. Look in the utility cabinet.
A. I did.
B. Oh! Wait a minute! I lent the **yardstick** to the neighbors.

[1–8, 23–26]
A. I'm going to the hardware store. Can you think of anything we need?
B. Yes. We need a/an _____.
A. Oh, that's right.

[9–22]
A. I'm going to the hardware store. Can you think of anything we need?
B. Yes. We need _____.
A. Oh, that's right.

What home supplies do you have? How and when do you use each one?

TOOLS AND HARDWARE
FERRAMENTAS E APARELHOS

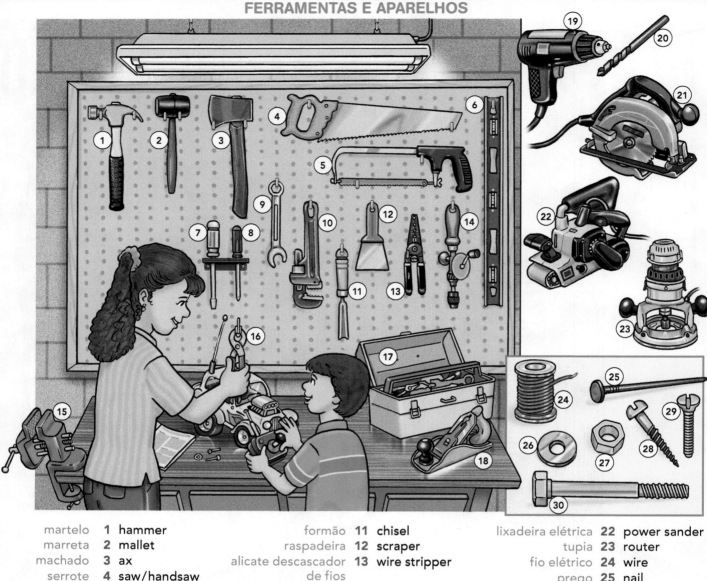

Português	#	English		Português	#	English		Português	#	English
martelo	1	hammer		formão	11	chisel		lixadeira elétrica	22	power sander
marreta	2	mallet		raspadeira	12	scraper		tupia	23	router
machado	3	ax		alicate descascador de fios	13	wire stripper		fio elétrico	24	wire
serrote	4	saw/handsaw		furadeira manual	14	hand drill		prego	25	nail
serra para metais	5	hacksaw		torno de bancada	15	vise		arruela	26	washer
nível	6	level		alicate	16	pliers		porca	27	nut
chave de fenda	7	screwdriver		caixa de ferramentas	17	toolbox		parafuso para madeira	28	wood screw
chave tipo phillips	8	Phillips screwdriver		plaina	18	plane		parafuso para metal/ parafuso de máquina	29	machine screw
chave de boca	9	wrench		furadeira elétrica	19	electric drill		parafuso soberbo	30	bolt
chave inglesa	10	monkey wrench/ pipe wrench		broca	20	(drill) bit				
				serra circular/ serra elétrica	21	circular saw/ power saw				

A. Can I borrow your **hammer**?
B. Sure.
A. Thanks.

* With 25–30, use: Could I borrow some _____ s?

[1–15, 17–24]
A. Where's the _____ ?
B. It's on/next to/near/over/under the _____ .

[16, 25–30]
A. Where are the _____ s?
B. They're on/next to/near/over/under the _____ .

Do you like to work with tools? What tools do you have in your home?

FERRAMENTAS E AÇÕES DE JARDINAGEM

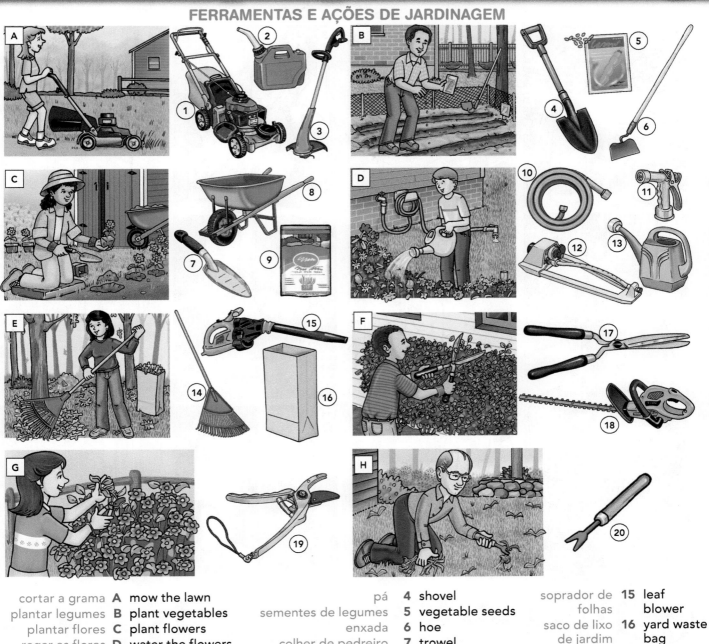

cortar a grama	**A**	mow the lawn
plantar legumes	**B**	plant vegetables
plantar flores	**C**	plant flowers
regar as flores	**D**	water the flowers
varrer as folhas	**E**	rake leaves
aparar a cerca viva	**F**	trim the hedge
aparar os arbustos	**G**	prune the bushes
erva daninha	**H**	weed

cortador de grama	**1**	lawnmower
galão de gasolina	**2**	gas can
aparador de grama	**3**	line trimmer

pá	**4**	shovel
sementes de legumes	**5**	vegetable seeds
enxada	**6**	hoe
colher de pedreiro	**7**	trowel
carrinho de mão/carriola	**8**	wheelbarrow
fertilizante	**9**	fertilizer
mangueira de jardim	**10**	(garden) hose
bico de mangueira	**11**	nozzle
aspersor	**12**	sprinkler
regador	**13**	watering can
vassoura para grama e jardim	**14**	rake

soprador de folhas	**15**	leaf blower
saco de lixo de jardim	**16**	yard waste bag
tesoura para cercas-vivas	**17**	(hedge) clippers
podador de cercas vivas	**18**	hedge trimmer
tesoura de podar	**19**	pruning shears
arrancador de ervas daninhas	**20**	weeder

[A–H]
A. Hi! Are you busy?
B. Yes. I'm **mow**ing **the lawn**.

[1–20]
A. What are you looking for?
B. The **lawnmower**.

[A–H]
A. What are you going to do tomorrow?
B. I'm going to _____.

[1–20]
A. Can I borrow your _____?
B. Sure.

Do you ever work with any of these tools? Which ones? What do you do with them?

LOCAIS PELA CIDADE I

padaria	**1**	**bakery**	revendedora de automóveis	**7**	**car dealership**
banco	**2**	**bank**	loja de cartões	**8**	**card store**
barbeiro	**3**	**barber shop**	creche	**9**	**child-care center / day-care center**
livraria	**4**	**book store**			
rodoviária	**5**	**bus station**	lavanderia / tinturaria	**10**	**cleaners / dry cleaners**
loja de doces e balas	**6**	**candy store**	clínica	**11**	**clinic**

loja de roupas	**12**	**clothing store**
lanchonete	**13**	**coffee shop**
loja de computadores	**14**	**computer store**
loja de conveniência	**15**	**convenience store**
loja de fotocópia	**16**	**copy center**

delicatessen/ loja de frios e laticínios	**17** delicatessen/ deli	ótica/óptica/ oculista	**23** eye-care center/ optician
loja de departamentos	**18** department store	lanchonete de fast-food	**24** fast-food restaurant
loja de desconto	**19** discount store	floricultura	**25** flower shop/florist
loja de donuts	**20** donut shop	loja de móveis	**26** furniture store
drogaria/farmácia	**21** drug store/pharmacy	posto de gasolina/ posto	**27** gas station/ service station
loja de eletrônicos	**22** electronics store	mercadinho/mercearia	**28** grocery store

A. Where are you going?
B. I'm going to the **bakery**.

A. Hi! How are you today?
B. Fine. Where are you going?
A. To the _____. How about you?
B. I'm going to the _____.

A. Oh, no! I can't find my wallet/purse!
B. Did you leave it at the _____?
A. Maybe I did.

Which of these places are in your neighborhood?
(In my neighborhood there's a/an ....)

cabeleireiro/ salão de beleza	**1**	**hair salon**
loja de ferragens	**2**	**hardware store**
academia de ginástica	**3**	**health club**
hospital	**4**	**hospital**
hotel	**5**	**hotel**
sorveteria	**6**	**ice cream shop**

joalheria	**7**	**jewelry store**
lavanderia automática	**8**	**laundromat**
biblioteca	**9**	**library**
loja de roupas para gestantes	**10**	**maternity shop**
motel	**11**	**motel**

cinema	**12**	**movie theater**
loja de música	**13**	**music store**
salão de manicure	**14**	**nail salon**
parque	**15**	**park**
loja de animais	**16**	**pet shop/ pet store**

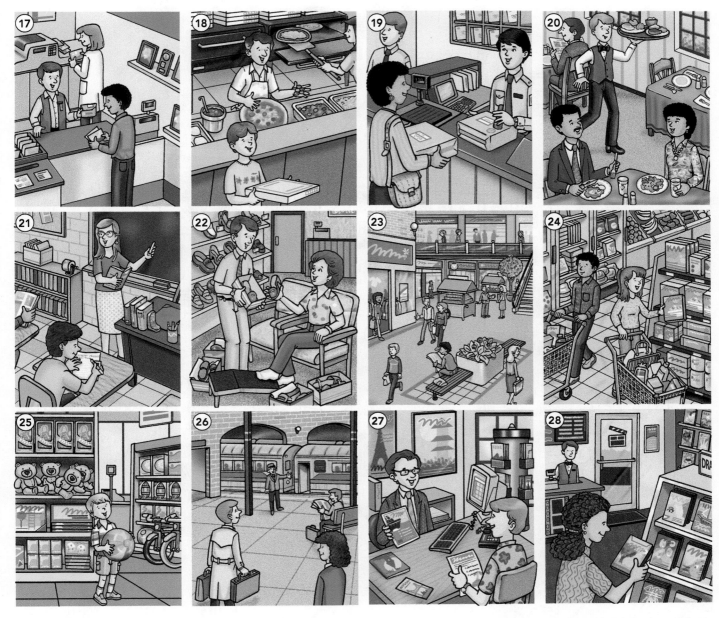

loja de fotografia	17	photo shop
pizzaria	18	pizza shop
correio	19	post office
restaurante	20	restaurant

escola	21	school
sapataria	22	shoe store
shopping center	23	(shopping) mall
supermercado	24	supermarket
loja de brinquedos	25	toy store

estação de trens/ estação ferroviária	26	train station
agência de viagens	27	travel agency
videolocadora	28	video store

A. Where's the **hair salon**?
B. It's right over there.

A. Is there a/an _____ nearby?
B. Yes. There's a/an _____ around the corner.
A. Thanks.

A. Excuse me. Where's the _____?
B. It's down the street, next to the _____.
A. Thank you.

Which of these places are in your neighborhood?
(In my neighborhood there's a/an ....)

A CIDADE

tribunal	1	courthouse
táxi	2	taxi/cab/taxicab
ponto de táxi	3	taxi stand
motorista de	4	taxi driver/
táxi		cab driver
hidrante	5	fire hydrant
lata de lixo	6	trash container
prefeitura	7	city hall
caixa de alarme	8	fire alarm box
de incêndio		

caixa de correio	9	mailbox
bueiro	10	sewer
delegacia de polícia	11	police station
cadeia	12	jail
calçada	13	sidewalk
rua	14	street
poste de	15	street light
iluminação pública/		
poste de luz		
estacionamento	16	parking lot

controladora de	17	meter maid
parquímetros		
parquímetro	18	parking meter
caminhão de lixo	19	garbage truck
metrô	20	subway
estação de metrô	21	subway station

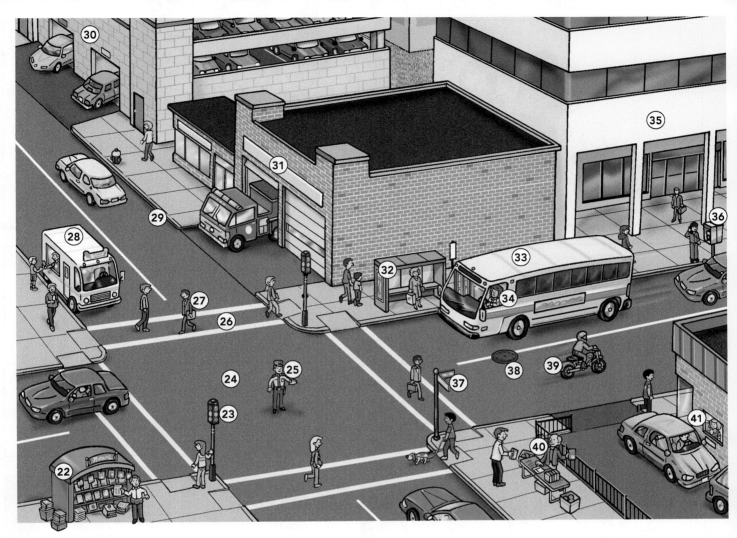

jornaleiro	**22**	newsstand
semáforo/	**23**	traffic light /
farol de trânsito/		traffic signal
sinal de trânsito		
cruzamento	**24**	intersection
policial	**25**	police officer
travessia de	**26**	crosswalk
pedestres/		
faixa de		
pedestres		

pedestre	**27**	pedestrian
caminhão de	**28**	ice cream truck
sorvete		
meio-fio/guia	**29**	curb
estacionamento	**30**	parking garage
quartel de	**31**	fire station
bombeiros		
ponto de ônibus	**32**	bus stop
ônibus	**33**	bus
motorista de	**34**	bus driver
ônibus		

edifício de	**35**	office building
escritórios		
telefone público	**36**	public
		telephone
placa de rua	**37**	street sign
tampão de inspeção	**38**	manhole
motocicleta	**39**	motorcycle
ambulante/camelô	**40**	street vendor
drive-thru	**41**	drive-through
		window

A. Where's the _____?
B. On/In/Next to/Between/Across from/ In front of/Behind/Under/Over the _____.

[An Election Speech]

If I am elected mayor, I'll take care of all the problems in our city. We need to do something about our _____s. We also need to do something about our _____s. And look at our _____s! We REALLY need to do something about THEM! We need a new mayor who can solve these problems. If I am elected mayor, we'll be proud of our _____s, _____s, and _____s again! Vote for me!

Go to an intersection in your city or town. What do you see? Make a list. Then tell about it.

PEOPLE AND PHYSICAL DESCRIPTIONS

DESCRIÇÕES DE PESSOAS E CARACTERÍSTICAS FÍSICAS

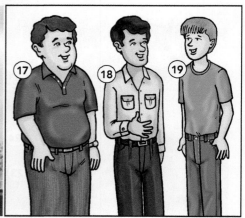

criança-crianças	**1**	**child-children**
bebê/nenê	**2**	**baby/infant**
criança pequena	**3**	**toddler**
menino	**4**	**boy**
menina	**5**	**girl**
adolescente	**6**	**teenager**
adulto	**7**	**adult**
homem–homens	**8**	**man–men**
mulher–mulheres	**9**	**woman–women**
idosa	**10**	**senior citizen/ elderly person**

idade	**age**	
jovem	**11**	**young**
pessoa de meia-idade	**12**	**middle-aged**
velho/idoso	**13**	**old/elderly**
altura	**height**	
alta	**14**	**tall**
altura média	**15**	**average height**
baixa	**16**	**short**
peso	**weight**	
pesado	**17**	**heavy**
peso médio/peso normal	**18**	**average weight**
magro	**19**	**thin/slim**
grávida	**20**	**pregnant**

deficiente físico	**21**	**physically challenged**
deficiente visual	**22**	**vision impaired**
deficiente auditivo	**23**	**hearing impaired**

Descrição de cabelos		Describing Hair
comprido	**24**	long
altura dos ombros	**25**	shoulder length
curto	**26**	short
liso	**27**	straight
ondulado	**28**	wavy
crespo	**29**	curly
preto	**30**	black

castanho	**31**	brown
louro	**32**	blond
ruivo	**33**	red
grisalho	**34**	gray
careca/calvo	**35**	bald
barba	**36**	beard
bigode	**37**	mustache

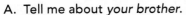

A. Tell me about *your brother.*
B. *He's a tall heavy boy* with *short curly brown* hair.

A. What does *your new boss* look like?
B. *She's average height,* and *she has long straight black* hair.

A. Can you describe *the person?*
B. *He's a tall thin middle-aged man.*
A. Anything else?
B. Yes. *He's bald,* and *he has a mustache.*

A. Can you describe *your grandmother?*
B. *She's a short thin elderly person* with *long wavy gray* hair.
A. Anything else?
B. Yes. *She's hearing impaired.*

Tell about yourself.

Tell about people in your family.

Tell about your favorite actor or actress or other famous person.

DESCRIÇÃO DE PESSOAS E COISAS

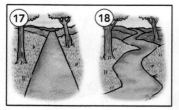

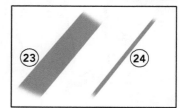

novo – velho	**1–2** new – old	escuro – claro	**25–26** dark – light
jovem – velho	**3–4** young – old	alta – baixa	**27–28** high – low
alta – baixa	**5–6** tall – short	frouxa/folgada – apertada	**29–30** loose – tight
comprido – curto	**7–8** long – short	bom – ruim/mau	**31–32** good – bad
grande – pequeno	**9–10** large/big – small/little	quente – gelado/frio	**33–34** hot – cold
rápido – lento/devagar	**11–12** fast – slow	arrumado – bagunçado	**35–36** neat – messy
encorpado/gordo – esguio/magro	**13–14** heavy/fat – thin/skinny	limpo – sujo	**37–38** clean – dirty
pesado – leve	**15–16** heavy – light	macio – duro	**39–40** soft – hard
reto – torto	**17–18** straight – crooked	fácil – difícil/rígido	**41–42** easy – difficult/hard
liso – crespo	**19–20** straight – curly	liso – áspero	**43–44** smooth – rough
larga – estreita	**21–22** wide – narrow	barulhento/alto – quieto	**45–46** noisy/loud – quiet
grosso – fino	**23–24** thick – thin	casada – solteira	**47–48** married – single

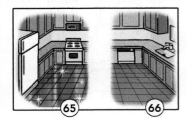

rico/abastado – pobre	**49–50**	rich/wealthy – poor
bonita/bela – feia	**51–52**	pretty/beautiful – ugly
bonito – feio	**53–54**	handsome – ugly
molhado – seco	**55–56**	wet – dry
aberta – fechada	**57–58**	open – closed
cheio – vazio	**59–60**	full – empty
caro – barato/em conta	**61–62**	expensive – cheap/inexpensive

sofisticado – simples	**63–64**	fancy – plain
brilhante – opaco	**65–66**	shiny – dull
afiada – cega/sem fio	**67–68**	sharp – dull
confortável – desconfortável	**69–70**	comfortable – uncomfortable
honesto – desonesto	**71–72**	honest – dishonest

[1–2]
A. Is your car **new**?
B. No. It's **old**.

1–2	Is your car _____?	25–26	Is the room _____?	49–50	Is your uncle _____?
3–4	Is he _____?	27–28	Is the bridge _____?	51–52	Is the witch _____?
5–6	Is your sister _____?	29–30	Are the pants _____?	53–54	Is the pirate _____?
7–8	Is his hair _____?	31–32	Are your neighbor's children _____?	55–56	Are the clothes _____?
9–10	Is their dog _____?	33–34	Is the water _____?	57–58	Is the door _____?
11–12	Is the train _____?	35–36	Is your desk _____?	59–60	Is the pitcher _____?
13–14	Is your friend _____?	37–38	Are the windows _____?	61–62	Is that restaurant _____?
15–16	Is the box _____?	39–40	Is the mattress _____?	63–64	Is the dress _____?
17–18	Is the road _____?	41–42	Is the homework _____?	65–66	Is your kitchen floor _____?
19–20	Is her hair _____?	43–44	Is your skin _____?	67–68	Is the knife _____?
21–22	Is the tie _____?	45–46	Is your neighbor _____?	69–70	Is the chair _____?
23–24	Is the line _____?	47–48	Is your sister _____?	71–72	Is he _____?

A. Tell me about your ....
B. He's/She's/It's/They're _____.

A. Do you have a/an _____ ....?
B. No. I have a/an _____ ....

Describe yourself.

Describe a person you know.

Describe some things in your home.

Describe some things in your community.

DESCRIÇÃO DE ESTADOS FÍSICOS E EMOÇÕES

cansada	**1**	tired	com fome/esfomeado	**7**	hungry	empolgada
sonolento	**2**	sleepy	com sede/sedenta	**8**	thirsty	desapontado
exausto	**3**	exhausted	satisfeito	**9**	full	muito chateada/
doente/enferma	**4**	sick / ill	feliz	**10**	happy	perturbada
com calor/calorento	**5**	hot	triste/infeliz	**11**	sad / unhappy	incomodado/
com frio	**6**	cold	infeliz/desconsolado	**12**	miserable	irritado

13	excited
14	disappointed
15	upset
16	annoyed

zangado/enraivecido	17	angry/mad
furioso	18	furious
indignada	19	disgusted
frustrado	20	frustrated
surpreso	21	surprised
chocada	22	shocked

solitário	23	lonely
com saudade de casa/da família	24	homesick
nervosos	25	nervous
preocupado	26	worried
assustada/com medo/amedrontada	27	scared/afraid

aborrecido	28	bored
orgulhoso	29	proud
embaraçado/com vergonha	30	embarrassed
invejoso	31	jealous
atrapalhado/confuso	32	confused

A. You look _____.
B. I am. I'm VERY _____.

A. Are you _____?
B. No. Why do you ask? Do I LOOK _____?
A. Yes. You do.

What makes you happy? sad? mad?

What do you do when you feel nervous? annoyed?

Do you ever feel embarrassed? When?

FRUTAS

maçã	**1** apple	figo	**12** fig	tangerina	**23** tangerine
pêssego	**2** peach	côco	**13** coconut	uvas	**24** grapes
pêra	**3** pear	abacate	**14** avocado	cerejas	**25** cherries
banana	**4** banana	melão cantalupo	**15** cantaloupe	ameixas secas	**26** prunes
banana-da-terra	**5** plantain	melão	**16** honeydew (melon)	tâmaras	**27** dates
ameixa	**6** plum	melancia	**17** watermelon	passas	**28** raisins
abricó	**7** apricot	abacaxi	**18** pineapple	nozes e castanhas	**29** nuts
nectarina	**8** nectarine	grapefruit	**19** grapefruit	framboesas	**30** raspberries
kiwi	**9** kiwi	limão siciliano	**20** lemon	mirtilos	**31** blueberries
papaia/mamão	**10** papaya	limão taiti	**21** lime	morangos	**32** strawberries
manga	**11** mango	laranja	**22** orange		

[1–23]
A. This **apple** is delicious! Where did you get it?
B. At *Sam's Supermarket*.

[24–32]
A. These **grapes** are delicious! Where did you get them?
B. At *Franny's Fruit Stand*.

A. I'm hungry. Do we have any fruit?
B. Yes. We have _____s* and _____s.*

A. Do we have any more _____s?†
B. No. I'll get some more when I go to the supermarket.

* With 15–19, use: We have _____ and _____.

† With 15–19, use: Do we have any more _____?

What are your favorite fruits?
Which fruits don't you like?

Which of these fruits grow where you live?

Name and describe other fruits you know.

LEGUMES

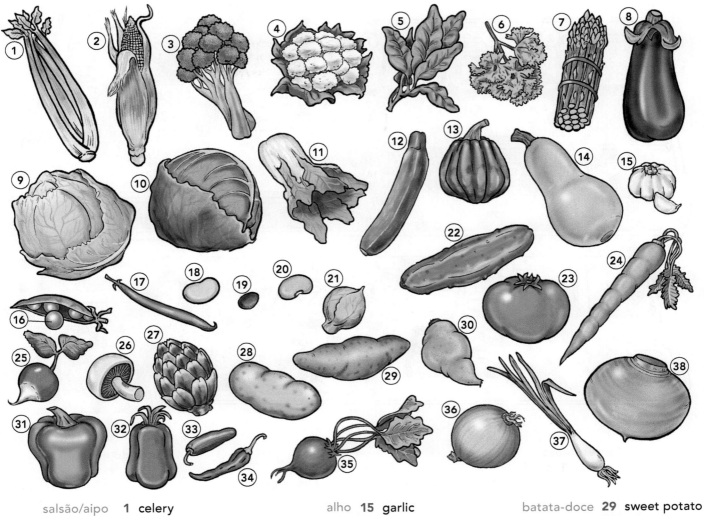

salsão/aipo	**1**	celery	alho	**15**	garlic
milho	**2**	corn	ervilha	**16**	pea
brócolis	**3**	broccoli	vagem/	**17**	string bean/
couve-flor	**4**	cauliflower	vagem macarrão		green bean
espinafre	**5**	spinach	feijão-de-lima	**18**	lima bean
salsinha	**6**	parsley	feijão preto	**19**	black bean
aspargos	**7**	asparagus	feijão-roxinho	**20**	kidney bean
berinjela	**8**	eggplant	couve-de-bruxelas	**21**	brussels sprout
alface	**9**	lettuce	pepino	**22**	cucumber
repolho	**10**	cabbage	tomate	**23**	tomato
acelga japonesa	**11**	bok choy	cenoura	**24**	carrot
abobrinha	**12**	zucchini	rabanete	**25**	radish
abóbora mogango	**13**	acorn squash	cogumelo	**26**	mushroom
abóbora butternut	**14**	butternut squash	alcachofra	**27**	artichoke
			batata	**28**	potato

batata-doce	**29**	sweet potato
batata-doce laranja	**30**	yam
pimentão verde/	**31**	green pepper/
pimentão		sweet pepper
pimentão vermelho	**32**	red pepper
pimenta jalapeno	**33**	jalapeño (pepper)
pimenta malagueta	**34**	chili pepper
beterraba	**35**	beet
cebola	**36**	onion
cebolinha	**37**	scallion/ green onion
nabo	**38**	turnip

A. What do we need from the supermarket?
B. We need **celery*** and **peas.**†

* 1–15   † 16–38

A. How do you like the
   ___[1–15]___ / ___[16–38]___ s?
B. It's/They're delicious.

A. *Bobby*? Finish your vegetables!
B. But you KNOW I hate
   ___[1–15]___ / ___[16–38]___ s!
A. I know. But it's/they're good for you!

Which vegetables do you like?
Which vegetables don't you like?

Which of these vegetables grow where you live?

Name and describe other vegetables you know.

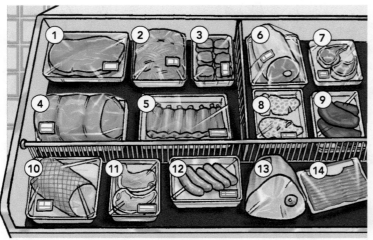

Carnes	**Meat**
bife	**1** steak
carne moída	**2** ground beef
carne para ensopado	**3** stewing beef
carne para rosbife	**4** roast beef
costela	**5** ribs
pernil de cordeiro	**6** leg of lamb
costeletas de cordeiro	**7** lamb chops
dobradinha	**8** tripe
fígado	**9** liver
porco	**10** pork
costeletas de porco	**11** pork chops
lingüiças	**12** sausages
presunto	**13** ham
bacon/ toucinho defumado	**14** bacon

Aves	**Poultry**
frango	**15** chicken
peito de frango	**16** chicken breasts
coxas de frango/ coxas	**17** chicken legs/ drumsticks
asas de frango	**18** chicken wings
sobrecoxas	**19** chicken thighs
peru	**20** turkey
pato	**21** duck

Frutos do mar	**Seafood**
PEIXE	**FISH**
salmão	**22** salmon
halibute/ linguado gigante	**23** halibut
hadoque	**24** haddock
peixe chato	**25** flounder
truta	**26** trout
catfish	**27** catfish
filé de linguado	**28** filet of sole
MARISCOS E CRUSTÁCEOS	**SHELLFISH**
camarão	**29** shrimp
vieiras	**30** scallops
caranguejo	**31** crabs
mariscos	**32** clams
mexilhões	**33** mussels
ostras	**34** oysters
lagosta	**35** lobster

A. I'm going to the supermarket. What do we need?
B. Please get some **steak**.
A. **Steak**? All right.

A. Excuse me. Where can I find _____?
B. Look in the _____ Section.
A. Thank you.

A. This/These _____ looks/ look very fresh!
B. Let's get some for dinner.

Do you eat meat, poultry, or seafood?
Which of these foods do you like?

Which of these foods are popular in your country

LATICÍNIOS, SUCOS E BEBIDAS

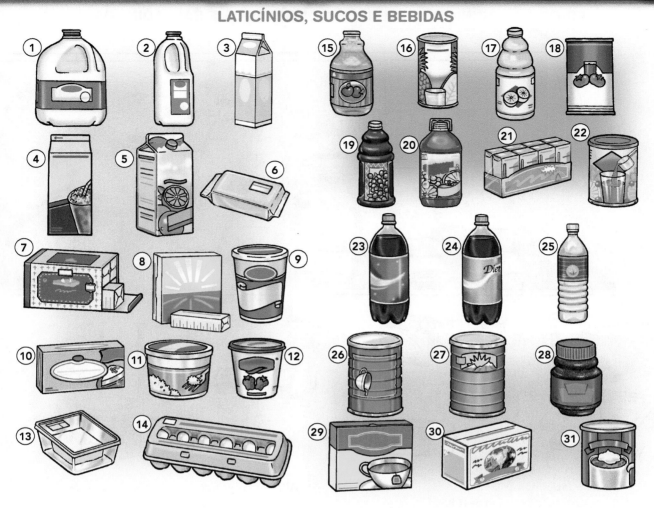

Laticínios		Dairy Products
leite	1	milk
leite com baixo teor de gordura	2	low-fat milk
leite desnatado	3	skim milk
leite achocolatado	4	chocolate milk
suco de laranja*	5	orange juice*
queijo	6	cheese
manteiga	7	butter
margarina	8	margarine
creme azedo	9	sour cream
cream cheese	10	cream cheese
queijo tipo cottage	11	cottage cheese
iogurte	12	yogurt

tofu*	13	tofu*
ovos	14	eggs

Sucos		Juices
suco de maçã	15	apple juice
suco de abacaxi	16	pineapple juice
suco de grapefruit	17	grapefruit juice
suco de tomate	18	tomato juice
suco de uva	19	grape juice
refresco de fruta	20	fruit punch
caixinhas de suco	21	juice paks
pó para refresco	22	powdered drink mix

Bebidas		Beverages
refrigerante	23	soda
refrigerante sem açúcar (light/diet)	24	diet soda
água mineral	25	bottled water

Café e chá		Coffee and Tea
café	26	coffee
café descafeinado	27	decaffeinated coffee/decaf
café solúvel	28	instant coffee
chá	29	tea
chá de ervas	30	herbal tea
mistura para chocolate quente	31	cocoa/hot chocolate mix

*Suco de laranja e tofu não são laticínios, mas costumam ser encontrados nesta seção.

A. I'm going to the supermarket to get some **milk**. Do we need anything else?
B. Yes. Please get some **apple juice**.

A. Excuse me. Where can I find _____?
B. Look in the _____ Section.
A. Thanks.

A. Look! _____ is/are on sale this week!
B. Let's get some!

Which of these foods do you like?

Which of these foods are good for you?

Which brands of these foods do you buy?

FRIOS E LATICÍNIOS, ALIMENTOS CONGELADOS E SALGADINHOS

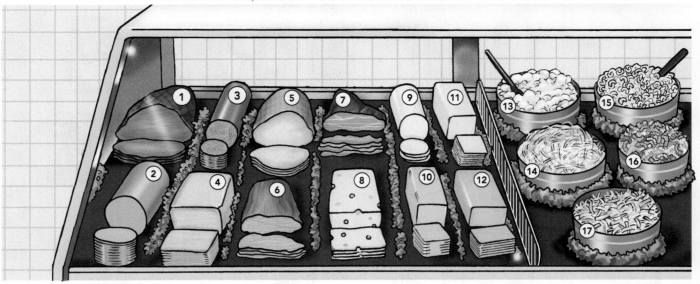

Frios e laticínios	Deli	
rosbife	1	roast beef
salsichão	2	bologna
salame	3	salami
presunto	4	ham
peru	5	turkey
carne em conserva	6	corned beef
pastrame	7	pastrami
queijo suíço	8	Swiss cheese
provolone	9	provolone
queijo processado	10	American cheese
muzarela	11	mozzarella
queijo tipo cheddar	12	cheddar cheese
salada de batata	13	potato salad
salada de repolho	14	cole slaw
salada de macarrão	15	macaroni salad
salada de macarrão	16	pasta salad
salada de frutos do mar	17	seafood salad

Alimentos congelados	Frozen Foods	
sorvete	18	ice cream
legumes congelados	19	frozen vegetables
pratos congelados	20	frozen dinners
limonada congelada	21	frozen lemonade
suco de laranja congelado	22	frozen orange juice

Salgadinhos	Snack Foods	
batatinhas fritas	23	potato chips
salgadinhos de tortilla	24	tortilla chips
pretzels	25	pretzels
nozes e castanhas	26	nuts
pipoca	27	popcorn

A. Should we get some **roast beef**?
B. Good idea. And let's get some **potato salad**.

[1–17]
A. May I help you?
B. Yes, please. I'd like some _____.

[1–27]
A. Excuse me. Where is/are _____?
B. It's/They're in the _____ Section.

What kinds of snack foods are popular in your country?

Are frozen foods common in your country? What kinds of foods are in the Frozen Foods Section?

PRODUTOS ALIMENTÍCIOS

Alimentos embalados	Packaged Goods
cereais	**1** cereal
biscoitos	**2** cookies
biscoitos salgados	**3** crackers
macarrão tortinho	**4** macaroni
talharim	**5** noodles
quebradinho	
espaguete	**6** spaghetti
arroz	**7** rice

Enlatados	Canned Goods
sopa	**8** soup
atum	**9** tuna (fish)
legumes enlatados	**10** (canned) vegetables
frutas enlatadas	**11** (canned) fruit

Geléias	Jams and Jellies
geléia	**12** jam
geléia	**13** jelly
pasta de amendoim/ manteiga de amendoim	**14** peanut butter

Condimentos	Condiments
ketchup	**15** ketchup
mostarda	**16** mustard
molho doce de pepinos em conserva	**17** relish
picles	**18** pickles
azeitonas	**19** olives
sal	**20** salt
pimenta-do-reino	**21** pepper
condimentos	**22** spices
molho de soja	**23** soy sauce
maionese	**24** mayonnaise
óleo (de cozinha)	**25** (cooking) oil
azeite	**26** olive oil

molho de tomate mexicano	**27** salsa
vinagre	**28** vinegar
molho para salada	**29** salad dressing

Produtos de padaria	Baked Goods
pão	**30** bread
pãezinhos	**31** rolls
english muffins	**32** English muffins
pão sírio	**33** pita bread
bolo	**34** cake

Produtos para pães e bolos	Baking Products
farinha	**35** flour
açúcar	**36** sugar
mistura para bolo	**37** cake mix

A. I got **cereal** and **soup**. What else is on the shopping list?
B. **Ketchup** and **bread**.

A. Excuse me. I'm looking for _____.
B. It's/They're next to the _____.

A. Pardon me. I'm looking for _____.
B. It's/They're between the _____ and the _____.

Which of these foods do you like?

Which brands of these foods do you buy?

PRODUTOS DOMÉSTICOS, PRODUTOS INFANTIS E ALIMENTOS PARA ANIMAIS

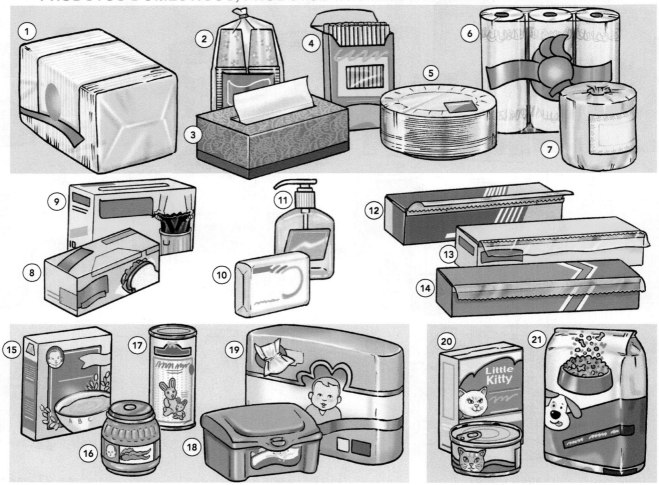

Artigos de papel	**Paper Products**
guardanapo	**1** napkins
copos de papel	**2** paper cups
lenços de papel	**3** tissues
canudos	**4** straws
pratos de papel	**5** paper plates
toalhas de papel	**6** paper towels
papel higiênico	**7** toilet paper

Produtos domésticos	**Household Items**
sacos plásticos para sanduíche	**8** sandwich bags
sacos para lixo	**9** trash bags
sabonete	**10** soap
sabonete líquido	**11** liquid soap
papel alumínio	**12** aluminum foil

filme plástico	**13** plastic wrap
papel de cera	**14** waxed paper

Produtos para bebês	**Baby Products**
cereal para bebês	**15** baby cereal
potinhos de alimento para bebês	**16** baby food
leite para bebês	**17** formula
lenços umedecidos	**18** wipes
fraldas descartáveis	**19** (disposable) diapers

Alimentos para animais	**Pet Food**
alimento para gatos	**20** cat food
alimento para cães	**21** dog food

A. Excuse me. Where can I find **napkins**?
B. **Napkins**? Look in Aisle *4*.

[7, 10–17, 20, 21]
A. We forgot to get _____!
B. I'll get it. Where is it?
A. It's in Aisle _____.

[1–6, 8, 9, 18, 19]
A. We forgot to get _____!
B. I'll get them. Where are they?
A. They're in Aisle _____.

What do you need from the supermarket?
Make a complete shopping list!

corredor	**1** aisle		empacotador	**14** bagger/packer
cliente	**2** shopper/customer		fila do caixa rápido	**15** express checkout (line)
cesta de compras	**3** shopping basket			
fila do caixa	**4** checkout line		tablóide	**16** tabloid (newspaper)
balcão do caixa	**5** checkout counter		revista	**17** magazine
esteira	**6** conveyor belt		scanner	**18** scanner
caixa registradora	**7** cash register		sacola plástica	**19** plastic bag
carrinho de compras	**8** shopping cart		frutas e verduras	**20** produce
chiclete/goma de mascar	**9** (chewing) gum		gerente	**21** manager
balas	**10** candy		balconista/funcionário	**22** clerk
cupons	**11** coupons		balança	**23** scale
caixa	**12** cashier		máquina para devolução de latas	**24** can-return machine
saco de papel	**13** paper bag		máquina para devolução de garrafas	**25** bottle-return machine

[1–8, 11–19, 21–25]
A. This is a gigantic supermarket!
B. It is! Look at all the **aisle**s!

[9, 10, 20]
A. This is a gigantic supermarket!
B. It is. Look at all the **produce**!

Where do you usually shop for food? Do you go to a supermarket, or do you go to a small grocery store? Describe the place where you shop.

Describe the differences between U.S. supermarkets and food stores in your country.

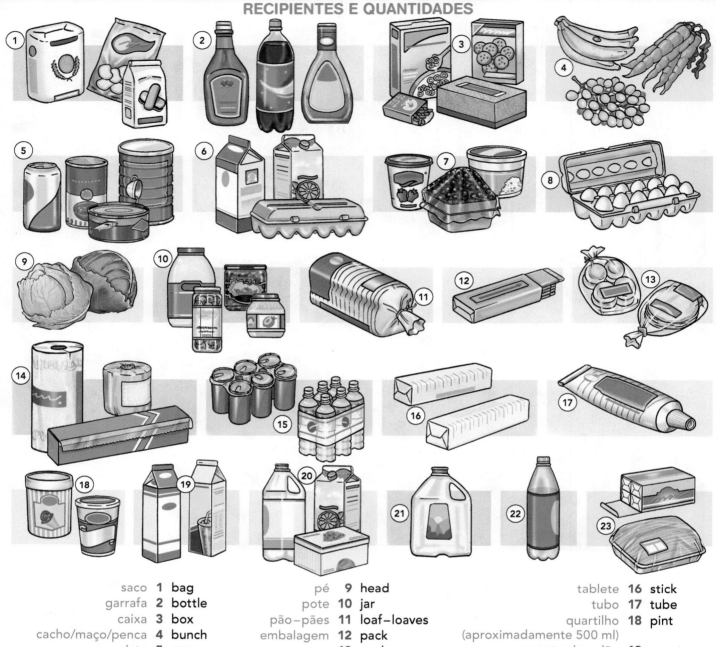

saco	1	bag
garrafa	2	bottle
caixa	3	box
cacho/maço/penca	4	bunch
lata	5	can
caixa	6	carton
embalagem/recipiente	7	container
dúzia*	8	dozen*

pé	9	head
pote	10	jar
pão–pães	11	loaf–loaves
embalagem	12	pack
pacote	13	package
rolo	14	roll
meia dúzia	15	six-pack

tablete	16	stick
tubo	17	tube
quartilho	18	pint
(aproximadamente 500 ml)		
quarto de galão	19	quart
meio galão	20	half-gallon
galão	21	gallon
litro	22	liter
libra	23	pound

* Diz-se "a dozen eggs" e NÃO "a dozen of eggs"

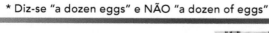

A. Please get a **bag** of *flour* when you go to the supermarket.
B. A **bag** of *flour*? Okay.

A. Please get two **bottles** of *ketchup* when you go to the supermarket.
B. Two **bottles** of *ketchup*? Okay.

[At home]
A. What did you get at the supermarket?
B. I got _____, _____, and _____.

[In a supermarket]
A. Is this the express checkout line?
B. Yes, it is. Do you have more than eight items?
A. No. I only have _____, _____, and _____.

Open your kitchen cabinets and refrigerator. Make a list of all the things you find.

What do you do with empty bottles, jars, and cans? Do you recycle them, reuse them, or throw them away?

UNIDADES DE MEDIDA

colher de chá **teaspoon**
tsp.

colher de sopa **tablespoon**
Tbsp.

onça fluida **1 (fluid) ounce**
1 fl. oz.

xícara **cup**
c.
8 fl. ozs.

quartilho **pint**
pt.
16 fl. ozs.

quarto de galão **quart**
qt.
32 fl. ozs.

galão **gallon**
gal.
128 fl. ozs.

A. How much water should I put in?
B. The recipe says to add one _____ of water.

A. This fruit punch is delicious! What's in it?
B. Two _____s of apple juice, three _____s
of orange juice, and a _____ of grape juice.

uma onça **an ounce**

oz.

um quarto **a quarter**
de libra **of a pound**
1/4 lb.
4 ozs.

meia **half a**
libra **pound**
1/2 lb.
8 ozs.

três quartos **three-quarters**
de libra **of a pound**
3/4 lb.
12 ozs.

libra **a pound**

lb.
16 ozs.

A. How much roast beef would you like?
B. I'd like _____, please.
A. Anything else?
B. Yes. Please give me _____ of Swiss cheese.

A. This chili tastes very good! What did you put
in it?
B. _____ of ground beef, _____ of beans, _____ of
tomatoes, and _____ of chili powder.

PREPARO DE ALIMENTOS E RECEITAS

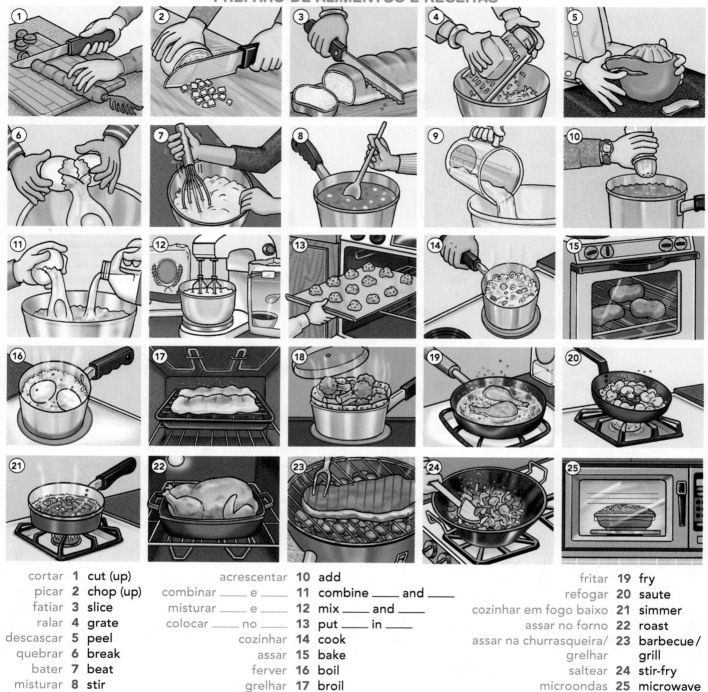

cortar **1** cut (up)	acrescentar **10** add	fritar **19** fry
picar **2** chop (up)	combinar ____ e ____ **11** combine ____ and ____	refogar **20** saute
fatiar **3** slice	misturar ____ e ____ **12** mix ____ and ____	cozinhar em fogo baixo **21** simmer
ralar **4** grate	colocar ____ no ____ **13** put ____ in ____	assar no forno **22** roast
descascar **5** peel	cozinhar **14** cook	assar na churrasqueira/ **23** barbecue/
quebrar **6** break	assar **15** bake	grelhar grill
bater **7** beat	ferver **16** boil	saltear **24** stir-fry
misturar **8** stir	grelhar **17** broil	microondas **25** microwave
derramar **9** pour	cozinhar no vapor **18** steam	

A. Can I help you?
B. Yes. Please **cut up** the vegetables.

[1–25]
A. What are you doing?
B. I'm _____ing the ....

[14–25]
A. How long should I _____ the ....?
B. _____ the .... for .... minutes/seconds.

What's your favorite recipe? Give instructions and use the units of measure on page 57. For example:

Mix a cup of flour and two tablespoons of sugar.
Add half a pound of butter.
Bake at 350° (degrees) for twenty minutes.

UTENSÍLIOS DE COZINHA

concha para sorvete	**1** ice cream scoop	cesta para cozimento a vapor	**14** steamer	forma para torta	**26** pie plate
abridor de latas	**2** can opener	faca	**15** knife	faquinha	**27** paring knife
abridor de garrafas	**3** bottle opener	espremedor de alho	**16** garlic press	tabuleiro	**28** cookie sheet
descascador de legumes	**4** (vegetable) peeler	ralador	**17** grater	cortador de biscoitos	**29** cookie cutter
batedeira de ovos	**5** (egg) beater	assadeira	**18** casserole dish	tigela	**30** (mixing) bowl
tampa	**6** lid/cover/top	assadeira de metal	**19** roasting pan	batedor de arame	**31** whisk
panela	**7** pot	grelha de assar	**20** roasting rack	medidor	**32** measuring cup
frigideira	**8** frying pan/skillet	faca para carne	**21** carving knife	colher medidora	**33** measuring spoon
banho-maria	**9** double boiler	panela	**22** saucepan	forma de bolo	**34** cake pan
wok	**10** wok	escorredor	**23** colander	colher de pau	**35** wooden spoon
concha	**11** ladle	minuteria	**24** kitchen timer		
peneira	**12** strainer	pau de macarrão	**25** rolling pin		
espátula/pão-duro	**13** spatula				

A. Could I possibly borrow your **ice cream scoop**?
B. Sure. I'll be happy to lend you my **ice cream scoop**.
A. Thanks.

A. What are you looking for?
B. I can't find the _____.
A. Look in that drawer/in that cabinet/ on the counter/next to the _____/ ....

[A Commercial]
Come to *Kitchen World*! We have everything you need for your kitchen, from _____s and _____s, to _____s and _____s. Are you looking for a new _____? Is it time to throw out your old _____? Come to *Kitchen World* today! We have everything you need!

What kitchen utensils and cookware do you have in your kitchen?

Which things do you use very often?

Which things do you rarely use?

FAST-FOOD

hambúrguer	**1**	**hamburger**
cheesebúrguer	**2**	**cheeseburger**
cachorro-quente	**3**	**hot dog**
sanduíche de peixe	**4**	**fish sandwich**
sanduíche de frango	**5**	**chicken sandwich**
frango frito	**6**	**fried chicken**
batatas fritas	**7**	**french fries**
nachos	**8**	**nachos**
taco	**9**	**taco**
burrito	**10**	**burrito**
fatia de pizza	**11**	**slice of pizza**
tigela de chili	**12**	**bowl of chili**
salada	**13**	**salad**
sorvete	**14**	**ice cream**

sorvete de iogurte	**15**	**frozen yogurt**
milkshake	**16**	**milkshake**
refrigerante	**17**	**soda**
tampas	**18**	**lids**
copos de papel	**19**	**paper cups**
canudos	**20**	**straws**
guardanapos	**21**	**napkins**
talheres de plástico	**22**	**plastic utensils**
ketchup	**23**	**ketchup**
mostarda	**24**	**mustard**
maionese	**25**	**mayonnaise**
molho doce de pepinos em conserva	**26**	**relish**
molho para salada	**27**	**salad dressing**

A. May I help you?
B. Yes. I'd like a/an ___[1–5, 9–17]___ / an order of ___[6–8]___ .

A. Excuse me. We're almost out of ___[18–27]___ .
B. I'll get some more from the supply room. Thanks for telling me.

Do you go to fast-food restaurants? Which ones? How often? What do you order?

Are there fast-food restaurants in your country? Are they popular? What foods do they have?

A LANCHONETE E SANDUÍCHES

donut	**1** donut
bolinho tipo muffin	**2** muffin
bagel	**3** bagel
pãozinho	**4** bun
pão doce	**5** danish/pastry
pão de minuto	**6** biscuit
croissant	**7** croissant
ovo	**8** eggs
panquecas	**9** pancakes
waffles	**10** waffles
torrada	**11** toast
bacon/toucinho defumado	**12** bacon
lingüiças	**13** sausages
batatas sauté estilo americano	**14** home fries
café	**15** coffee
café descafeinado	**16** decaf coffee
chá	**17** tea
chá gelado	**18** iced tea
limonada	**19** lemonade

chocolate quente	**20** hot chocolate
leite	**21** milk
sanduíche de atum	**22** tuna fish sandwich
sanduíche de ovos com maionese	**23** egg salad sandwich
sanduíche de salada de frango	**24** chicken salad sandwich
sanduíche de presunto e queijo	**25** ham and cheese sandwich
sanduíche de carne em conserva	**26** corned beef sandwich
sanduíche de bacon, alface e tomate	**27** BLT/bacon, lettuce, and tomato sandwich
sanduíche de rosbife	**28** roast beef sandwich
pão branco	**29** white bread
pão de trigo integral	**30** whole wheat bread
pão sírio	**31** pita bread
pão de centeio pumpernickel	**32** pumpernickel
pão de centeio	**33** rye bread
pãozinho	**34** a roll
pão para sanduíche tipo submarino	**35** a submarine roll

A. May I help you?
B. Yes. I'd like a ___[1–7]___/an order of ___[8–14]___, please.
A. Anything to drink?
B. Yes. I'll have a small/medium-size/large/extra-large ___[15–21]___.

A. I'd like a ___[22–28]___ on ___[29–35]___, please.
B. What do you want on it?
A. Lettuce/tomato/mayonnaise/mustard/. . .

Do you like these foods? Which ones? Where do you get them? How often do you have them?

levar os clientes à mesa	A	seat the customers
servir água	B	pour the water
anotar os pedidos	C	take the order
servir os pratos/servir a refeição	D	serve the meal
hostess/recepcionista de restaurante	1	hostess
host/recepcionista de restaurante	2	host
freguês/cliente	3	diner/patron/customer
mesa com bancos	4	booth
mesa	5	table
cadeirão/cadeira de criança	6	high chair
assento para criança	7	booster seat
menu/cardápio	8	menu
cesta de pães	9	bread basket
auxiliar de garçom	10	busperson
garçonete	11	waitress/server
garçom	12	waiter/server
bufê de saladas	13	salad bar
salão do restaurante	14	dining room
cozinha	15	kitchen
chef	16	chef

[4–9]
A. Would you like a **booth**?
B. Yes, please.

[10–12]
A. Hello. My name is *Julie*, and I'll be your **waitress** this evening.
B. Hello.

[1, 2, 13–16]
A. This restaurant has a wonderful **salad bar**.
B. I agree.

tirar a mesa	E clear the table
pagar a conta	F pay the check
deixar uma gorjeta	G leave a tip
arrumar a mesa	H set the table

copa	17 dishroom
lavador de pratos	18 dishwasher
bandeja	19 tray
carrinho de sobremesas	20 dessert cart
conta	21 check
gorjeta	22 tip
prato de salada	23 salad plate
prato de pão/prato de manteiga	24 bread-and-butter plate
prato de mesa	25 dinner plate

prato fundo	26 soup bowl
copo de água	27 water glass
copo de vinho	28 wine glass
xícara	29 cup
pires	30 saucer
guardanapo	31 napkin

talheres silverware
garfo de salada	32 salad fork
garfo de mesa	33 dinner fork
faca	34 knife
colher de chá	35 teaspoon
colher de sopa	36 soup spoon
faca de manteiga	37 butter knife

[A–H]
A. Please _____.
B. All right. I'll _____ right away.

[23–37]
A. Excuse me. Where does the _____ go?
B. It goes
to the left of the _____.
to the right of the _____.
on the _____.
between the _____ and the _____.

[1, 2, 10–12, 16, 18]
A. Do you have any job openings?
B. Yes. We're looking for a _____.

[23–37]
A. Excuse me. I dropped my _____.
B. That's okay. I'll get you another _____ from the kitchen.

Tell about a restaurant you know. Describe the place and the people. (Is the restaurant large or small? How many tables are there? How many people work there? Is there a salad bar? . . .)

A RESTAURANT MENU

UM CARDÁPIO DE RESTAURANTE

salada de frutas	**1**	fruit cup/ fruit cocktail	bolo de carne	**12**	meatloaf	bolo de chocolate	**24** chocolate cake
suco de tomate	**2**	tomato juice	rosbife	**13**	roast beef/prime rib	torta de maçã	**25** apple pie
coquetel de camarão	**3**	shrimp cocktail	frango assado	**14**	baked chicken	sorvete	**26** ice cream
asas de frango	**4**	chicken wings	peixe grelhado	**15**	broiled fish	gelatina	**27** jello
nachos	**5**	nachos	espaguete com almôndegas	**16**	spaghetti and meatballs	pudim	**28** pudding
aperitivo de cascas de batata	**6**	potato skins	costeleta de vitela	**17**	veal cutlet	sundae	**29** ice cream sundae
salada mista	**7**	tossed salad/ garden salad	batata assada	**18**	a baked potato		
salada grega	**8**	Greek salad	purê de batata	**19**	mashed potatoes		
salada de espinafre	**9**	spinach salad	batatas fritas	**20**	french fries		
prato de antepasto	**10**	antipasto (plate)	arroz	**21**	rice		
salada César	**11**	Caesar salad	macarrão	**22**	noodles		
			legumes mistos	**23**	mixed vegetables		

[Ordering dinner]
A. May I take your order?
B. Yes, please. For the appetizer, I'd like the ___[1–6]___.
A. And what kind of salad would you like?
B. I'll have the ___[7–11]___.
A. And for the main course?
B. I'd like the ___[12–17]___, please.
A. What side dish would you like with that?
B. Hmm. I think I'll have ___[18–23]___.

[Ordering dessert]
A. Would you care for some dessert?
B. Yes. I'll have ___[24–28]___/an ___[29]___.

Tell about the food at a restaurant you know. What's on the menu?

What are some typical foods on the menus of restaurants in your country?

CORES

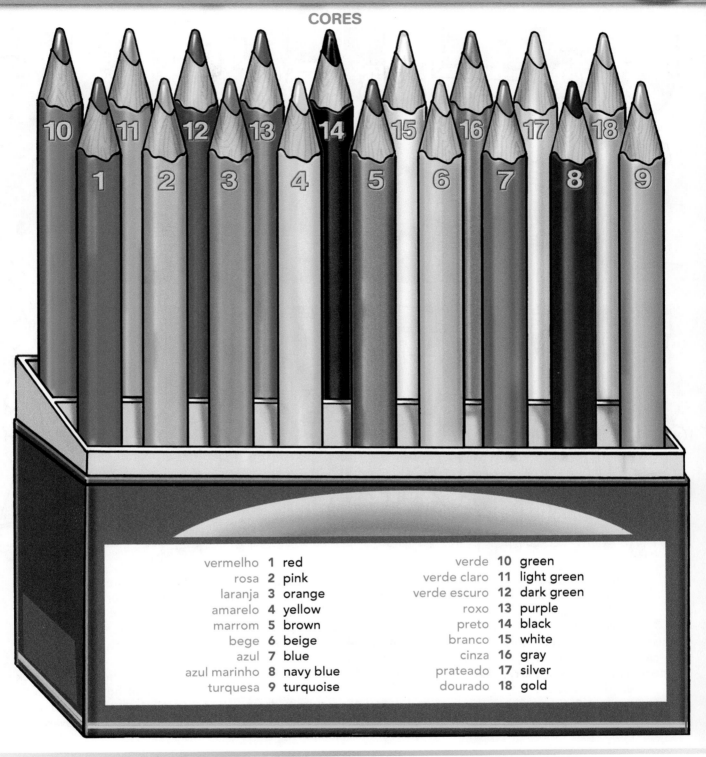

vermelho	1	red		verde	10	green
rosa	2	pink		verde claro	11	light green
laranja	3	orange		verde escuro	12	dark green
amarelo	4	yellow		roxo	13	purple
marrom	5	brown		preto	14	black
bege	6	beige		branco	15	white
azul	7	blue		cinza	16	gray
azul marinho	8	navy blue		prateado	17	silver
turquesa	9	turquoise		dourado	18	gold

A. What's your favorite color?
B. **Red.**

A. I like your _____ shirt.
   You look very good in _____.
B. Thank you. _____ is my
   favorite color.

A. My TV is broken.
B. What's the matter with it?
A. People's faces are _____,
   the sky is _____, and the
   grass is _____!

Do you know the flags of different countries?
What are the colors of flags you know?

What color makes you happy? What color
makes you sad? Why?

ROUPAS

blusa	**1** blouse	paletó/	**11** sport coat/	colete	**20** vest
saia	**2** skirt	jaqueta	sport jacket/jacket	vestido jumper	**21** jumper
camisa	**3** shirt	tailleur	**12** suit	blazer/japona	**22** blazer
calça	**4** pants/slacks	terno	**13** three-piece suit	túnica	**23** tunic
camisa esporte	**5** sport shirt	gravata	**14** tie/necktie	legging	**24** leggings
calça jeans	**6** jeans	uniforme	**15** uniform	macacão	**25** overalls
camisa pólo	**7** knit shirt/jersey	camiseta	**16** T-shirt	gola olímpica	**26** turtleneck
vestido	**8** dress	short/bermuda	**17** shorts	smoking	**27** tuxedo
suéter/malha	**9** sweater	vestido de	**18** maternity dress	gravata borboleta	**28** bow tie
jaqueta/blazer	**10** jacket	gestante		longo	**29** (evening) gown
		macacão	**19** jumpsuit		

A. I think I'll wear my new **blouse** today.
B. Good idea!

A. I really like your _____.
B. Thank you.
A. Where did you get it/them?
B. At ....

A. Oh, no! I just ripped
my _____!
B. What a shame!

What clothing items in this lesson do you wear?

What color clothing do you like to wear?

What do you wear at work or at school? at parties? at weddings?

CASACOS E AGASALHOS

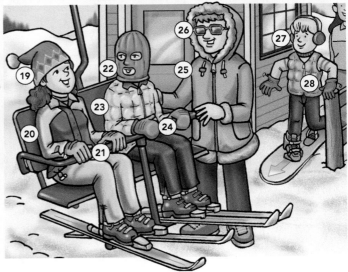

casaco	**1**	coat	boné	**10**	baseball cap	jaqueta de esqui	**20** ski jacket
sobretudo	**2**	overcoat	blusão	**11**	windbreaker	luvas	**21** gloves
chapéu	**3**	hat	capa de chuva	**12**	raincoat	máscara de esqui	**22** ski mask
jaqueta/casaco	**4**	jacket	chapéu de chuva	**13**	rain hat	jaqueta acolchoada	**23** down jacket
cachecol	**5**	scarf/muffler	casaco trench coat	**14**	trench coat	luvas sem dedos	**24** mittens
casaco de malha	**6**	sweater jacket	guarda-chuva	**15**	umbrella	parka	**25** parka
collant	**7**	tights	poncho	**16**	poncho	óculos escuros/	**26** sunglasses
boné	**8**	cap	jaqueta de chuva	**17**	rain jacket	óculos de sol	
jaqueta de couro/	**9**	leather jacket	botas de chuva	**18**	rain boots	protetores de orelha	**27** ear muffs
casaco de couro			gorro	**19**	ski hat	colete acolchoado	**28** down vest

A. What's the weather like today?
B. It's cool/cold/raining/snowing.
A. I think I'll wear my _____.

[1–6, 8–17, 19, 20, 22, 23, 25, 28]
A. May I help you?
B. Yes, please. I'm looking for a/an _____.

[7, 18, 21, 24, 26, 27]
A. May I help you?
B. Yes, please. I'm looking for _____.

What do you wear outside when the weather is cool?/when it's raining?/when it's very cold?

ROUPAS DE DORMIR E ROUPAS ÍNTIMAS

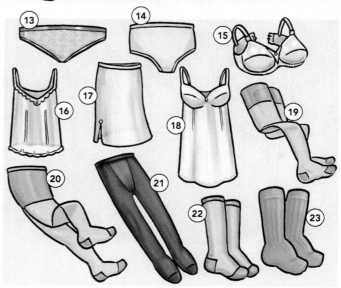

pijama	**1**	pajamas
camisola longa	**2**	nightgown
camisola curta	**3**	nightshirt
roupão/robe	**4**	bathrobe/robe
pantufas/chinelos	**5**	slippers
macacão de dormir	**6**	blanket sleeper
camiseta	**7**	undershirt/T-shirt
sunga/cueca	**8**	(jockey) shorts/underpants/briefs

cueca samba-canção	**9**	boxer shorts/boxers
suporte atlético	**10**	athletic supporter/jockstrap
ceroulas/minhocão	**11**	long underwear/long johns
meias	**12**	socks
biquíni	**13**	(bikini) panties
calcinha	**14**	briefs/underpants

sutiã	**15**	bra
corpete	**16**	camisole
anágua	**17**	half slip
combinação	**18**	(full) slip
meias	**19**	stockings
meia-calça	**20**	pantyhose
collant	**21**	tights
meia três-quartos	**22**	knee-highs
meia soquete	**23**	knee socks

A. I can't find my new _____.
B. Did you look in the bureau/dresser/closet?
A. Yes, I did.
B. Then it's/they're probably in the wash.

What sleepwear items do you wear? What sleepwear items do people in your family wear?

camiseta regata	**1**	tank top	calção de banho	**11**	swimming trunks/ swimsuit/ bathing suit	basquete/ tênis de basquete	**20** high-tops/ high-top sneakers
short de corrida	**2**	running shorts	calção			sandálias	**21** sandals
testeira	**3**	sweatband	malha de ginástica	**12**	leotard	chineloś/	**22** thongs/ flip-flops
jogging/ agasalho esportivo/ conjunto jogging	**4**	jogging suit/ running suit/ warm-up suit	sapatos	**13**	shoes	sandálias de dedo/ sandálias estilo havaianas	
camiseta	**5**	T-shirt	sapatos de salto alto/escarpim	**14**	(high) heels	botas	**23** boots
bermuda de lycra/ bermuda de ciclismo	**6**	lycra shorts/ bike shorts	sapatos de salto baixo	**15**	pumps	botas de trabalho	**24** work boots
blusão de moletom	**7**	sweatshirt	mocassim	**16**	loafers	botas de caminhada	**25** hiking boots
calça de moleton	**8**	sweatpants	tênis	**17**	sneakers/ athletic shoes	botas de caubói	**26** cowboy boots
saída de praia	**9**	cover-up	tênis	**18**	tennis shoes	mocassim	**27** moccasins
maiô/ calção de banho	**10**	swimsuit/ bathing suit	tênis de corrida	**19**	running shoes		

[1–12]
A. Excuse me. I found this/these _____ in the dryer. Is it/Are they yours?
B. Yes. It's/They're mine. Thank you.

[13–27]
A. Are those new _____?
B. Yes, they are.
A. They're very nice.
B. Thanks.

Do you exercise? What do you do? What kind of clothing do you wear when you exercise?

What kind of shoes do you wear when you go to work or to school? when you exercise? when you relax at home? when you go out with friends or family members?

JÓIAS E ACESSÓRIOS

anel	**1** ring	relógio/relógio de pulso	**15** watch/wrist watch
anel de noivado	**2** engagement ring	lenço	**16** handkerchief
anel de casamento/aliança	**3** wedding ring/wedding band	chaveiro	**17** key ring/key chain
brincos	**4** earrings	porta-moedas	**18** change purse
colar	**5** necklace	carteira	**19** wallet
colar de pérolas	**6** pearl necklace/pearls/ string of pearls	cinto	**20** belt
		bolsa	**21** purse/handbag/pocketbook
corrente	**7** chain	bolsa tiracolo	**22** shoulder bag
colar de contas	**8** beads	sacola	**23** tote bag
broche	**9** pin/brooch	pasta com alça tiracolo	**24** book bag
medalhão	**10** locket	mochila necessaire/bolsinha	**25** backpack
pulseira/bracelete	**11** bracelet	bolsa para maquillaje/	**26** makeup bag
fivela	**12** barrette	necessaire de maquiagem	
abotoaduras	**13** cuff links	pasta para documentos/	**27** briefcase
suspensórios	**14** suspenders	maleta para documentos	

A. Oh, no! I think I lost my **ring**!
B. I'll help you look for it.

A. Oh, no! I think I lost my **earrings**!
B. I'll help you look for them.

[In a store]
A. Excuse me. Is this/Are these
   _____ on sale this week?
B. Yes. It's/They're half price.

[On the street]
A. Help! Police! Stop that man/woman!
B. What happened?!
A. He/She just stole my _____
   and my _____!

Do you like to wear jewelry? What jewelry do you have?

In your country, what do men, women, and children use to carry their things?

DESCRIÇÃO DE ROUPAS

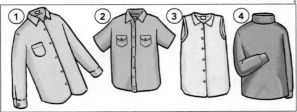
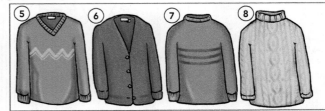

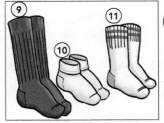

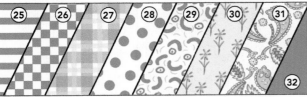

Tipos de roupas		Types of Clothing
camisa de manga comprida	1	long-sleeved shirt
camisa de manga curta	2	short-sleeved shirt
camisa sem manga	3	sleeveless shirt
camisa com gola olímpica/	4	turtleneck (shirt)
camisa com gola rulê		
malha com gola em V	5	V-neck sweater
casaco de malha com botões	6	cardigan sweater
malha com decote redondo	7	crewneck sweater
malha com gola olímpica/	8	turtleneck sweater
malha com gola rulê		
meias três-quartos	9	knee-high socks
meias curtas	10	ankle socks
meias soquete	11	crew socks
brincos de orelha furada	12	pierced earrings
brincos de pressão	13	clip-on earrings

Tipos de material		Types of Material
calças de veludo cotelê	14	corduroy pants
botas de couro	15	leather boots
meias de náilon	16	nylon stockings
camiseta de algodão	17	cotton T-shirt
jaqueta jeans	18	denim jacket

camisa de flanela	19	flannel shirt
blusa de poliéster	20	polyester blouse
vestido de linho	21	linen dress
lenço de seda/	22	silk scarf
echarpe de seda		
malha de lã	23	wool sweater
chapéu de palha	24	straw hat

Padrões		Patterns
listado	25	striped
quadriculado	26	checked
xadrez	27	plaid
bolinhas	28	polka-dotted
estampado	29	patterned/print
florido/floral	30	flowered/floral
desenho de cachemira	31	paisley
azul liso	32	solid blue

Tamanhos		Sizes
extrapequeno	33	extra-small
pequeno	34	small
médio	35	medium
grande	36	large
extragrande	37	extra-large

[1–24]
A. May I help you?
B. Yes, please. I'm looking for a *shirt*.*
A. What kind?
B. I'm looking for a *long-sleeved shirt*.

* With 9–16: I'm looking for _____ .

[25–32]
A. How do you like this _____ tie/shirt/skirt?
B. Actually, I prefer that _____ one.

[33–37]
A. What size are you looking for?
B. _____ .

Describe your favorite clothing items. For each item, tell about the color, the type of material, the size, and the pattern.

PROBLEMAS E REFORMAS DE ROUPAS

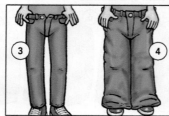
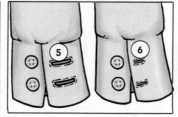
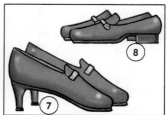

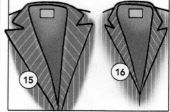
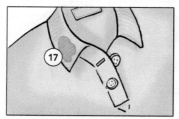

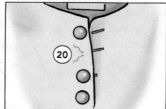
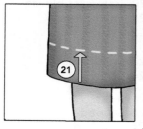

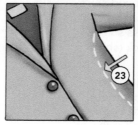

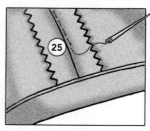

comprido – curto	**1–2**	long – short
estreito – frouxo/folgado	**3–4**	tight – loose/baggy
largo/grande – pequeno/estreito	**5–6**	large/big – small
alto – baixo	**7–8**	high – low
sofisticado – simples	**9–10**	fancy – plain
pesado – leve	**11–12**	heavy – light
escuro – claro	**13–14**	dark – light
largo – estreito	**15–16**	wide – narrow

colarinho manchado	**17**	stained *collar*
bolso rasgado	**18**	ripped/torn *pocket*
zíper quebrado	**19**	broken *zipper*
botão faltando	**20**	missing *button*
encurtar a *saia*	**21**	shorten the *skirt*
encompridar as *mangas*	**22**	lengthen the *sleeves*
estreitar a *jaqueta*	**23**	take in the *jacket*
alargar as *calças*	**24**	let out the *pants*
consertar/refazer a *costura*	**25**	fix/repair the *seam*

[1–2]
A. Are the sleeves too **long**?
B. No. They're too **short**.

1–2 Are the sleeves too _____?
3–4 Are the pants too _____?
5–6 Are the buttonholes too _____?
7–8 Are the heels too _____?

9–10 Are the buttons too _____?
11–12 Is the coat too _____?
13–14 Is the color too _____?
15–16 Are the lapels too _____?

[17–20]
A. What's the matter with it?
B. It has a **stained** *collar*.

[21–25]
A. Please **shorten** the *skirt*.
B. **Shorten** the *skirt*? Okay.

Tell about the differences between clothing people wear now and clothing people wore a long time ago.

LAVANDERIA

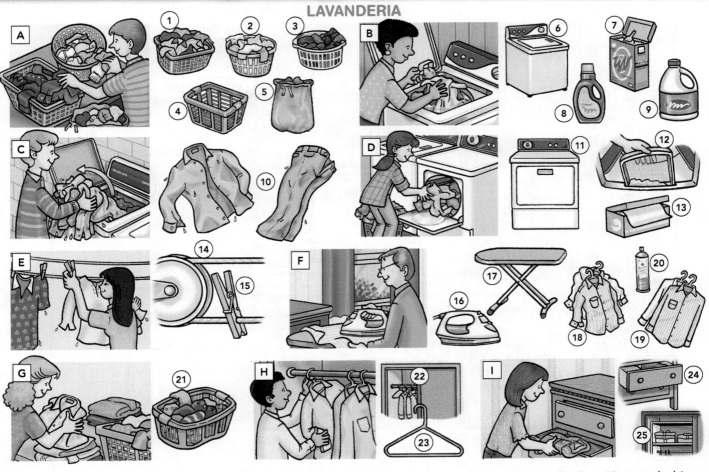

separar as roupas para lavar	**A**	sort the laundry	roupas molhadas	**10** wet clothing
colocar na lavadora/máquina de lavar roupa	**B**	load the washer	secadora/secadora de roupas	**11** dryer
tirar da lavadora/máquina de lavar roupa	**C**	unload the washer	filtro	**12** lint trap
colocar na secadora	**D**	load the dryer	lenços antiestática	**13** static cling remover
pendurar as roupas no varal	**E**	hang clothes on the clothesline	varal	**14** clothesline
ferro de passar	**F**	iron	pregador	**15** clothespin
dobrar as roupas	**G**	fold the laundry	ferro de passar	**16** iron
pendurar as roupas	**H**	hang up clothing	mesa de passar	**17** ironing board
guardar	**I**	put things away	roupas amassadas	**18** wrinkled clothing
lavanderia	**1**	laundry	roupas passadas	**19** ironed clothing
roupas claras	**2**	light clothing	pulverizador de goma	**20** spray starch
roupas escuras	**3**	dark clothing	roupas limpas	**21** clean clothing
cesto de roupas	**4**	laundry basket	armário	**22** closet
sacola de roupas	**5**	laundry bag	cabide	**23** hanger
lavadora/máquina de lavar roupa	**6**	washer/washing machine	gaveta	**24** drawer
sabão em pó	**7**	laundry detergent	prateleira-prateleiras	**25** shelf-shelves
amaciante	**8**	fabric softener		
alvejante	**9**	bleach		

[A–I]
A. What are you doing?
B. I'm _____ing.

[4–6, 11, 14–17, 23]
A. Excuse me. Do you sell _____s?
B. Yes. They're at the back of the store.
A. Thank you.

[7–9, 13, 20]
A. Excuse me. Do you sell _____?
B. Yes. It's at the back of the store.
A. Thank you.

Who does the laundry in your home? What things does this person use?

A LOJA DE DEPARTAMENTOS

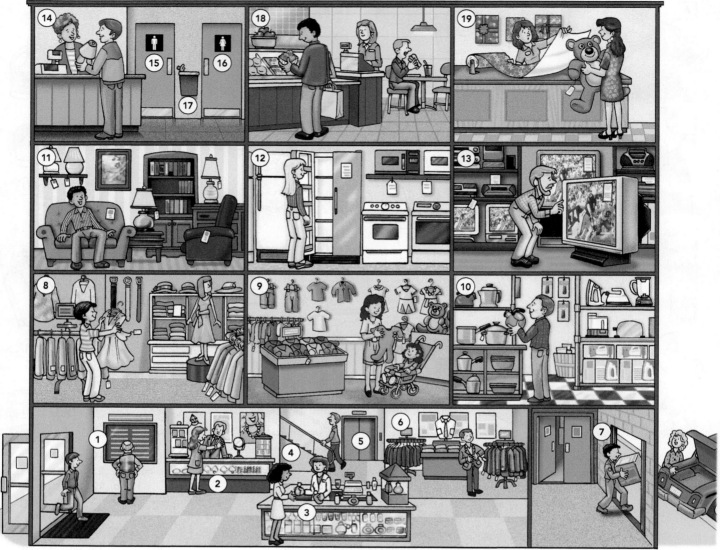

diretório da loja	**1**	**(store) directory**	Seção de utensílios domésticos	**10** Housewares Department
Balcão de jóias	**2**	**Jewelry Counter**	Seção de móveis/	**11** Furniture Department/
Balcão de perfumaria	**3**	**Perfume Counter**	Seção de mobiliário	Home Furnishings Department
escada rolante	**4**	**escalator**	Seção de aparelhos domésticos	**12** Household Appliances Department
elevador	**5**	**elevator**	Seção de aparelhos eletrônicos	**13** Electronics Department
Seção de roupas masculinas	**6**	**Men's Clothing Department**	Balcão de atendimento a clientes/ Balcão de serviço a clientes	**14** Customer Assistance Counter/ Customer Service Counter
Área de carregamento dos clientes	**7**	**customer pickup area**	banheiro masculino	**15** men's room
Seção de roupas femininas	**8**	**Women's Clothing Department**	banheiro feminino	**16** ladies' room
			bebedouro	**17** water fountain
Seção de roupas infantis	**9**	**Children's Clothing Department**	lanchonete	**18** snack bar
			Balcão de embalagens de presente	**19** Gift Wrap Counter

A. Excuse me. Where's the **store directory**?
B. It's over there, next to the **Jewelry Counter**.
A. Thanks.
B. You're welcome.

A. Excuse me. Do you sell *ties**?
B. Yes. You can find *ties** in the ___[6, 8–13]___ /at the ___[2, 3]___
on the first/second/third/fourth floor.
A. Thank you.

**ties/bracelets/dresses/toasters/. . .*

Describe a department store you know. Tell what is on each floor.

COMPRAS

comprar	**A**	buy
devolver	**B**	return
trocar	**C**	exchange
experimentar	**D**	try on
pagar	**E**	pay for
obter	**F**	get some
informações		information
sobre		about

cartaz de desconto	**1**	sale sign
etiqueta	**2**	label
etiqueta de preço	**3**	price tag
recibo	**4**	receipt
desconto	**5**	discount
tamanho	**6**	size
tecido	**7**	material

instruções de lavagem	**8**	care instructions
preço normal	**9**	regular price
preço de liquidação	**10**	sale price
preço	**11**	price
imposto de venda	**12**	sales tax
preço total	**13**	total price

A. May I help you?
B. Yes, please. I want to ___[A–F]___ this item.
A. Certainly. I'll be glad to help you.

A. { What's the ___[5–7, 9–13]___ ?
{ What are the ___[8]___ ?
B. _____.
A. Are you sure?
B. Yes. Look at the ___[1–4]___ !

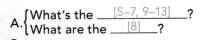

Which stores in your area have sales? How often?

Tell about something you bought on sale.

EQUIPAMENTO DE VÍDEO E ÁUDIO

TV/televisão	**1**	**TV/television**	sistema estéreo/	**19**	**stereo system/**
TV de plasma	**2**	**plasma TV**	sistema de som		**sound system**
TV de LCD	**3**	**LCD TV**	disco	**20**	**record**
TV de projeção	**4**	**projection TV**	toca-discos	**21**	**turntable**
TV portátil	**5**	**portable TV**	CD	**22**	**CD/compact disc**
controle remoto	**6**	**remote (control)**	aparelho de CD	**23**	**CD player**
DVD	**7**	**DVD**	sintonizador	**24**	**tuner**
aparelho de DVD	**8**	**DVD player**	fita de áudio/fita cassete de áudio	**25**	**(audio)tape/(audio)cassette**
vídeo/videocassete/	**9**	**video/videocassette/**	toca-fitas	**26**	**tape deck/cassette deck**
fita de vídeo		**videotape**	alto-falantes	**27**	**speakers**
VCR/	**10**	**VCR/videocassette**	aparelho de som portátil/	**28**	**portable stereo system/**
gravador de videocassete		**recorder**	som portátil		**boombox**
filmadora/	**11**	**camcorder/**	toca-CD portátil/	**29**	**portable/personal**
câmara de vídeo		**video camera**	CD player portátil		**CD player**
bateria	**12**	**battery pack**	toca-fitas portátil	**30**	**portable/personal cassette**
carregador de bateria	**13**	**battery charger**			**player**
rádio	**14**	**radio**	fones de ouvido	**31**	**headphones**
rádio relógio	**15**	**clock radio**	aparelho de MP3	**32**	**portable/personal digital**
rádio de ondas curtas	**16**	**shortwave radio**			**audio player**
gravador/	**17**	**tape recorder/**	sistema de videogame	**33**	**video game system**
gravador de videocassete		**cassette recorder**	videogame	**34**	**video game**
microfone	**18**	**microphone**	videogame portátil	**35**	**hand-held video game**

A. May I help you?
B. Yes, please. I'm looking for a **TV**.

* With 27 & 31, use: I'm looking for _____

A. I like your new _____.
Where did you get it/them?

B. At .....(name of store)....

A. Which company makes the best
_____?

B. In my opinion, the best _____
is/are made by ....

What video and audio equipment do you
have or want?

In your opinion, which brands of video and
audio equipment are the best?

TELEFONES E CÂMERAS

telefone	1	telephone/phone
telefone sem fio	2	cordless phone
celular/telefone celular	3	cell phone/cellular phone
bateria	4	battery
carregador de bateria	5	battery charger
secretária eletrônica	6	answering machine
pager	7	pager
PDA/ organizador pessoal	8	PDA/electronic personal organizer
equipamento de fax	9	fax machine
calculadora de bolso	10	(pocket) calculator
calculadora	11	adding machine
regulador de tensão	12	voltage regulator

carregador	13	adapter
câmera de 35 milímetros	14	(35 millimeter) camera
lente	15	lens
filme	16	film
lente zoom	17	zoom lens
câmera digital	18	digital camera
disco de memória	19	memory disk
tripé	20	tripod
flash	21	flash (attachment)
estojo da câmera	22	camera case
projetor de slides	23	slide projector
tela	24	(movie) screen

A. Can I help you?
B. Yes. I want to buy a **telephone.***

* With 16, use: I want to buy _____.

A. Excuse me. Do you sell _____s?*
B. Yes. We have a large selection of _____s.

* With 16, use the singular.

A. Which _____ is the best?
B. This one here. It's made by
    ....(company).....

What kind of telephone do you use?

Do you have a camera? What kind is it?
What do you take pictures of?

Does anyone you know have an answering machine?
When you call, what message do you hear?

COMPUTADORES

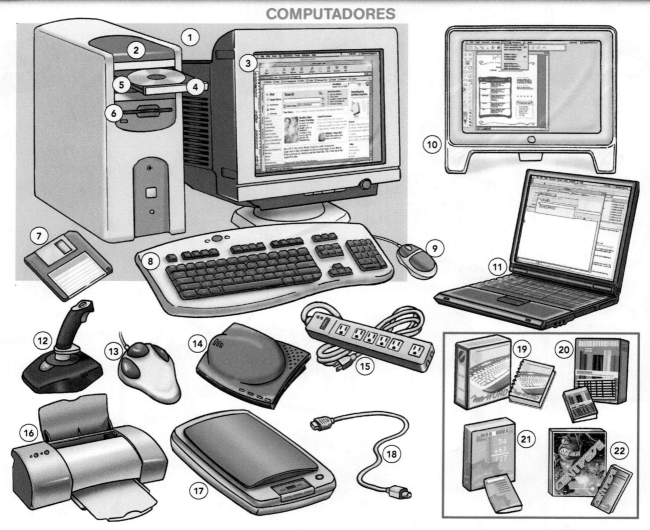

Equipamentos de computador/hardware	Computer Hardware
computador de mesa	1 (desktop) computer
CPU/unidade central de processamento	2 CPU/central processing unit
monitor/tela	3 monitor/screen
unidade de CD-ROM	4 CD-ROM drive
CD-ROM	5 CD-ROM
unidade de disco	6 disk drive
disquete	7 (floppy) disk
teclado	8 keyboard
mouse	9 mouse
tela plana/ tela de LCD	10 flat panel screen/ LCD screen
computador notebook	11 notebook computer

joystick	12 joystick
track ball	13 track ball
modem	14 modem
protetor contra surtos	15 surge protector
impressora	16 printer
scanner	17 scanner
cabo	18 cable

software de computador	Computer Software
programa de processador de texto	19 word-processing program
programa de planilha	20 spreadsheet program
software educativo	21 educational software program
jogo de computador	22 computer game

A. Can you recommend a good **computer**?
B. Yes. This **computer** here is excellent.

A. Is that a new _____?
B. Yes.
A. Where did you get it?
B. At ....*(name of store)*....

A. May I help you?
B. Yes, please. Do you sell _____s?
A. Yes. We carry a complete line of _____s.

Do you use a computer? When?

In your opinion, how have computers changed the world?

A LOJA DE BRINQUEDOS

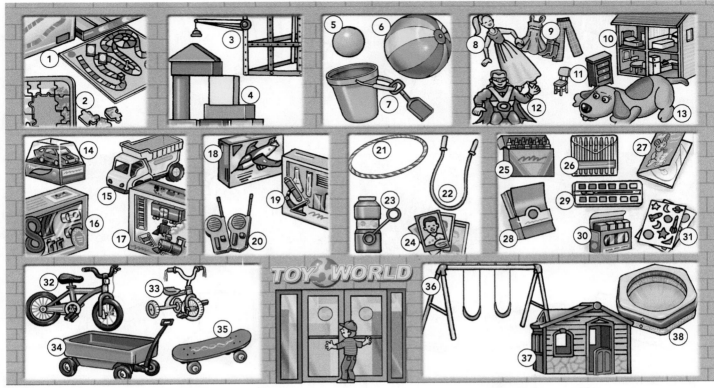

jogo de tabuleiro	1	board game
quebra-cabeça	2	(jigsaw) puzzle
conjunto de construção	3	construction set
blocos de construção	4	(building) blocks
bola de borracha	5	rubber ball
bola de praia	6	beach ball
balde e pá	7	pail and shovel
boneca	8	doll
roupas de boneca	9	doll clothing
casa de boneca	10	doll house
móveis de casa de boneca	11	doll house furniture
bonequinho/boneco	12	action figure
bichinho de pelúcia	13	stuffed animal
carrinho em miniatura	14	matchbox car
caminhão de brinquedo	15	toy truck
autorama	16	racing car set
conjunto de trem	17	train set
modelo	18	model kit
conjunto de ciência	19	science kit
jogo de rádios comunicadores	20	walkie-talkie (set)

bambolê	21	hula hoop
corda de pular	22	jump rope
bolinha de sabão	23	bubble soap
figurinhas	24	trading cards
lápis de cera	25	crayons
canetas hidrográficas	26	(color) markers
álbum de colorir	27	coloring book
papel criativo	28	construction paper
jogo de pintura	29	paint set
massinha de modelar	30	(modeling) clay
adesivos	31	stickers
bicicleta	32	bicycle
triciclo	33	tricycle
carrinho de puxar	34	wagon
skate	35	skateboard
conjunto de balanço	36	swing set
casinha de brinquedo	37	play house
piscina infantil/ piscina inflável	38	kiddie pool/ inflatable pool

A. Excuse me. I'm looking for (a/an) _____(s) for my *grandson*.*
B. Look in the next aisle.
A. Thank you.

* *grandson/granddaughter/. . .*

A. I don't know what to get my ....-year-old son/daughter for his/her birthday.
B. What about (a) _____?
A. Good idea! Thanks.

A. Mom/Dad? Can we buy this/these _____?
B. No, *Johnny*. Not today.

What toys are most popular in your country?

What were your favorite toys when you were a child?

O BANCO

fazer um depósito	A make a deposit		cheque de viagem	4 traveler's check
fazer uma retirada	B make a withdrawal		talão de cheques	5 bankbook/passbook
descontar um cheque	C cash a check		cartão de banco	6 ATM card
comprar cheques de viagem	D get traveler's checks		cartão de crédito	7 credit card
abrir uma conta	E open an account		caixa-forte do banco	8 (bank) vault
pedir um empréstimo	F apply for a loan		cofre	9 safe deposit box
câmbio de moeda	G exchange currency		caixa	10 teller
			guarda de segurança	11 security guard
formulário de depósito	1 deposit slip		caixa eletrônico/	12 ATM (machine)/
formulário de retirada	2 withdrawal slip		caixa automático	cash machine
cheque	3 check		gerente do banco	13 bank officer

[A–G]
A. Where are you going?
B. I'm going to the bank.
I have to _____.

[5–7]
A. What are you looking for?
B. My _____. I can't find it anywhere!

[8–13]
A. How many _____s does the State Street Bank have?
B. ....

Do you have a bank account? What kind? Where? What do you do at the bank?

Do you ever use traveler's checks? When?

Do you have a credit card? What kind? When do you use it?

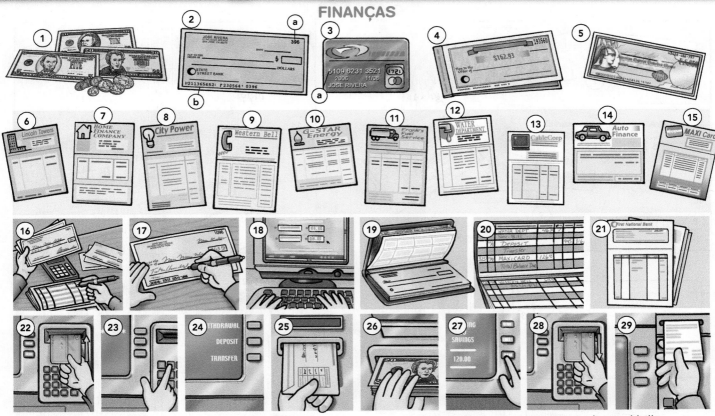

Formas de pagamento	Forms of Payment
dinheiro	**1** cash
cheque	**2** check
número do cheque	**a** check number
número da conta	**b** account number
cartão de crédito	**3** credit card
número do cartão de crédito	**a** credit card number
ordem de pagamento	**4** money order
cheque de viagem	**5** traveler's check

Contas domésticas	Household Bills
aluguel	**6** rent
pagamento da hipoteca	**7** mortgage payment
conta de luz	**8** electric bill
conta de telefone	**9** telephone bill
conta de gás	**10** gas bill
conta do óleo de aquecimento/ conta de aquecimento	**11** oil bill/ heating bill
conta de água	**12** water bill
conta da TV a cabo	**13** cable TV bill
pagamento do carro	**14** car payment

conta do cartão de crédito	**15** credit card bill

Finanças da família	Family Finances
conferir o saldo	**16** balance the checkbook
fazer um cheque	**17** write a check
operações bancárias on-line	**18** bank online
talão de cheque	**19** checkbook
canhoto do cheque	**20** check register
extrato mensal	**21** monthly statement

Usar um caixa eletrônico	Using an ATM Machine
colocar o cartão do banco	**22** insert the ATM card
digitar a senha	**23** enter your PIN number/ personal identification number
escolher a transação	**24** select a transaction
fazer um depósito	**25** make a deposit
fazer uma retirada/pegar o dinheiro	**26** withdraw/get cash
transferir dinheiro	**27** transfer funds
retirar o cartão	**28** remove your card
pegar o comprovante/ pegar o recibo	**29** take your transaction slip/receipt

---

A. Can I pay by ___[1, 2]___ / with a ___[3–5]___ ?
B. Yes. We accept ___[1]___ / ___[2–5]___ s.

A. What are you doing?
B. { I'm paying the ___[6–15]___ .
    I'm ___[16–18]___ ing.
    I'm looking for the ___[19–21]___ .

A. What should I do?
B. ___[22–29]___ .

What household bills do you receive? How much do you pay for the different bills?

Who takes care of the finances in your household? What does that person do?

Do you use ATM machines? If you do, how do you use them?

O CORREIO

carta	**1**	letter	formulário de mudança de endereço	**15**	change-of-address form
cartão postal	**2**	postcard	formulário de alistamento militar	**16**	selective service registration form
carta aérea/ aerograma	**3**	air letter/ aerogramme	formulário de solicitação de passaporte	**17**	passport application form
pacote	**4**	package/parcel	envelope	**18**	envelope
primeira classe	**5**	first class	endereço do remetente	**19**	return address
serviço de entrega prioritária	**6**	priority mail	endereço do destinatário	**20**	mailing address
serviço de entrega expressa/ serviço de entrega até a manhã seguinte	**7**	express mail/ overnight mail	código de endereçamento postal	**21**	zip code
			carimbo do correio	**22**	postmark
remessa postal/ encomenda postal	**8**	parcel post	selo/franquia	**23**	stamp/postage
carta registrada	**9**	certified mail	fenda para correspondência	**24**	mail slot
selo	**10**	stamp	funcionária do correio	**25**	postal worker/postal clerk
folha de selos	**11**	sheet of stamps	balança	**26**	scale
rolo de selos	**12**	roll of stamps	máquina de selos	**27**	stamp machine
cartela de selos	**13**	book of stamps	carteiro	**28**	letter carrier/mail carrier
vale postal	**14**	money order	caminhão do correio	**29**	mail truck
			caixa de correio	**30**	mailbox

[1–4]
A. Where are you going?
B. To the post office. I have to mail a/an _____.

[5–9]
A. How do you want to send it?
B. _____, please.

[10–17]
A. Next!
B. I'd like a _____, please.
A. Here you are.

[19–21, 23]
A. Do you want me to mail this letter?
B. Yes, thanks.
A. Oops! You forgot the _____!

A BIBLIOTECA

catálogo bibliográfico eletrônico	**1**	online catalog	seção de periódicos	**10**	periodical section	seção de livros de referência	**23**	reference section

catálogo bibliográfico eletrônico | **1** online catalog
catálogo bibliográfico de fichas | **2** card catalog
autor | **3** author
título | **4** title
cartão de biblioteca | **5** library card
fotocopiadora/ copiadora | **6** copier/ photocopier/ copy machine
estantes | **7** shelves
seção infantil | **8** children's section
livro infantil | **9** children's books

seção de periódicos | **10** periodical section
periódicos | **11** journals
revistas | **12** magazines
jornais | **13** newspapers
seção de fitas/ cds e dvds | **14** media section
áudio-livro | **15** books on tape
fitas de áudio | **16** audiotapes
CDs | **17** CDs
fitas de vídeo | **18** videotapes
software de computador | **19** (computer) software
DVDs | **20** DVDs
seção de línguas estrangeiras | **21** foreign language section
livros em línguas estrangeiras | **22** foreign language books

seção de livros de referência | **23** reference section
microfilme | **24** microfilm
leitor de microfilme | **25** microfilm reader
dicionário | **26** dictionary
enciclopédia | **27** encyclopedia
atlas | **28** atlas
balcão de consultas | **29** reference desk
bibliotecária de consultas | **30** (reference) librarian
balcão de atendimento | **31** checkout desk
auxiliar de biblioteca | **32** library clerk

[1, 2, 6–32]
A. Excuse me. Where's/Where are the _____?
B. Over there, at/near/next to the _____.

[8–23, 26–28]
A. Excuse me. Where can I find a/an __[26–28]__ / __[9, 11–13, 15–20, 22]__?
B. Look in the __[8, 10, 14, 21, 23]__ over there.

A. I'm having trouble finding a book.
B. Do you know the __[3–4]__?
A. Yes. ....

A. Excuse me. I'd like to check out this __[26–28]__ /these __[11–13]__.
B. I'm sorry. It/They must remain in the library.

Do you go to a library? Where? What does this library have?

Tell about how you use the library.

INSTITUIÇÕES COMUNITÁRIAS

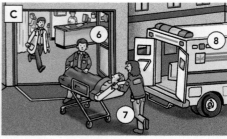

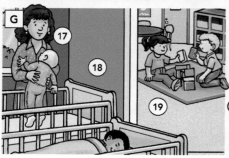

delegacia de polícia	A	police station
quartel de bombeiros	B	fire station
hospital	C	hospital
prefeitura	D	town hall/city hall
centro recreativo	E	recreation center
aterro sanitário	F	dump
creche	G	child-care center
centro de idosos	H	senior center
igreja	I	church
sinagoga	J	synagogue
mesquita	K	mosque
templo	L	temple
telefonista de chamadas de emergência	1	emergency operator
policial	2	police officer
viatura policial	3	police car
caminhão de bombeiro	4	fire engine
bombeiro	5	firefighter
pronto-socorro	6	emergency room
paramédico	7	EMT/paramedic
ambulância	8	ambulance
prefeito	9	mayor/city manager
sala de reuniões	10	meeting room
ginásio	11	gym
diretor de atividades	12	activities director
sala de jogos	13	game room
piscina	14	swimming pool
lixeiro	15	sanitation worker
centro de reciclagem	16	recycling center
funcionária de creche	17	child-care worker
berçário	18	nursery
sala de brinquedos	19	playroom
funcionária de casa de idosos	20	eldercare worker/senior care worker

[A–L]
A. Where are you going?
B. I'm going to the _____.

[1, 2, 5, 7, 12, 15, 17, 20]
A. What do you do?
B. I'm a/an _____.

[3, 4, 8]
A. Do you hear a siren?
B. Yes. There's a/an _____ coming up behind us.

What community institutions are in your city or town? Where are they located?

Which community institutions do you use? When?

CRIME E EMERGÊNCIAS

acidente de carro	1	car accident
incêndio	2	fire
explosão	3	explosion
roubo	4	robbery
furto	5	burglary
assalto	6	mugging
seqüestro	7	kidnapping
criança perdida	8	lost child
roubo de automóvel	9	car jacking
assalto a banco	10	bank robbery
assalto	11	assault
assassinato	12	murder
apagão/blecaute/falta de energia	13	blackout/power outage
vazamento de gás	14	gas leak
cano de água estourado	15	water main break
fio elétrico caído	16	downed power line
derramamento de produto químico	17	chemical spill
descarrilhamento de trem	18	train derailment
vandalismo	19	vandalism
violência de gangues	20	gang violence
dirigir embriagado	21	drunk driving
tráfico de drogas	22	drug dealing

[1–13]
A. I want to report a/an _____.
B. What's your location?
A. ....

[14–18]
A. Why is this street closed?
B. It's closed because of a _____.

[19–22]
A. I'm very concerned about the amount of _____ in our community.
B. I agree. _____ is a very serious problem.

Is there much crime in your community? Tell about it.

Have you ever experienced a crime or emergency? What happened?

O CORPO

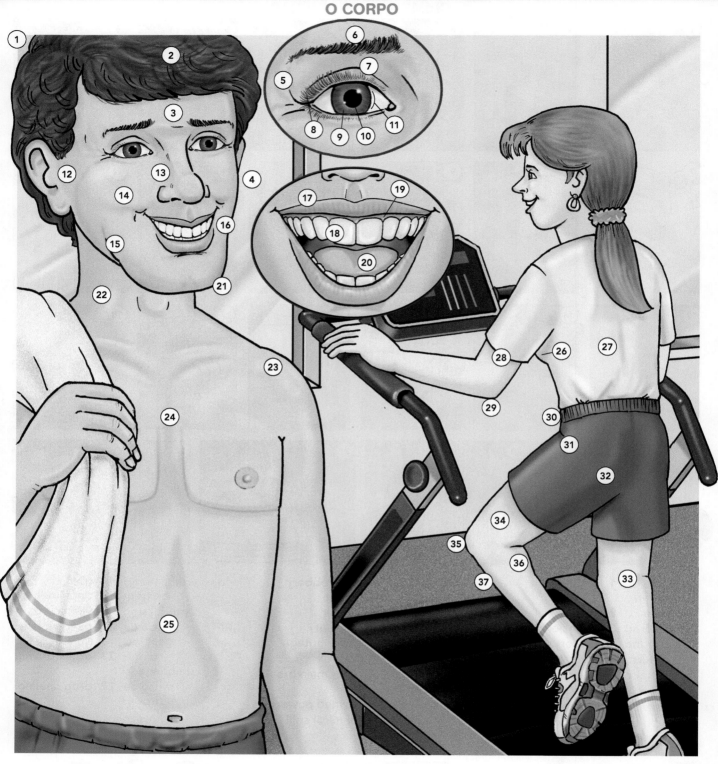

cabeça	**1**	head	córnea	**11**	cornea	queixo	**21**	chin	cintura	**30**	waist
cabelo	**2**	hair	orelha	**12**	ear	pescoço	**22**	neck	quadril	**31**	hip
testa	**3**	forehead	nariz	**13**	nose	ombro	**23**	shoulder	nádegas	**32**	buttocks
rosto	**4**	face	bochecha	**14**	cheek	peito	**24**	chest	perna	**33**	leg
olho	**5**	eye	maxilar	**15**	jaw	abdome/	**25**	abdomen	coxa	**34**	thigh
sobrancelha	**6**	eyebrow	boca	**16**	mouth	abdômen			joelho	**35**	knee
pálpebra	**7**	eyelid	lábio	**17**	lip	seio	**26**	breast	barriga da	**36**	calf
cílios	**8**	eyelashes	dente-dentes	**18**	tooth–teeth	costas	**27**	back	perna/		
íris	**9**	iris	gengiva	**19**	gums	braço	**28**	arm	panturrilha		
pupila	**10**	pupil	língua	**20**	tongue	cotovelo	**29**	elbow	canela	**37**	shin

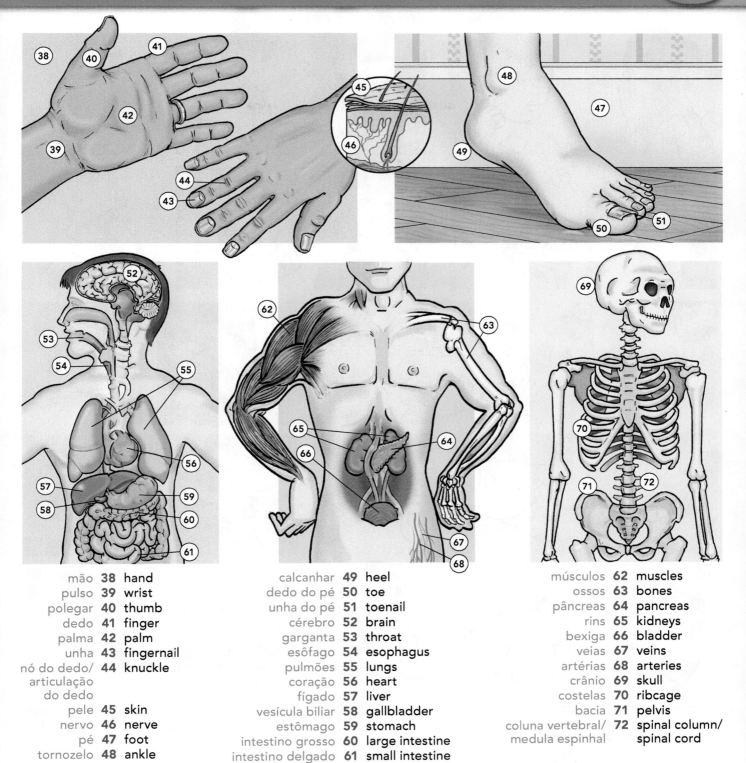

mão	**38**	hand	calcanhar	**49**	heel	músculos	**62**	muscles
pulso	**39**	wrist	dedo do pé	**50**	toe	ossos	**63**	bones
polegar	**40**	thumb	unha do pé	**51**	toenail	pâncreas	**64**	pancreas
dedo	**41**	finger	cérebro	**52**	brain	rins	**65**	kidneys
palma	**42**	palm	garganta	**53**	throat	bexiga	**66**	bladder
unha	**43**	fingernail	esôfago	**54**	esophagus	veias	**67**	veins
nó do dedo/	**44**	knuckle	pulmões	**55**	lungs	artérias	**68**	arteries
articulação			coração	**56**	heart	crânio	**69**	skull
do dedo			fígado	**57**	liver	costelas	**70**	ribcage
pele	**45**	skin	vesícula biliar	**58**	gallbladder	bacia	**71**	pelvis
nervo	**46**	nerve	estômago	**59**	stomach	coluna vertebral/	**72**	spinal column/
pé	**47**	foot	intestino grosso	**60**	large intestine	medula espinhal		spinal cord
tornozelo	**48**	ankle	intestino delgado	**61**	small intestine			

A. My doctor checked my **head** and said everything is okay.
B. I'm glad to hear that.

[1, 3–7, 12–29, 31–51]

A. Ooh!
B. What's the matter?
{ My _____ hurts!
{ My _____ s hurt!

[52–72]

A. My doctor wants me to have some tests.
B. Why?
A. She's concerned about my _____.

Describe yourself as completely as you can.

Which parts of the body are most important at school? at work? when you play your favorite sport?

DOENÇAS, SINTOMAS E FERIMENTOS

  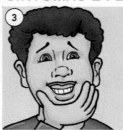  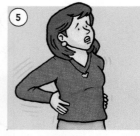

   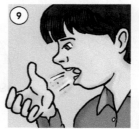 

  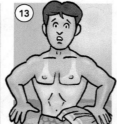   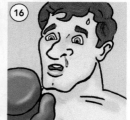

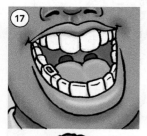 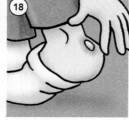 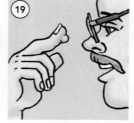  

dor de cabeça	1	headache
dor de ouvido	2	earache
dor de dente	3	toothache
dor de barriga	4	stomachache
dor nas costas	5	backache
dor de garganta	6	sore throat
febre/ temperatura alta	7	fever/ temperature
resfriado	8	cold
tosse	9	cough
infecção	10	infection
erupção cutânea	11	rash
picada de inseto	12	insect bite
queimadura de sol	13	sunburn
torcicolo	14	stiff neck
coriza	15	runny nose
sangramento nasal	16	bloody nose
cárie	17	cavity
bolha	18	blister
verruga	19	wart
soluço	20	(the) hiccups
calafrio	21	(the) chills
cólica	22	cramps
diarréia	23	diarrhea
dor torácica/ dor no peito	24	chest pain
falta de ar/ dispnéia	25	shortness of breath
laringite	26	laryngitis

A. What's the matter?
B. I have a/an ____[1–19]____.

A. What's the matter?
B. I have ____[20–26]____.

desmaio	**27**	faint	arrotar	**36**	burp	machucar–dor	**44**	hurt–hurt
vertigem/tontura (com)	**28**	dizzy	vomitar	**37**	vomit/	cortar–corte	**45**	cut–cut
nauseado/enjoado	**29**	nauseous			throw up	entorse	**46**	sprain
distensão abdominal (com)	**30**	bloated	sangrar	**38**	bleed	deslocar	**47**	dislocate
congestão nasal (com)	**31**	congested	torcer	**39**	twist	quebrar–	**48**	break–
exausto	**32**	exhausted	arranhão	**40**	scratch	quebrado		broke
tossir	**33**	cough	ralar	**41**	scrape	inchado	**49**	swollen
espirrar	**34**	sneeze	machucar	**42**	bruise	coceira (com)	**50**	itchy
chiar	**35**	wheeze	queimar	**43**	burn			

A. What's the problem?

B. { I feel [27–30] .
I'm [31–32] .
I've been [33–38] ing a lot.

A. What happened?

B. { I [39–45] ed my ....
I think I [46–48] ed my ....
My .... is/are [49–50] .

A. How do you feel?

B. Not so good./Not very well./Terrible!

A. What's the matter?

B. ...., ..., and ....

A. I'm sorry to hear that.

Tell about the last time you didn't feel well. What was the matter?

Tell about a time you hurt yourself. What happened? How? What did you do about it?

What do you do when you have a cold? a stomachache? an insect bite? the hiccups?

PRIMEIROS SOCORROS

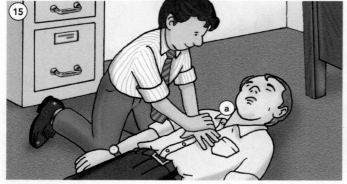

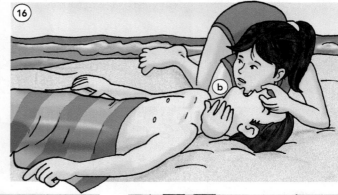

manual de primeiros socorros	**1**	**first-aid manual**	analgésico sem aspirina	**14 non-aspirin pain reliever**
estojo de primeiros socorros	**2**	**first-aid kit**	RCP (reanimação cardiopulmonar)	**15 CPR (cardiopulmonary resuscitation)**
curativo adesivo/ Band-Aid™	**3**	**(adhesive) bandage/ Band-Aid™**	sem pulso	**a has no pulse**
lenço antisséptico de limpeza	**4**	**antiseptic cleansing wipe**	respiração de resgate	**16 rescue breathing**
compressa para curativo estéril	**5**	**sterile (dressing) pad**	não está respirando/ sem respiração	**b isn't breathing**
água oxigenada	**6**	**hydrogen peroxide**	manobra de Heimlich	**17 the Heimlich maneuver**
pomada antibiótica	**7**	**antibiotic ointment**	está engasgando	**c is choking**
gaze	**8**	**gauze**	tala	**18 splint**
esparadrapo	**9**	**adhesive tape**	quebrou um dedo	**d broke a finger**
pinça	**10**	**tweezers**	torniquete	**19 tourniquet**
creme anti-histamínico	**11**	**antihistamine cream**	está sangrando	**e is bleeding**
atadura elástica/ atadura Ace™	**12**	**elastic bandage/ Ace™ bandage**		
aspirina	**13**	**aspirin**		

A. Do we have any ___[3–5, 12]___ s/ ___[6–11, 13, 14]___ ?
B. Yes. Look in the first-aid kit.

A. Help! My friend ___[a–e]___ !
B. I can help!
{ I know how to do ___[15–17]___.
{ I can make a ___[18, 19]___.

Do you have a first-aid kit? If you do, what's in it? If you don't, where can you buy one?

Tell about a time when you gave or received first aid.

Where can a person learn first aid in your community?

machucado/ferido	**1**	hurt/injured
em choque	**2**	in shock
inconsciente	**3**	unconscious
hiperpirexia do calor	**4**	heatstroke
geladura	**5**	frostbite
ataque cardíaco	**6**	heart attack
reação alérgica	**7**	allergic reaction
tomar veneno/ingerir veneno	**8**	swallow poison
overdose/superdosagem	**9**	overdose on drugs
queda/cair–caiu	**10**	fall–fell
sofrer um choque elétrico	**11**	get–got an electric shock
gripe/influenza	**12**	the flu/influenza
infecção de ouvido	**13**	an ear infection
infecção de garganta	**14**	strep throat

sarampo	**15**	measles
cachumba	**16**	mumps
catapora	**17**	chicken pox
asma	**18**	asthma
câncer	**19**	cancer
depressão	**20**	depression
diabetes	**21**	diabetes
doença cardíaca	**22**	heart disease
pressão alta/pressão arterial alta/hipertensão	**23**	high blood pressure/hypertension
tuberculose	**24**	TB/tuberculosis
AIDS*	**25**	AIDS*
* Síndrome da Imunodeficiência Adquirida		* Acquired Immune Deficiency Syndrome

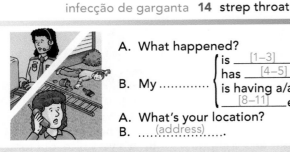

A. What happened?
B. My .... { is _____[1–3]_____. }
{ has _____[4–5]_____. }
{ is having a/an _____[6–7]_____. }
{ _____[8–11]____ed. }
A. What's your location?
B. ......(address)......

A. My .... is sick.
B. What's the matter?
A. He/She has _____[12–25]_____.
B. I'm sorry to hear that.

Tell about a medical emergency that happened to you or someone you know.

Which illnesses in this lesson are you familiar with?

O EXAME MÉDICO

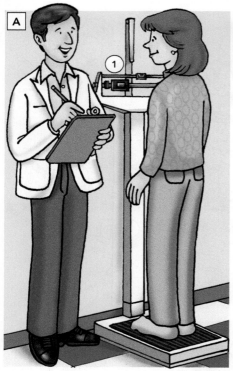

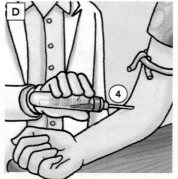
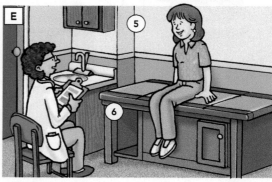

medir *seu* peso e altura	**A**	**measure** *your* **height and weight**	
medir *sua* temperatura	**B**	take *your* temperature	
medir *sua* pressão arterial	**C**	check *your* blood pressure	
coletar sangue	**D**	draw some blood	
fazer-*lhe* algumas perguntas sobre a *sua* saúde	**E**	ask *you* some questions about *your* health	
examinar *seus* olhos, ouvidos, nariz e garganta	**F**	examine *your* eyes, ears, nose, and throat	
ascultar *seu* coração	**G**	listen to *your* heart	
fazer uma radiografia do tórax	**H**	take a chest X-ray	

balança	**1**	scale	
termômetro	**2**	thermometer	
manômetro de pressão arterial/medidor de pressão	**3**	blood pressure gauge	
agulha/seringa	**4**	needle/syringe	
sala de exame	**5**	examination room	
mesa de exames	**6**	examination table	
cartaz de letras/ carta de Snellen	**7**	eye chart	
estetoscópio	**8**	stethoscope	
aparelho de raio X	**9**	X-ray machine	

[A–H]
A. Now I'm going to **measure your height and weight**.
B. All right.

[A–H]
A. What did the doctor/nurse do during the examination?
B. She/He **measured my height and weight**.

[1–3, 5–9]
A. So, how do you like our new **scale?**
B. It's very nice, doctor.

How often do you have a medical exam? What does the doctor/nurse do?

PROCEDIMENTOS MÉDICOS E ODONTOLÓGICOS

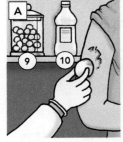
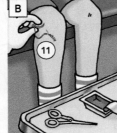
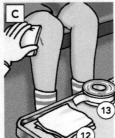

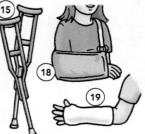

limpar o ferimento	**A** clean the wound	sala de espera	**1** waiting room	unidade de gelo	**16** ice pack
fechar o ferimento/ suturar o ferimento	**B** close the wound	recepcionista	**2** receptionist	prescrição médica/ receita médica	**17** prescription
colocar curativo no ferimento	**C** dress the wound	cartão do seguro	**3** insurance card		
		formulário de histórico clínico	**4** medical history form	tipóia	**18** sling
limpar seus dentes	**D** clean *your* teeth	sala de exame	**5** examination room	gesso	**19** cast
examinar seus dentes	**E** examine *your* teeth	médico	**6** doctor/physician	suporte/ ortose	**20** brace
aplicar uma injeção de anestésico/ anestesia/ procaína (Novocaine™)	**F** give *you* a shot of anesthetic/ Novocaine™	paciente	**7** patient	higienista dental	**21** dental hygienist
		enfermeira	**8** nurse	máscara	**22** mask
		chumaços de algodão	**9** cotton balls	luvas	**23** gloves
		álcool	**10** alcohol	dentista	**24** dentist
perfurar com broca a cárie	**G** drill the cavity	pontos/sutura	**11** stitches	assistente de dentista	**25** dental assistant
obturar o dente	**H** fill the tooth	gaze	**12** gauze	broca	**26** drill
		esparadrapo	**13** tape	obturação	**27** filling
		injeção	**14** injection/shot		
		muletas	**15** crutches		

A. Now I'm going to {
___[A–H]___.
give you (a/an) ___[14–17]___.
put your .... in a ___[18–20]___.
}

B. Okay.

A. I need {
___[9, 10, 12, 13, 23]___.
a ___[22, 26]___.
}

B. Here you are.

Tell about a personal experience you had with a medical or dental procedure.

CONSELHOS MÉDICOS

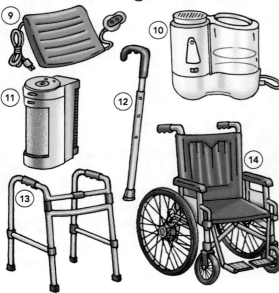

ficar de cama/repousar no leito	1	rest in bed		bengala	12	cane
ingerir líquidos	2	drink fluids		andador	13	walker
gargarejar	3	gargle		cadeira de rodas	14	wheelchair
fazer dieta/fazer regime	4	go on a diet		exames de sangue/	15	blood work/
fazer exercício/exercitar-se	5	exercise		exame de sangue		blood tests
tomar vitaminas	6	take vitamins		testes	16	tests
consultar um especialista	7	see a specialist		fisioterapia	17	physical therapy
fazer acupuntura	8	get acupuncture		cirurgia	18	surgery
almofada térmica	9	heating pad		aconselhamento	19	counseling
umidificador	10	humidifier		aparelho	20	braces
purificador de ar	11	air purifier				

A. I think { you should _____ [1–8] .
              you should use a/an _____ [9–14] .
              you need _____ [15–20] .
B. I see.

A. What did the doctor say?
B. The doctor thinks { I should _____ [1–8] .
                        I should use a/an _____ [9–14] .
                        I need _____ [15–20] .

Tell about medical advice a doctor gave you. What did the doctor say? Did you follow the advice?

REMÉDIOS

aspirina	**1** aspirin	pastilhas contra tosse	**6** cough drops
comprimidos contra gripe	**2** cold tablets	pastilhas para dor de garganta	**7** throat lozenges
vitaminas	**3** vitamins	comprimidos de antiácido	**8** antacid tablets
xarope contra tosse	**4** cough syrup	spray descongestionante nasal	**9** decongestant spray/ nasal spray
analgésico sem aspirina	**5** non-aspirin pain reliever	colírio	**10** eye drops
		pomada	**11** ointment
		creme	**12** cream/creme

loção	**13** lotion
pílula	**14** pill
comprimido	**15** tablet
cápsula	**16** capsule
tablete	**17** caplet
colher de chá	**18** teaspoon
colher de sopa	**19** tablespoon

[1–13]

A. What did the doctor say?

B. { She/He told me to take _____[1–4]_____ / a _____[5]_____.
{ She/He told me to use _____[6–13]_____.

[14–19]

A. What's the dosage?

B. One _____ every four hours.

What medicines in this lesson do you have at home? What other medicines do you have?

What do you take or use for a fever? a headache? a stomachache? a sore throat? a cold? a cough?

Tell about any medicines in your country that are different from the ones in this lesson.

MEDICAL SPECIALISTS
ESPECIALISTAS MÉDICOS

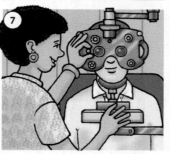

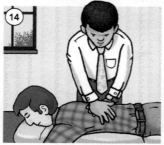

cardiologista	**1**	**cardiologist**	audiologista **9**	**audiologist**
ginecologista	**2**	**gynecologist**	fisioterapeuta **10**	**physical therapist**
pediatra	**3**	**pediatrician**	conselheiro/terapeuta **11**	**counselor/therapist**
gerontologista	**4**	**gerontologist**	psiquiatra **12**	**psychiatrist**
alergista	**5**	**allergist**	gastroenterologista **13**	**gastroenterologist**
ortopedista	**6**	**orthopedist**	quiroprático **14**	**chiropractor**
oftalmologista	**7**	**ophthalmologist**	acupunturista **15**	**acupuncturist**
otorrinolaringologista	**8**	**ear, nose, and throat (ENT) specialist**	ortodontista **16**	**orthodontist**

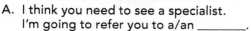

A. I think you need to see a specialist.
   I'm going to refer you to a/an _____.
B. A/An _____?
A. Yes.

A. When is your next appointment with the _____?
B. It's at ......(time)...... on .....(date)........

Do you or members of your family see any of these medical specialists? Which ones?

quarto do paciente/ quarto de hospital	**A patient's room**	enfermeira cirúrgica	**16 surgical nurse**
paciente	**1 patient**	anestesista	**17 anesthesiologist**
camisola de hospital	**2 hospital gown**	**sala de espera**	**D waiting room**
cama de hospital	**3 hospital bed**	voluntária	**18 volunteer**
controle da cama	**4 bed control**	**sala de parto**	**E birthing room/ delivery room**
botão para chamar enfermeira	**5 call button**	obstetra	**19 obstetrician**
soro	**6 I.V.**	parteira/enfermeira obstetra	**20 midwife/nurse-midwife**
monitor de sinais vitais	**7 vital signs monitor**	**pronto-socorro/ PS**	**F emergency room/ ER**
mesa para refeição	**8 bed table**	técnico de enfermagem de emergências/paramédico	**21 emergency medical technician/EMT**
comadre	**9 bed pan**	maca	**22 gurney**
prontuário	**10 medical chart**	**departamento de radiologia**	**G radiology department**
médico	**11 doctor/physician**	técnico de raio x	**23 X-ray technician**
posto de enfermagem	**B nurse's station**	radiologista	**24 radiologist**
enfermeiro	**12 nurse**	**laboratório**	**H laboratory/lab**
nutricionista	**13 dietitian**	técnico de laboratório	**25 lab technician**
atendente de enfermagem	**14 orderly**		
sala cirúrgica	**C operating room**		
cirurgião	**15 surgeon**		

A. This is your _____[2–10]_____.
B. I see.

A. Do you work here?
B. Yes. I'm a/an ____[11–21, 23–25]____.

A. Where's the ____[11–21, 23–25]____?
B. She's/He's { in the ____[A, C–H]____.
at the ____[B]____.

Tell about an experience you or a family member had in the hospital.

HIGIENE PESSOAL

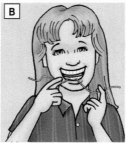

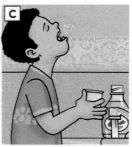

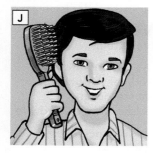

escovar *meus* dentes	A	brush *my* teeth	
escova de dente	1	toothbrush	
pasta de dente	2	toothpaste	
passar fio dental nos *meus* dentes	B	floss *my* teeth	
fio dental	3	dental floss	
gargarejar	C	gargle	
enxágüe bucal	4	mouthwash	
branquear *meus* dentes	D	whiten *my* teeth	
branqueador de dentes	5	teeth whitener	
tomar banho/ tomar banho de banheira	E	bathe/take a bath	
sabonete	6	soap	
banho de espumas	7	bubble bath	
tomar banho de chuveiro	F	take a shower	
touca de banho	8	shower cap	
lavar *meu* cabelo	G	wash *my* hair	
shampoo	9	shampoo	
condicionador/creme rinse	10	conditioner/rinse	
secar *meu* cabelo	H	dry *my* hair	
secador de cabelo/ secador de cabelos/secador	11	hair dryer/ blow dryer	
pentear *meu* cabelo	I	comb *my* hair	
pente	12	comb	
escovar *meu* cabelo	J	brush *my* hair	
escova de cabelos	13	(hair) brush	
arrumar *meu* cabelo	K	style *my* hair	
modelador/ modelador de cabelos	14	hot comb/ curling iron	
spray fixador/laquê	15	hairspray	
gel para cabelos	16	hair gel	
grampo	17	bobby pin	
fivela	18	barrette	
fivela do tipo piranha	19	hairclip	

barbear-se	**L**	**shave**
creme de barbear	**20**	shaving cream
aparelho de barbear	**21**	razor
lâmina de barbear	**22**	razor blade
barbeador elétrico	**23**	electric shaver
lápis hemostático	**24**	styptic pencil
loção pós-barba	**25**	aftershave (lotion)
fazer *minhas* unhas	**M**	**do *my* nails**
lixa de unha de metal	**26**	nail file
lixa de unha	**27**	emery board
cortador de unha	**28**	nail clipper
escova de unha	**29**	nail brush
tesoura	**30**	scissors
esmalte de unha	**31**	nail polish
removedor de esmalte	**32**	nail polish remover
passar . . .	**N**	**put on . . .**
desodorante	**33**	deodorant
loção para as mãos	**34**	hand lotion

loção para o corpo	**35**	body lotion
talco	**36**	powder
colônia/perfume	**37**	cologne/perfume
protetor solar	**38**	sunscreen
colocar a maquiagem	**O**	**put on makeup**
blush/ruge	**39**	blush/rouge
base	**40**	foundation/base
hidratante	**41**	moisturizer
pó de arroz	**42**	face powder
delineador	**43**	eyeliner
sombra	**44**	eye shadow
rímel	**45**	mascara
lápis de sobrancelha	**46**	eyebrow pencil
batom	**47**	lipstick
engraxar *meus* sapatos	**P**	**polish *my* shoes**
graxa para sapato	**48**	shoe polish
cadarços	**49**	shoelaces

[A–M, N (33–38), O, P]
A. What are you doing?
B. I'm _____ing.

[1, 8, 11–14, 17–19, 21–24, 26–30, 46, 49]
A. Excuse me. Where can I find _____(s)?
B. They're in the next aisle.

[2–7, 9, 10, 15, 16, 20, 25, 31–45, 47, 48]
A. Excuse me. Where can I find _____?
B. It's in the next aisle.

Which of these personal care products do you use?

You're going on a trip. Make a list of the personal care products you need to take with you.

CUIDADOS DO BEBÊ

alimentar	**A**	**feed**
potinho de alimento para bebês	**1**	baby food
babador	**2**	bib
mamadeira	**3**	bottle
bico de mamadeira	**4**	nipple
leite para bebês	**5**	formula
vitaminas líquidas	**6**	(liquid) vitamins
mudar a fralda do bebê	**B**	**change the baby's diaper**
fralda descartável	**7**	disposable diaper
fralda de pano	**8**	cloth diaper
alfinete de fralda	**9**	diaper pin
lenços umedecidos	**10**	(baby) wipes
talco de bebê	**11**	baby powder
fralda-calça infantil	**12**	training pants
pomada	**13**	ointment
dar banho	**C**	**bathe**
shampoo de bebê	**14**	baby shampoo

haste flexível/cotonete	**15**	cotton swab
loção de bebê	**16**	baby lotion
segurar no colo	**D**	**hold**
chupeta	**17**	pacifier
mordedor	**18**	teething ring
amamentar	**E**	**nurse**
vestir	**F**	**dress**
embalar	**G**	**rock**
creche	**19**	child-care center
funcionária de creche	**20**	child-care worker
cadeira de balanço	**21**	rocking chair
ler para	**H**	**read to**
prateleira	**22**	cubby
brincar com	**I**	**play with**
brinquedos	**23**	toys

A. What are you doing?
B. { I'm _____[A, C–I]_____ing the baby.
{ I'm _____[B]_____ing.

A. Do we need anything from the store?
B. Yes. We need some more { _____[2–4, 7–9, 15, 17, 18]_____s
{ _____[1, 5, 6, 10–14, 16]_____.

In your opinion, which are better: cloth diapers or disposable diapers? Why?   Tell about baby products in your country.

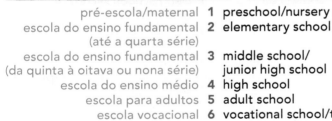

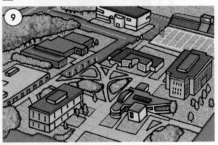

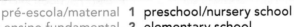

pré-escola/maternal	**1**	preschool/nursery school	faculdade equivalente aos dois primeiros anos de estudos superiores	**7** community college
escola do ensino fundamental (até a quarta série)	**2**	elementary school	'college'/instituição de ensino superior	**8** college
escola do ensino fundamental (da quinta à oitava ou nona série)	**3**	middle school/ junior high school	universidade	**9** university
escola do ensino médio	**4**	high school	pós-graduação	**10** graduate school
escola para adultos	**5**	adult school	faculdade de direito	**11** law school
escola vocacional	**6**	vocational school/trade school	faculdade de medicina	**12** medical school

A. Are you a student?
B. Yes. I'm in _____[1–4, 8, 10–12]_____.

A. Are you a student?
B. Yes. I go to a/an _____[5–7, 9]_____.

A. Is this apartment building near a/an _____?
B. Yes. _____(name of school)_____ is nearby.

A. Tell me about your previous education.
B. I went to _____(name of school)_____
A. Did you like it there?
B. Yes. It was an excellent _____.

What types of schools are there in your community? What are their names, and where are they located?

What types of schools have you gone to?

Where? When? What did you study?

A ESCOLA

secretaria	**A** (main) office	biblioteca	**M** library
diretoria	**B** principal's office	funcionária/secretária da escola	**1** clerk/(school) secretary
enfermaria	**C** nurse's office	diretor	**2** principal
sala de orientação	**D** guidance office	enfermeira da escola	**3** (school) nurse
pedagógica		orientador pedagógico	**4** (guidance) counselor
sala de aula	**E** classroom	professora	**5** teacher
corredor	**F** hallway	assistente de diretor/vice-diretor	**6** assistant principal/vice-principal
armário	**a** locker	guarda de segurança	**7** security officer
laboratório	**G** science lab	professor de ciências	**8** science teacher
ginásio	**H** gym/gymnasium	professor de educação física	**9** P.E. teacher
vestiário	**a** locker room	técnico	**10** coach
pista de atletismo	**I** track	zelador	**11** custodian
arquibancada	**a** bleachers	funcionária do refeitório	**12** cafeteria worker
campo	**J** field	monitor da hora do almoço	**13** lunchroom monitor
auditório	**K** auditorium	bibliotecária da escola	**14** (school) librarian
refeitório	**L** cafeteria		

A. Where are you going?
B. I'm going to the ____[A–D, G–M]____ .
A. Do you have a hall pass?
B. Yes. Here it is.

A. Where's the ____[1–14]____ ?
B. He's/She's in the ____[A–M]____ .

Describe the school where you study English. Tell about the rooms, offices, and people.

Tell about differences between the school in this lesson and schools in your country.

MATÉRIAS ESCOLARES

matemática	**1**	math/mathematics	ciências da computação	**11**	computer science
inglês	**2**	English	espanhol	**12**	Spanish
história	**3**	history	francês	**13**	French
geografia	**4**	geography	economia doméstica	**14**	home economics
governo	**5**	government	artes industriais/oficina	**15**	industrial arts/shop
ciências	**6**	science	comércio	**16**	business education
biologia	**7**	biology	educação física	**17**	physical education/P.E.
química	**8**	chemistry	curso de direção	**18**	driver's education/driver's ed
física	**9**	physics	arte	**19**	art
saúde	**10**	health	música	**20**	music

A. What do you have next period?
B. **Math**. How about you?
A. **English**.
B. There's the bell. I've got to go.

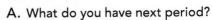

What is/was your favorite subject? Why?

In your opinion, what's the most interesting subject? the most difficult subject? Why do you think so?

banda	**1**	**band**		jornal da escola	**9**	**school newspaper**
orquestra	**2**	**orchestra**		livro do ano	**10**	**yearbook**
coral/coro	**3**	**choir/chorus**		revista literária	**11**	**literary magazine**
teatro	**4**	**drama**		equipe de áudio e vídeo	**12**	**A.V. crew**
futebol americano	**5**	**football**		clube de debates	**13**	**debate club**
animação da torcida	**6**	**cheerleading/pep squad**		clube de computação	**14**	**computer club**
diretório acadêmico estudantil	**7**	**student government**		clube internacional	**15**	**international club**
serviço comunitário	**8**	**community service**		clube de xadrez	**16**	**chess club**

A. Are you going home right after school?

B. { No. I have ____[1–6]____ practice.
{ No. I have a ____[7–16]____ meeting.

What extracurricular activities do/did you participate in?

Which extracurricular activities in this lesson are there in schools in your country? What other activities are there?

MATEMÁTICA

Arithmetic   Aritmética

$$2+1=3 \qquad 8-3=5 \qquad 4\times2=8 \qquad 10\div2=5$$

soma **addition**	subtração **subtraction**	multiplicação **multiplication**	divisão **division**
2 **plus** 1 **equals*** 3.	8 **minus** 3 **equals*** 5.	4 **times** 2 **equals*** 8.	10 **divided by** 2 **equals*** 5.

*You can also say: **is**

A. How much is *two plus one?*
B. *Two plus one* equals / is *three.*

Make conversations for the arithmetic problems above and others.

Fractions   Frações

1/4	1/3	1/2	2/3	3/4
one quarter / one fourth	one third	one half / half	two thirds	three quarters / three fourths

A. Is this on sale?
B. Yes. It's _____ off the regular price.

A. Is the gas tank almost empty?
B. It's about _____ full.

Percents   Porcentagem

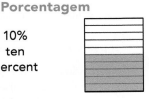

10% ten percent	50% fifty percent	75% seventy-five percent	100% one-hundred percent

A. How did you do on the test?
B. I got _____ percent of the answers right.

A. What's the weather forecast?
B. There's a _____ percent chance of rain.

Types of Math   Tipos de matemática

$$5y-5y+3=$$

$$\sin(y)=x$$

$$\int_{2}^{6} g(x)\,dx$$

algebra	geometry	trigonometry	calculus	statistics
álgebra	geometria	trigonometria	cálculo	estatística

A. What math course are you taking this year?
B. I'm taking _____.

Are you good at math?

What math courses do / did you take in school?

Tell about something you bought on sale. How much off the regular price was it?

Research and discuss: What percentage of people in your country live in cities? live on farms? work in factories? vote in general elections?

MEDIDAS E FORMAS GEOMÉTRICAS

Medidas	Measurements
altura	**1** height
largura	**2** width
profundidade	**3** depth
comprimento	**4** length
polegada	**5** inch
pé	**6** foot–feet
jarda	**7** yard
centímetro	**8** centimeter
metro	**9** meter
distância	**10** distance
milha	**11** mile
quilômetro	**12** kilometer

Linhas	**Lines**
linha reta	**13** straight line
linha curva	**14** curved line

linhas paralelas	**15** parallel lines
linhas perpendiculares	**16** perpendicular lines

Formas geométricas	**Geometric Shapes**
quadrado	**17** square
lado	**a** side
retângulo	**18** rectangle
comprimento	**a** length
largura	**b** width
diagonal	**c** diagonal
triângulo reto	**19** right triangle
vértice	**a** apex
ângulo reto	**b** right angle
base	**c** base
hipotenusa	**d** hypotenuse

triângulo isósceles	**20** isosceles triangle
ângulo agudo	**a** acute angle
ângulo obtuso	**b** obtuse angle
círculo	**21** circle
centro	**a** center
raio	**b** radius
diâmetro	**c** diameter
circunferência	**d** circumference
elipse/oval	**22** ellipse/oval

Sólidos	**Solid Figures**
cubo	**23** cube
cilindro	**24** cylinder
esfera	**25** sphere
cone	**26** cone
pirâmide	**27** pyramid

[1–9]
A. What's the _____ [1–4] ?
B. .... _____ [5–9] (s).

[11–12]
A. What's the distance?
B. .... _____ (s).

1 inch (1")	=	2.54 centimeters (cm)
1 foot (1')	=	0.305 meters (m)
1 yard (1 yd.)	=	0.914 meters (m)
1 mile (mi.)	=	1.6 kilometers (km)

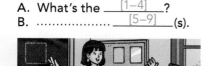

[17–22]
A. Who can tell me what shape this is?
B. I can. It's a/an _____.

[23–27]
A. Who knows what figure this is?
B. I do. It's a/an _____.

[13–27]
A. This painting is magnificent!
B. Hmm. I don't think so. It just looks like a lot of _____s and _____s to me!

Types of Sentences & Parts of Speech   **Tipos de orações e classes gramaticais**

A Students study in the new library.
① ② ③ ④ ⑤

B Do they study hard?
⑥ ⑦

C Read page nine.

D This cake is fantastic!

afirmativa	**A** declarative	
interrogativa	**B** interrogative	
imperativa	**C** imperative	
exclamativa	**D** exclamatory	

substantivo	**1** noun
verbo	**2** verb
preposição	**3** preposition
artigo	**4** article

adjetivo	**5** adjective
pronome	**6** pronoun
advérbio	**7** adverb

A. What type of sentence is this?
B. It's a/an ___[A–D]___ sentence.

A. What part of speech is this?
B. It's a/an ___[1–7]___.

Punctuation Marks & the Writing Process   **Sinais de pontuação e o processo de redação**

ponto final	**8** period	
ponto de interrogação	**9** question mark	
ponto de exclamação	**10** exclamation point	
vírgula	**11** comma	
apóstrofe	**12** apostrophe	
aspas	**13** quotation marks	
dois pontos	**14** colon	
ponto e vírgula	**15** semi-colon	

gerar idéias	**16** brainstorm ideas
organizar minhas idéias	**17** organize *my* ideas
escrever o primeiro rascunho	**18** write a first draft
título	**a** title
parágrafo	**b** paragraph
fazer correções/revisar	**19** make corrections/revise/edit
obter opiniões/feedback	**20** get feedback
escrever a versão final/reescrever	**21** write a final copy/rewrite

A. Did you find any mistakes?
B. Yes. You forgot to put a/an ___[8–15]___ in this sentence.

A. Are you working on your composition?
B. Yes. I'm ___[16–21]___ing.

LITERATURA E ESCRITA

ficção	**1**	fiction	ensaio	**8**	essay	bilhete	**15**	note
romance	**2**	novel	relatório	**9**	report	convite	**16**	invitation
conto	**3**	short story	artigo de revista	**10**	magazine article	bilhete de agradecimento	**17**	thank-you note
poesia/poemas	**4**	poetry/poems	artigo de jornal	**11**	newspaper article			
não-ficção	**5**	non-fiction	editorial	**12**	editorial	memorando	**18**	memo
biografia	**6**	biography	carta	**13**	letter	e-mail	**19**	e-mail
autobiografia	**7**	autobiography	cartão postal	**14**	postcard	mensagem instantânea	**20**	instant message

A. What are you doing?

B. I'm writing { [1, 4, 5] .

                 a/an   [2, 3, 6–20] .

What kind of literature do you like to read? What are some of your favorite books? Who is your favorite author?

Do you like to read newspapers and magazines? Which ones do you read?

Do you sometimes send or receive letters, postcards, notes, e-mail, or instant messages? Tell about the people you communicate with, and how.

GEOGRAFIA

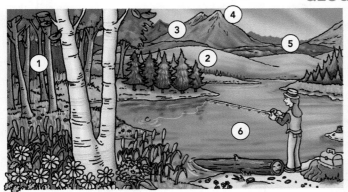

floresta/bosque	**1** forest/woods	riacho/córrego	**9** stream/brook	baía	**17** bay
colina	**2** hill	lagoa	**10** pond	oceano	**18** ocean
cordilheira	**3** mountain range	planalto	**11** plateau	ilha	**19** island
pico da montanha	**4** mountain peak	canhão/garganta	**12** canyon	península	**20** peninsula
vale	**5** valley	duna/duna de areia	**13** dune/sand dune	floresta pluvial	**21** rainforest
lago	**6** lake	deserto	**14** desert	rio	**22** river
planície	**7** plains	selva	**15** jungle	cachoeira	**23** waterfall
campina/prado	**8** meadow	litoral/beira-mar/costa	**16** seashore/shore		

A. { Isn't this a beautiful _____?!
 Aren't these beautiful _____s?!
B. Yes. It's / They're magnificent!

Tell about the geography of your country. Describe the different geographic features.

Have you seen some of the geographic features in this lesson? Which ones? Where?

CIÊNCIAS

Equipamento de ciência — Science Equipment

microscópio	1	microscope
computador	2	computer
lâmina	3	slide
placa de Petri	4	Petri dish
frasco	5	flask
funil	6	funnel
béquer	7	beaker
tubo de ensaio	8	test tube
fórceps	9	forceps
pinça para cadinho	10	crucible tongs
bico de Bunsen	11	Bunsen burner
cilindro graduado	12	graduated cylinder
ímã	13	magnet
prisma	14	prism
conta-gotas	15	dropper
produtos químicos	16	chemicals
balança	17	balance
balança	18	scale

Método científico (o) — The Scientific Method

definir o problema	A	state the problem
formar uma hipótese	B	form a hypothesis
planejar um procedimento	C	plan a procedure
executar um procedimento	D	do a procedure
fazer/registrar observações	E	make/record observations
chegar a conclusões	F	draw conclusions

A. What do we need to do this procedure?
B. We need a/an/the ____ [1–18].

A. How is your experiment coming along?
B. I'm getting ready to ____ [A–F].

Do you have experience with the scientific equipment in this lesson? Tell about it.

What science courses do/did you take in school?

Think of an idea for a science experiment.
What question about science do you want to answer? State the problem.
What do you think will happen in the experiment? Form a hypothesis.
How can you test your hypothesis? Plan a procedure.

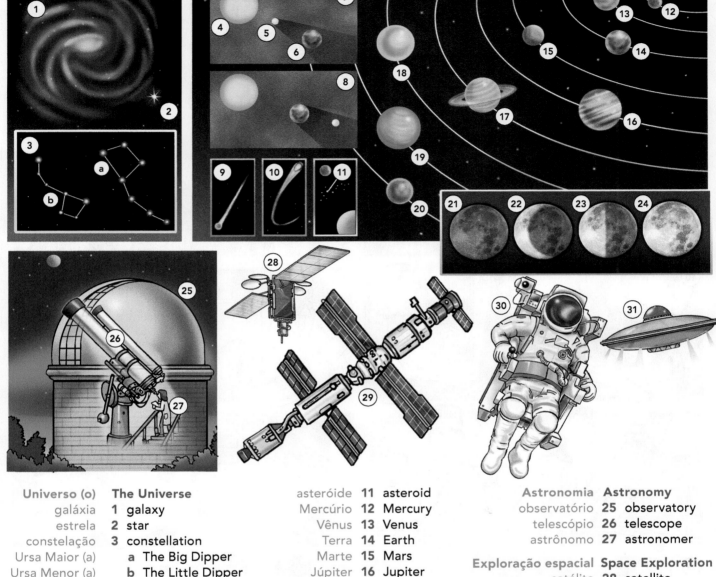

Universo (o)	The Universe
galáxia	**1** galaxy
estrela	**2** star
constelação	**3** constellation
Ursa Maior (a)	**a** The Big Dipper
Ursa Menor (a)	**b** The Little Dipper

Sistema solar (o)	The Solar System
sol	**4** sun
lua	**5** moon
planeta	**6** planet
eclipse solar	**7** solar eclipse
eclipse lunar	**8** lunar eclipse
meteoro	**9** meteor
cometa	**10** comet

asteróide	**11** asteroid
Mercúrio	**12** Mercury
Vênus	**13** Venus
Terra	**14** Earth
Marte	**15** Mars
Júpiter	**16** Jupiter
Saturno	**17** Saturn
Urano	**18** Uranus
Netuno	**19** Neptune
Plutão	**20** Pluto
lua nova	**21** new moon
lua crescente	**22** crescent moon
quarto minguante	**23** quarter moon
lua cheia	**24** full moon

Astronomia	Astronomy
observatório	**25** observatory
telescópio	**26** telescope
astrônomo	**27** astronomer

Exploração espacial	Space Exploration
satélite	**28** satellite
estação espacial	**29** space station
astronauta	**30** astronaut
OVNI/ Objeto Voador Não-Identificado/ disco voador	**31** U.F.O./ Unidentified Flying Object/ flying saucer

[1–24]
A. Is that (a/an/the) _____?
B. I'm not sure. I think it might be (a/an/the) _____.

[28–30]
A. Is the _____ ready for tomorrow's launch?
B. Yes. "All systems are go!"

Pretend you are an astronaut traveling in space. What do you see?

Draw and name a constellation you are familiar with.

Do you think space exploration is important? Why?

Have you ever seen a U.F.O.? Do you believe there is life in outer space? Why?

OCUPAÇÕES I

contador	**1**	accountant
ator	**2**	actor
atriz	**3**	actress
arquiteto	**4**	architect
artista	**5**	artist
operário	**6**	assembler
babysitter	**7**	babysitter
padeiro	**8**	baker
barbeiro	**9**	barber
pedreiro	**10**	bricklayer/mason
homem de negócios	**11**	businessman
mulher de negócios	**12**	businesswoman
açougueiro	**13**	butcher
carpinteiro	**14**	carpenter
caixa	**15**	cashier
chef/cozinheiro	**16**	chef/cook
funcionária de creche	**17**	child day-care worker
engenheiro de software	**18**	computer software engineer
trabalhadora de construção civil	**19**	construction worker
zelador	**20**	custodian/janitor
representante de atendimento ao cliente	**21**	customer service representative
digitador de dados	**22**	data entry clerk

entregadora	**23**	delivery person	
estivador	**24**	dockworker	
engenheira	**25**	engineer	
operário	**26**	factory worker	
fazendeiro	**27**	farmer	
bombeiro	**28**	firefighter	
pescador	**29**	fisher	
funcionário de restaurante	**30**	food-service worker	
supervisor	**31**	foreman	

jardineira/paisagista	**32**	gardener/landscaper
operário têxtil	**33**	garment worker
cabeleireira	**34**	hairdresser
auxiliar/atendente de enfermagem	**35**	health-care aide/attendant
atendente de cuidados domiciliares/ cuidador domiciliar	**36**	home health aide/ home attendant
responsável pelo trabalho doméstico/dono-de-casa	**37**	homemaker
camareira	**38**	housekeeper

A. What do you do?
B. I'm an **accountant**. How about you?
A. I'm a **carpenter**.

[At a job interview]
A. Are you an experienced _____?
B. Yes. I'm a very experienced _____.

A. How long have you been a/an _____?
B. I've been a/an _____ for .... months/years.

Which of these occupations do you think are the most interesting? the most difficult? Why?

OCUPAÇÕES II

jornalista/repórter	**1**	journalist/reporter
advogada	**2**	lawyer
operador de máquina	**3**	machine operator
carteira	**4**	mail carrier/letter carrier
gerente	**5**	manager
manicure	**6**	manicurist
mecânica	**7**	mechanic
auxiliar médico	**8**	medical assistant/physician assistant
mensageira/entregadora	**9**	messenger/courier
funcionário de empresa de mudanças	**10**	mover
músico	**11**	musician
pintora	**12**	painter
farmacêutico	**13**	pharmacist
fotógrafa	**14**	photographer
aviadora/piloto de avião	**15**	pilot
policial	**16**	police officer
funcionário do correio	**17**	postal worker
recepcionista	**18**	receptionist
técnico de reparos	**19**	repairperson
vendedora	**20**	salesperson

lixeira/ coletora de lixo	21	sanitation worker/ trash collector	professor/instrutor	30 teacher/instructor
secretário	22	secretary	funcionário de telemarketing	31 telemarketer
guarda de segurança	23	security guard	tradutor/intérprete	32 translator/interpreter
recruta	24	serviceman	agente de viagens	33 travel agent
recruta	25	servicewoman	motorista de caminhão/ caminhoneiro	34 truck driver
estoquista	26	stock clerk	veterinário	35 veterinarian/vet
dono de loja/lojista	27	store owner/shopkeeper	garçom	36 waiter/server
supervisor	28	supervisor	garçonete	37 waitress/server
alfaiate	29	tailor	soldador	38 welder

A. What's your occupation?
B. I'm a **journalist**.
A. A **journalist**?
B. Yes. That's right.

A. Are you still a _____?
B. No. I'm a _____.
A. Oh. That's interesting.

A. What kind of job would you like in the future?
B. I'd like to be a _____.

Do you work? What's your occupation?

What are the occupations of people in your family?

HABILIDADES PROFISSIONAIS E ATIVIDADES DE TRABALHO

atuar	**1**	act
montar *componentes*	**2**	assemble *components*
ajudar *pacientes*	**3**	assist *patients*
assar	**4**	bake
construir *coisas*	**5**	build *things*/construct *things*
limpar	**6**	clean
cozinhar	**7**	cook
entregar *pizzas*	**8**	deliver *pizzas*
projetar *edifícios*	**9**	design *buildings*
desenhar	**10**	draw

dirigir *um caminhão*	**11**	drive *a truck*
arquivar	**12**	file
pilotar *um avião*	**13**	fly *an airplane*
cultivar *legumes*	**14**	grow *vegetables*
vigiar *edifícios*	**15**	guard *buildings*
gerenciar *um restaurante*	**16**	manage *a restaurant*
cortar *grama*	**17**	mow *lawns*
operar *equipamento*	**18**	operate *equipment*
pintar	**19**	paint
tocar *piano*	**20**	play the *piano*

Por favor complete esto.

Да. Yes.

preparar *comida*	**21**	**prepare** *food*
fazer *reparos*/consertar *coisas*	**22**	**repair** *things*/**fix** *things*
vender *carros*	**23**	**sell** *cars*
servir *comida*	**24**	**serve** *food*
costurar	**25**	**sew**
cantar	**26**	**sing**
falar *espanhol*	**27**	**speak** *Spanish*
supervisionar *pessoas*	**28**	**supervise** *people*

cuidar *de pessoas idosas*	**29**	**take care of** *elderly people*
controlar estoque	**30**	**take inventory**
ensinar	**31**	**teach**
traduzir	**32**	**translate**
datilografar/digitar	**33**	**type**
usar *uma máquina registradora*	**34**	**use** *a cash register*
lavar *pratos*	**35**	**wash** *dishes*
escrever	**36**	**write**

A. Can you **act**?
B. Yes, I can.

A. Do you know how to _____?
B. Yes. I've been _____ing for years.

A. Tell me about your skills.
B. I can _____, and I can _____.

Tell about your job skills.
What can you do?

PROCURA DE EMPREGO

CASHIERS
FT & PT positions avail. $11/hr.
④ ⑤ ⑥ ⑦
M-F. Days & eves. Prev. exper. req.
⑧ ⑨ ⑩ ⑪ ⑫
Excel. salary. Save-Mart, 2540 Central Ave.
⑬

Tipos de anúncios de emprego	Types of Job Ads
cartaz de vaga de emprego	1 help wanted sign
anúncio de emprego	2 job notice/job announcement
anúncio classificado/ classificado de emprego	3 classified ad/want ad

Abreviações de classificados de emprego	Job Ad Abbreviations
período integral	4 full-time
meio-período	5 part-time
disponível	6 available
hora	7 hour
de segunda a sexta-feira	8 Monday through Friday
noites	9 evenings
anterior	10 previous
experiência	11 experience
exigida	12 required
excelente	13 excellent

Procura de emprego	Job Search
responder a um anúncio	A respond to an ad
pedir informações	B request information
pedir uma entrevista	C request an interview
preparar um currículo	D prepare a resume
vestir-se adequadamente	E dress appropriately
preencher um formulário de pedido de emprego	F fill out an application (form)
comparecer a uma entrevista	G go to an interview
falar sobre suas qualificações e habilidades profissionais	H talk about your skills and qualifications
falar sobre sua experiência	I talk about your experience
perguntar sobre o salário	J ask about the salary
perguntar sobre os benefícios	K ask about the benefits
escrever um bilhete de agradecimento	L write a thank-you note
ser contratado	M get hired

A. How did you find your job?
B. I found it through a ___[1–3]___.

A. How was your job interview?
B. It went very well.
A. Did you ___[D–F, H–M]___?
B. Yes, I did.

Tell about a job you are familiar with. What are the skills and qualifications required for the job? What are the hours? What is the salary?

Tell about how people you know found their jobs.

Tell about your own experience with a job search or a job interview.

O LOCAL DE TRABALHO

recepção	**A**	reception area	máquina de franquear	**7**	postage meter
sala de reuniões	**B**	conference room	auxiliar de escritório	**8**	office assistant
sala de correspondência	**C**	mailroom	caixa postal	**9**	mailbox
área de trabalho	**D**	work area	cubículo de trabalho	**10**	cubicle
escritório	**E**	office	poltrona giratória	**11**	swivel chair
sala de estoque	**F**	supply room	máquina de escrever	**12**	typewriter
almoxarifado	**G**	storage room	calculadora	**13**	adding machine
sala dos funcionários	**H**	employee lounge	copiadora/ fotocopiadora	**14**	copier/ photocopier
cabide de casacos	**1**	coat rack	trituradora de papéis	**15**	paper shredder
armário de casacos	**2**	coat closet	guilhotina	**16**	paper cutter
recepcionista	**3**	receptionist	arquivista	**17**	file clerk
mesa de reuniões	**4**	conference table	arquivo	**18**	file cabinet
cartaz de apresentação	**5**	presentation board	secretária	**19**	secretary
balança postal	**6**	postal scale	estação de trabalho	**20**	computer workstation
			patrão/chefe	**21**	employer/boss

assistente administrativo	**22**	administrative assistant
gerente de escritório	**23**	office manager
almoxarifado	**24**	supply cabinet
armário	**25**	storage cabinet
máquina de auto-serviço	**26**	vending machine
bebedouro	**27**	water cooler
máquina de café	**28**	coffee machine
quadro de avisos	**29**	message board
pegar um recado	**a**	take a message
fazer uma apresentação	**b**	give a presentation
distribuir a correspondência	**c**	sort the mail
fazer fotocópias	**d**	make copies
arquivar	**e**	file
digitar uma carta	**f**	type a letter

[A–H]
A. Where's ......(name)......?
B. He's/She's in the _____.

[1–29]
A. What do you think of the new _____?
B. He's/She's/It's very nice.

[a–f]
A. What's ......(name)...... doing?
B. He's/She's _____ing.

Describe a workplace you are familiar with. Tell about the rooms, the areas, and the employees.

MATERIAIS E EQUIPAMENTOS DE ESCRITÓRIO

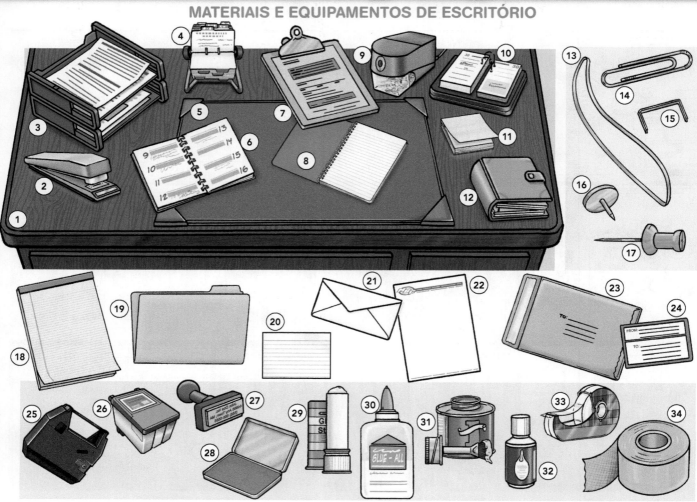

escrivaninha	1 desk	elástico	13 rubber band	cartucho de tinta	26 ink cartridge
grampeador	2 stapler	clipe	14 paper clip	carimbo	27 rubber stamp
bandeja para correspondência	3 letter tray/ stacking tray	grampo	15 staple	almofada para carimbo	28 ink pad
fichário rotativo	4 rotary card file	tachinha/ percevejo	16 thumbtack	bastão de cola	29 glue stick
protetor de mesa	5 desk pad	tachinha	17 pushpin	cola/cola branca	30 glue
agenda	6 appointment book	bloco de papel	18 legal pad	cola de borracha	31 rubber cement
prancha	7 clipboard	pasta de arquivo	19 file folder	corretivo líquido	32 correction fluid
caderno de anotações	8 note pad/ memo pad	ficha	20 index card	fita adesiva transparente	33 cellophane tape/ clear tape
apontador elétrico	9 electric pencil sharpener	envelope	21 envelope	fita adesiva para empacotamento de papel/ fita parda para empacotamento	34 packing tape/ sealing tape
calendário de mesa	10 desk calendar	papel de carta/ papel timbrado	22 stationery/ letterhead (paper)		
bloco auto-adesivo Post-It	11 Post-It note pad	envelope saco	23 mailer		
organizador/ agenda pessoal	12 organizer/ personal planner	etiqueta para correspondência	24 mailing label		
		cartucho de fita para máquina de escrever	25 typewriter cartridge		

A. My desk is a mess! I can't find my __[2–12]__ !
B. Here it is next to your __[2–12]__ .

A. Could you get some more __[13–21, 23–29]__ s/ __[22, 30–34]__ from the supply room?
B. Some more __[13–21, 23–29]__ s/ __[22, 30–34]__ ? Sure. I'd be happy to.

Which supplies and equipment do you use? What do you use them for?

Which supplies in this lesson do you have at home? at school?

A FÁBRICA

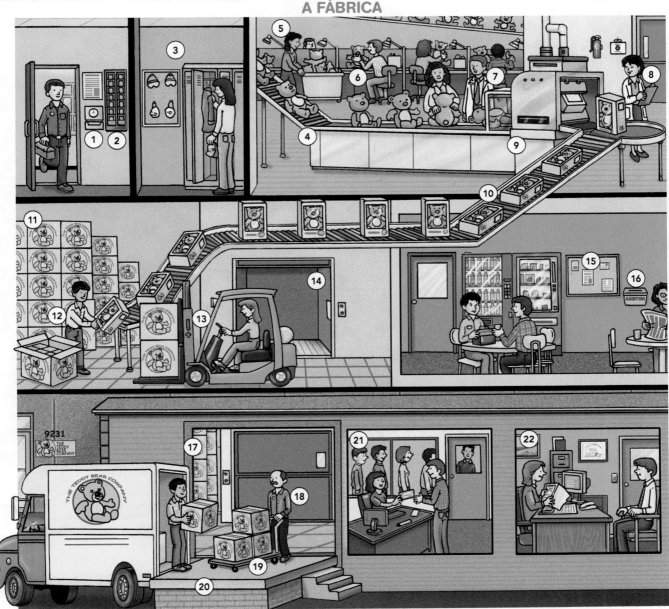

relógio de ponto	1	time clock
cartões de ponto	2	time cards
vestiário	3	locker room
linha de montagem	4	(assembly) line
operária	5	(factory) worker
estação de trabalho	6	work station
supervisor de linha	7	line supervisor
supervisora do controle de qualidade	8	quality control supervisor
máquina	9	machine
esteira transportadora	10	conveyor belt
armazém/depósito	11	warehouse
empacotador/embalador	12	packer
empilhadeira	13	forklift
elevador de carga	14	freight elevator
aviso do sindicato	15	union notice
caixa de sugestões	16	suggestion box
departamento de expedição	17	shipping department
funcionário da expedição	18	shipping clerk
carrinho de plataforma/carrinho	19	hand truck/dolly
cais de carga	20	loading dock
departamento de folha de pagamento	21	payroll office
departamento pessoal	22	personnel office

A. Excuse me. I'm a new employee.
   Where's/Where are the _____?
B. Next to/Near/In/On the _____.

A. Have you seen *Tony*?
B. Yes. *He's* in/on/at/next to/near
   the _____.

Are there any factories where you live? What kind?
What are the working conditions there?

What products do factories in your country produce?

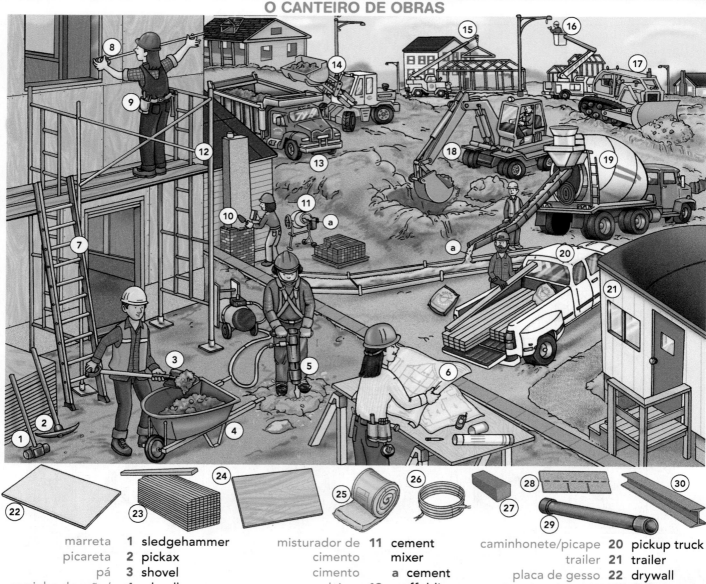

marreta	**1**	**sledgehammer**	misturador de cimento	**11**	**cement mixer**	caminhonete/picape	**20**	**pickup truck**

marreta · **1** **sledgehammer**
picareta · **2** **pickax**
pá · **3** **shovel**
carrinho de mão/ carriola · **4** **wheelbarrow**
britadeira/ martelo pneumático · **5** **jackhammer/ pneumatic drill**
plantas · **6** **blueprints**
escada · **7** **ladder**
fita métrica · **8** **tape measure**
cinturão de ferramentas · **9** **toolbelt**
colher de pedreiro · **10** **trowel**

misturador de cimento · **11** **cement mixer**
cimento · **a** **cement**
andaime · **12** **scaffolding**
caminhão basculante · **13** **dump truck**
carregadeira frontal · **14** **front-end loader**
guindaste · **15** **crane**
caminhão com cesta aérea · **16** **cherry picker**
buldôzer · **17** **bulldozer**
retroescavadeira · **18** **backhoe**
caminhão-betoneira · **19** **concrete mixer truck**
concreto · **a** **concrete**

caminhonete/picape · **20** **pickup truck**
trailer · **21** **trailer**
placa de gesso · **22** **drywall**
madeira/madeira de construção · **23** **wood/ lumber**
compensado/madeira compensada · **24** **plywood**
isolamento · **25** **insulation**
fio elétrico · **26** **wire**
tijolo · **27** **brick**
telha · **28** **shingle**
cano · **29** **pipe**
longarina/viga · **30** **girder/beam**

A. Could you get me that/those ___[1–10]___ ?
B. Sure.

A. Watch out for that ___[11–21]___ !
B. Oh! Thanks for the warning!

A. Do we have enough ___[22–26]___ / ___[27–30]___ s?
B. I think so.

What building materials is your home made of?
When was it built?

Describe a construction site near your home or school.
Tell about the construction equipment and the materials.

SEGURANÇA NO TRABALHO

capacete	1	hard hat/ helmet
protetores de ouvido	2	earplugs
óculos de proteção	3	goggles
colete de segurança	4	safety vest
botas de segurança	5	safety boots
protetor de dedos	6	toe guard
cinturão abdominal lombar	7	back support
abafador de ruídos/ protetor auricular tipo concha	8	safety earmuffs
rede para cabelo	9	hairnet
máscara	10	mask
luvas de látex	11	latex gloves
respirador	12	respirator
óculos de segurança	13	safety glasses
inflamável	14	flammable
venenoso/tóxico	15	poisonous
corrosivo	16	corrosive
radioativo	17	radioactive
perigoso	18	dangerous
área de risco	19	hazardous
biorrisco	20	biohazard
risco de choque elétrico	21	electrical hazard
estojo de primeiros socorros	22	first-aid kit
extintor de incêndio	23	fire extinguisher
desfibrilador	24	defibrillator
saída de emergência	25	emergency exit

A. Don't forget to wear your ___[1–13]___!
B. Thanks for reminding me.

A. Be careful!
That material is ___[14–17]___!
That machine is ___[18]___!
That work area is ___[19]___!
That's a ___[20]___!/That's an ___[21]___!
B. Thanks for the warning.

A. Where's the ___[22–25]___?
B. It's over there.

Have you ever used any of the safety equipment in this lesson? What have you used? When? Where?

Where do you see people using safety equipment in your community?

TRANSPORTE PÚBLICO

ônibus	**A**	**bus**
ponto de ônibus	**1**	bus stop
caminho do ônibus/ rota do ônibus	**2**	bus route
passageiro	**3**	passenger/rider
passagem de ônibus	**4**	(bus) fare
bilhete para transferência	**5**	transfer
motorista de ônibus	**6**	bus driver
rodoviária	**7**	bus station
balcão de passagens	**8**	ticket counter
passagem	**9**	ticket
bagageiro	**10**	baggage compartment/ luggage compartment

trem	**B**	**train**
estação de trens/ estação ferroviária	**11**	train station
guichê de passagens	**12**	ticket window
quadro de chegadas e partidas	**13**	arrival and departure board
balcão de informações	**14**	information booth
horário	**15**	schedule/ timetable
plataforma	**16**	platform
trilhos	**17**	track
condutor	**18**	conductor

metrô	**C**	**subway**
estação de metrô	**19**	subway station
ficha do metrô	**20**	(subway) token
catraca	**21**	turnstile
bilhete	**22**	fare card
máquina de bilhetes	**23**	fare card machine

táxi	**D**	**taxi**
ponto de táxi	**24**	taxi stand
táxi	**25**	taxi/cab/taxicab
taxímetro	**26**	meter
motorista de táxi	**27**	cab driver/ taxi driver

| balsa | **E** | **ferry** |

[A–E]
A. How are you going to get there?
B. { I'm going to take the ___[A–C, E]___ .
{ I'm going to take a ___[D]___ .

[1, 7, 8, 10–19, 21, 23–25]
A. Excuse me. Where's the _____?
B. Over there.

How do you get to different places in your community? Describe public transportation where you live.

In your country, can you travel far by train or by bus? Where can you go? How much do tickets cost? Describe the buses and trains.

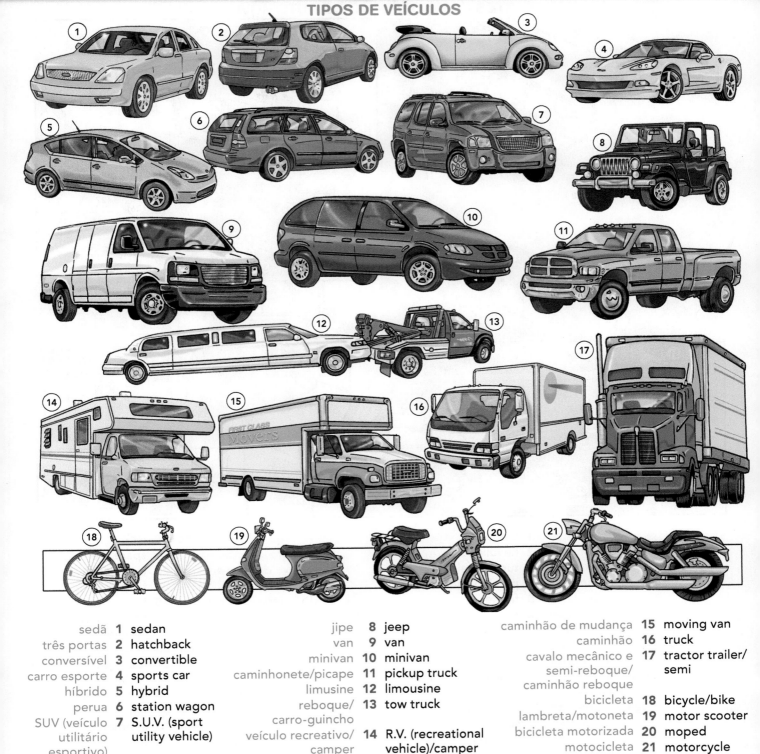

sedã	**1**	sedan	jipe	**8**	jeep	caminhão de mudança **15** moving van
três portas	**2**	hatchback	van	**9**	van	caminhão **16** truck
conversível	**3**	convertible	minivan	**10**	minivan	cavalo mecânico e **17** tractor trailer/
carro esporte	**4**	sports car	caminhonete/picape	**11**	pickup truck	semi-reboque/ semi
híbrido	**5**	hybrid	limusine	**12**	limousine	caminhão reboque
perua	**6**	station wagon	reboque/	**13**	tow truck	bicicleta **18** bicycle/bike
SUV (veículo	**7**	S.U.V. (sport	carro-guincho			lambreta/motoneta **19** motor scooter
utilitário		utility vehicle)	veículo recreativo/	**14**	R.V. (recreational	bicicleta motorizada **20** moped
esportivo)			camper		vehicle)/camper	motocicleta **21** motorcycle

A. What kind of vehicle are you looking for?
B. I'm looking for a **sedan**.

A. Do you drive a/an _____?
B. No. I drive a/an _____.

A. I just saw an accident between a/an _____ and a/an _____!
B. Was anybody hurt?
A. No. Fortunately, nobody was hurt.

What are the most common types of vehicles in your country?

What's your favorite type of vehicle? Why? In your opinion, which company makes the best one?

PARTES E MANUTENÇÃO DE AUTOMÓVEL

pára-choque	**1** bumper	macaco	**26** jack
farol dianteiro	**2** headlight	pneu sobressalente/estepe	**27** spare tire
pisca-pisca/indicador de direção	**3** turn signal	chave de roda em cruz	**28** lug wrench
luz de estacionamento	**4** parking light	tocha	**29** flare
pára-lama	**5** fender	cabo de bateria para chupeta	**30** jumper cables
pneu	**6** tire	velas de ignição	**31** spark plugs
calota	**7** hubcap	filtro de ar	**32** air filter
capô	**8** hood	motor	**33** engine
pára-brisa	**9** windshield	sistema de injeção de combustível	**34** fuel injection system
limpadores de pára-brisa	**10** windshield wipers	radiador	**35** radiator
espelho lateral	**11** side mirror	mangueira de radiador	**36** radiator hose
bagageiro de teto	**12** roof rack	correia da ventoinha	**37** fan belt
teto solar	**13** sunroof	alternador	**38** alternator
antena	**14** antenna	vareta de óleo	**39** dipstick
janela traseira	**15** rear window	bateria	**40** battery
desembaçador traseiro	**16** rear defroster	bomba de ar	**41** air pump
porta-malas	**17** trunk	bomba de gasolina	**42** gas pump
farol traseiro	**18** taillight	bico	**43** nozzle
luz de freio	**19** brake light	tampa do tanque de combustível	**44** gas cap
luz de ré	**20** backup light	gasolina	**45** gas
placa de automóvel	**21** license plate	óleo	**46** oil
escape/cano de escapamento	**22** tailpipe/exhaust pipe	líquido de resfriamento/	**47** coolant
silenciador	**23** muffler	fluido para radiador	
transmissão	**24** transmission	ar	**48** air
tanque de combustível	**25** gas tank		

air bag/airbag	49	air bag
pára-sol	50	visor
espelho retrovisor	51	rearview mirror
painel de instrumentos	52	dashboard/ instrument panel
indicador de temperatura	53	temperature gauge
indicador do nível de combustível	54	gas gauge/ fuel gauge
velocímetro	55	speedometer
odômetro	56	odometer
luzes de advertência	57	warning lights
pisca-pisca/ indicador de direção	58	turn signal
volante	59	steering wheel
buzina	60	horn
ignição	61	ignition

entrada de ar	62	vent
sistema de navegação	63	navigation system
rádio	64	radio
aparelho de CD	65	CD player
aquecedor	66	heater
ar condicionado	67	air conditioning
desembaçador	68	defroster
tomada elétrica	69	power outlet
porta-luvas	70	glove compartment
freio de emergência	71	emergency brake
pedal do freio	72	brake (pedal)
acelerador/ pedal do acelerador	73	accelerator/ gas pedal

câmbio automático	74	automatic transmission
alavanca de mudança de marcha	75	gearshift
câmbio manual	76	manual transmission
alavanca de mudança de marcha manual	77	stickshift
embreagem	78	clutch
trava da porta	79	door lock
maçaneta da porta	80	door handle
cinto de segurança diagonal	81	shoulder harness
apoio do braço	82	armrest
apoio de cabeça	83	headrest
assento	84	seat
cinto de segurança	85	seat belt

[2, 3, 9–16, 24, 35–39, 49–85]
A. What's the matter with your car?
B. The _____(s) is/are broken.

[45–48]
A. Can I help you?
B. { Yes. My car needs __[45–47]__.
{ Yes. My tires need __[48]__.

[1, 2, 4–15, 17–23, 25]
A. I was just in a car accident!
B. Oh, no! Were you hurt?
A. No. But my _____(s) was/were damaged.

In your opinion, what are the most important features to look for when you buy a car?

Do you own a car? What kind? Tell about any repairs your car has needed.

ESTRADAS E RUAS

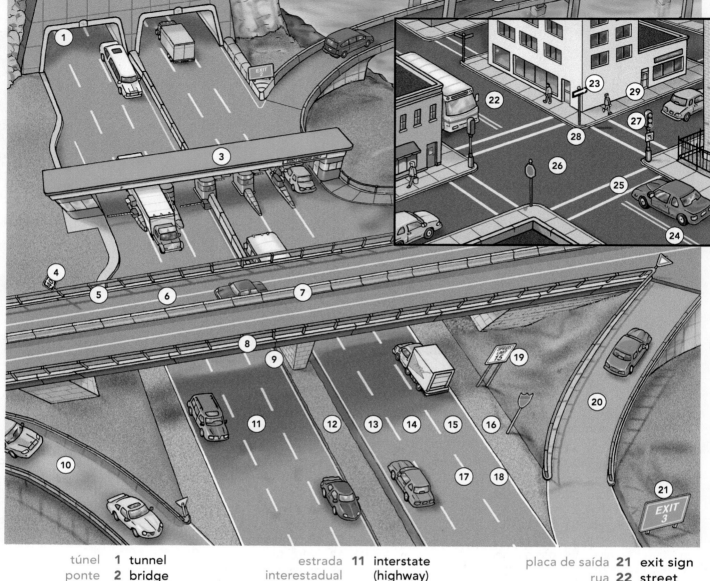

túnel	**1**	tunnel
ponte	**2**	bridge
pedágio	**3**	tollbooth
sinal rodoviário	**4**	route sign
rodovia	**5**	highway
estrada	**6**	road
divisória/ separador central	**7**	divider/ barrier
viaduto	**8**	overpass
passagem inferior	**9**	underpass
rampa	**10**	entrance ramp/ on ramp

estrada interestadual	**11**	interstate (highway)
canteiro central	**12**	median
faixa da esquerda	**13**	left lane
faixa central	**14**	middle lane/ center lane
faixa da direita	**15**	right lane
acostamento	**16**	shoulder
faixa seccionada	**17**	broken line
faixa contínua	**18**	solid line
placa de velocidade	**19**	speed limit sign
rampa de saída	**20**	exit (ramp)

placa de saída	**21**	exit sign
rua	**22**	street
rua de mão única	**23**	one-way street
faixa dupla contínua	**24**	double yellow line
travessia de pedestres/ faixa de pedestres	**25**	crosswalk
cruzamento	**26**	intersection
semáforo/ farol de trânsito	**27**	traffic light/ traffic signal
esquina	**28**	corner
quarteirão	**29**	block

[1–28]
A. Where's the accident?
B. It's on/in/at/near the _____.

Describe a highway you travel on.

Describe an intersection near where you live.

In your area, on which highways and streets do most accidents occur? Why are these places dangerous?

PREPOSIÇÕES DE MOVIMENTO

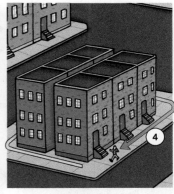

sobre	**1** over	para lá	**5** up	dentro	**9** on
sob	**2** under	para cá	**6** down	fora	**10** off
através	**3** through	no outro lado	**7** across	para dentro	**11** into
ao redor	**4** around	além	**8** past	para fora	**12** out of
				em direção a	**13** onto

[1–8]
A. Go **over** the bridge.
B. **Over** the bridge?
A. Yes.

[9–13]
A. I can't talk right now. I'm getting **on** a train.
B. You're getting **on** a train?
A. Yes. I'll call you later.

What places do you go past on your way to school?   Tell how to get to different places from your home or your school.

Sinais de trânsito	Traffic Signs				
parada obrigatória	**1** stop	dê a preferência	**13** yield	Instruções para	Road Test
proibido virar à esquerda	**2** no left turn	desvio	**14** detour	o exame de	Instructions
proibido virar à direita	**3** no right turn	pista escorregadia	**15** slippery	motorista	
proibido retornar	**4** no U-turn	quando molhada	when wet	Vire à esquerda.	**21** Turn left.
vire à direita	**5** right turn only	estacionamento	**16** handicapped	Vire à direita.	**22** Turn right.
entrada proibida	**6** do not enter	exclusivo para	parking only	Vá em frente.	**23** Go straight.
sentido único	**7** one way	deficientes físicos		Faça baliza.	**24** Parallel park.
rua sem saída/sem saída	**8** dead end/no outlet			Fazer uma	**25** Make a
passagem de pedestres	**9** pedestrian crossing	**Pontos**	**Compass**	conversão	3-point turn.
passagem de nível	**10** railroad crossing	**cardeais**	**Directions**	de 3 pontos.	
passagem de escolares	**11** school crossing	norte	**17** north	Usar sinais	**26** Use hand
confluência	**12** merging traffic	sul	**18** south	de mão.	signals.
		oeste	**19** west		
		leste	**20** east		

[1–16]
A. Careful! That sign says "**stop**"!
B. Oh. Thanks.

[17–20]
A. Which way should I go?
B. Go **north**.

[21–26]
A. Turn **right**.
B. Turn **right**?
A. Yes.

Which of these traffic signs are in your neighborhood?
What other traffic signs do you usually see?

Describe any differences between traffic signs in
different countries you know.

O AEROPORTO

Fazer o check-in/fazer o registro para o vôo	**A**	**Check-In**
passagem	**1**	ticket
balcão de passagens	**2**	ticket counter
agente de passagens	**3**	ticket agent
mala	**4**	suitcase
monitor de chegadas e partidas	**5**	arrival and departure monitor
Segurança	**B**	**Security**
inspeção de segurança	**6**	security checkpoint
detector de metais	**7**	metal detector
guarda de segurança/ agente de proteção da aviação civil	**8**	security officer
aparelho de raio X	**9**	X-ray machine
bagagem de mão	**10**	carry-on bag
Portão (o)	**C**	**The Gate**
balcão de check-in	**11**	check-in counter
cartão de embarque	**12**	boarding pass
portão	**13**	gate
área de embarque	**14**	boarding area
Recebimento de bagagem	**D**	**Baggage Claim**
área de recebimento de bagagem	**15**	baggage claim (area)
esteira de bagagens	**16**	baggage carousel
bagagem	**17**	baggage
carrinho de bagagem	**18**	baggage cart/luggage cart
carrinho de mala	**19**	luggage carrier
porta-ternos etiqueta	**20**	garment bag
de destino da bagagem	**21**	baggage claim check
Alfândega e imigração	**E**	**Customs and Immigration**
alfândega	**22**	customs
funcionário da alfândega	**23**	customs officer
formulário de declaração alfandegária	**24**	customs declaration form
imigração	**25**	immigration
funcionário da imigração	**26**	immigration officer
passaporte	**27**	passport
visto	**28**	visa

[2, 3, 5–9, 11, 13–16, 22, 23, 25, 26]
A. Excuse me. Where's the _____?*
B. Right over there.

* With 22 and 25, use: Excuse me. Where's _____?

[1, 4, 10, 12, 17–21, 24, 27, 28]
A. Oh, no! I think I've lost my _____!
B. I'll help you look for it.

Describe an airport you are familiar with. Tell about the check-in area, the security area, the gates, and the baggage claim area.

Have you ever gone through Customs and Immigration? Tell about your experience.

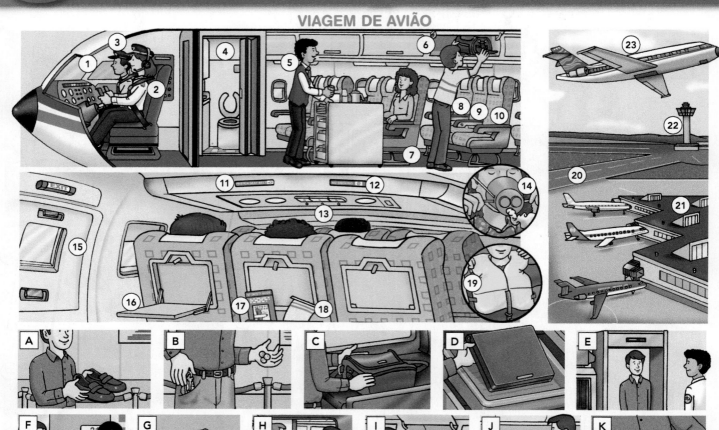

cabina de pilotagem/ cabina de comando	**1**	cockpit
piloto/capitão	**2**	pilot/captain
co-piloto	**3**	co-pilot
lavatório/banheiro	**4**	lavatory/bathroom
comissário de bordo	**5**	flight attendant
compartimento de bagagem	**6**	overhead compartment
corredor	**7**	aisle
assento da janela	**8**	window seat
assento do meio	**9**	middle seat
assento do corredor	**10**	aisle seat
aviso de apertar os cintos	**11**	Fasten Seat Belt sign
aviso de não fumar	**12**	No Smoking sign
botão para chamar o comissário de bordo	**13**	call button
máscara de oxigênio	**14**	oxygen mask
saída de emergência	**15**	emergency exit
mesinha	**16**	tray (table)
cartão com instruções de emergência	**17**	emergency instruction card
saquinho para enjôo	**18**	air sickness bag

colete salva-vidas	**19**	life vest/life jacket
pista	**20**	runway
edifício do terminal	**21**	terminal (building)
torre de controle	**22**	control tower
avião/jato	**23**	airplane/plane/jet
tirar os sapatos	**A**	take off your shoes
esvaziar os bolsos	**B**	empty your pockets
colocar a mala na esteira transportadora	**C**	put your bag on the conveyor belt
colocar o computador na bandeja	**D**	put your computer in a tray
passar pelo detector de metais	**E**	walk through the metal detector
fazer o check-in no portão de embarque	**F**	check in at the gate
pegar o cartão de embarque	**G**	get your boarding pass
embarcar no avião	**H**	board the plane
guardar a bagagem de mão no compartimento	**I**	stow your carry-on bag
encontrar seu assento	**J**	find your seat
apertar o cinto de segurança	**K**	fasten your seat belt

[1–23]
A. Where's the _____?
B. In/On/Next to/Behind/In front of/ Above/Below the _____.

[A–K]
A. Please _____.
B. All right. Certainly.

Have you ever flown in an airplane? Tell about a flight you took.

Be an airport security officer! Give passengers instructions as they go through the security area. Now, be a flight attendant! Give passengers instructions before take-off.

O HOTEL

porteiro	1 doorman
estacionamento com manobrista	2 valet parking
manobrista	3 parking attendant
mensageiro de hotel	4 bellhop
carrinho de bagagem	5 luggage cart
supervisor dos mensageiros do hotel	6 bell captain

sagüão	7 lobby
recepção	8 front desk
recepcionista	9 desk clerk
hóspede	10 guest
balcão de informações	11 concierge desk
encarregado do balcão de informações	12 concierge
restaurante	13 restaurant
sala de reuniões	14 meeting room
loja de presentes	15 gift shop

piscina	16 pool
sala de ginástica	17 exercise room
elevador	18 elevator
máquina de gelo	19 ice machine
corredor	20 hall/hallway
chave do quarto	21 room key
carrinho da governanta	22 housekeeping cart
camareira	23 housekeeper
quarto de hóspede	24 guest room
serviço de quarto	25 room service

A. Where do you work?
B. I work at the *Grand* Hotel.
A. What do you do there?
B. I'm a/an _____ [1, 3, 4, 6, 9, 12, 23] _____.

A. Excuse me. Where's the _____ [1–19, 22, 23] _____?
B. Right over there.
A. Thanks.

Tell about a hotel you are familiar with. Describe the place and the people.

In your opinion, which hotel employee has the most interesting job? the most difficult job? Why?

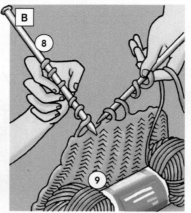
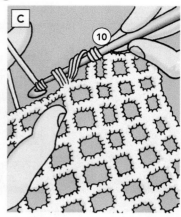
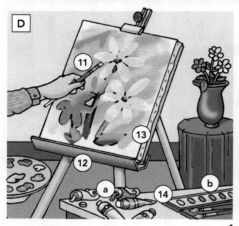

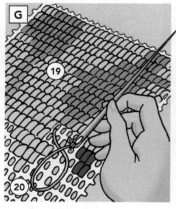

costurar	**A**	**sew**
máquina de costura	1	sewing machine
alfinete	2	pin
almofada de alfinetes	3	pin cushion
carretel de linha	4	(spool of) thread
agulha de costura	5	(sewing) needle
dedal	6	thimble
alfinete de segurança	7	safety pin
tricotar	**B**	**knit**
agulha de tricô	8	knitting needle
fio	9	yarn

fazer crochê	**C**	**crochet**
agulha de crochê	10	crochet hook
pintar	**D**	**paint**
pincel	11	paintbrush
cavalete	12	easel
tela	13	canvas
tinta	14	paint
tinta a óleo		**a** oil paint
aquarela		**b** watercolor
desenhar	**E**	**draw**
caderno de esboços	15	sketch book
conjunto de lápis de cor	16	(set of) colored pencils
lápis para desenho	17	drawing pencil

bordar	**F**	**do embroidery**
bordado	18	embroidery
fazer tapeçaria	**G**	**do needlepoint**
trabalho com agulha	19	needlepoint
molde	20	pattern
fazer trabalho em madeira	**H**	**do woodworking**
kit de trabalho em madeira	21	woodworking kit
fazer origami	**I**	**do origami**
papel para origami	22	origami paper
fazer cerâmica	**J**	**make pottery**
argila	23	clay
torno de cerâmica	24	potter's wheel

  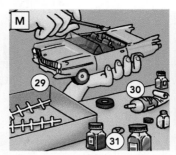 

 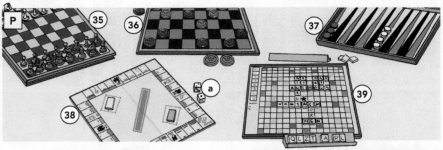

colecionar selos **K collect stamps**	jogar cartas/ **O play cards**	jogo de palavras **39 Scrabble**
álbum de selos **25 stamp album**	jogar baralho	cruzadas Scrabble
lupa **26 magnifying glass**	baralho **34 (deck of) cards**	
	de cartas	entrar na rede/ **Q go online/**
colecionar moedas **L collect coins**	paus **a club**	conectar-se/ **browse the Web/**
catálogo de moedas **27 coin catalog**	ouros **b diamond**	navegar **"surf" the net**
coleção de moedas **28 coin collection**	copas **c heart**	pela internet/
	espadas **d spade**	usar a internet
construir modelos **M build models**		navegador **40 web browser**
modelo **29 model kit**	jogar jogos **P play board**	de internet
cola **30 glue**	de tabuleiro **games**	endereço de **41 web address/**
tinta acrílico **31 acrylic paint**	xadrez **35 chess**	internet/URL **URL**
	damas **36 checkers**	
observar pássaros **N go bird-watching**	gamão **37 backgammon**	fotografia **R photography**
binóculos **32 binoculars**	Banco **38 Monopoly**	câmara **42 camera**
guia de campo **33 field guide**	Imobiliário	
	dados **a dice**	astronomia **S astronomy**
		telescópio **43 telescope**

A. What do you like to do in your free time?
B. { I like to ___[A–Q]___.
     I enjoy ___[R, S]___.

A. May I help you?
B. Yes, please. I'd like to buy (a/an) ___[1–34, 42, 43]___.

A. What do you want to do?
B. Let's play ___[35–39]___.
A. Good idea!

Do you like to do any of these activities in your free time? Which ones?

What games are popular in your country? Describe how to play one.

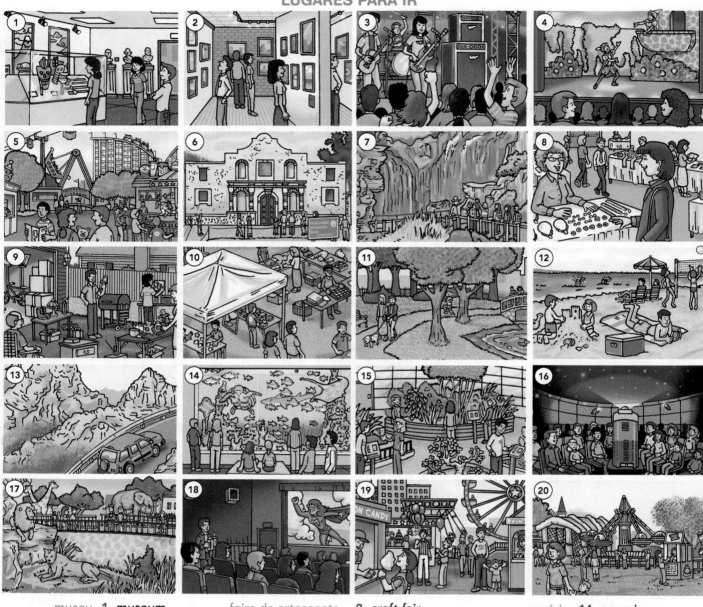

museu	**1** museum	feira de artesanato	**8** craft fair
galeria de arte	**2** art gallery	venda de objetos usados	**9** yard sale
concerto	**3** concert	feira de trocas/ mercado de pulgas	**10** swap meet/ flea market
peça	**4** play	parque	**11** park
parque de diversões	**5** amusement park	praia	**12** beach
local histórico	**6** historic site	montanhas	**13** mountains
parque nacional	**7** national park		

aquário	**14** aquarium		
jardim botânico	**15** botanical gardens		
planetário	**16** planetarium		
zoológico	**17** zoo		
cinema	**18** movies		
parque de diversões	**19** carnival		
exposição	**20** fair		

A. What do you want to do today?
B. Let's go to { a/an ____ [1–9] . the ____ [10–20] .

A. What did you do over the weekend?
B. I went to { a/an ____ [1–9] . the ____ [10–20] .

A. What are you going to do on your day off?
B. I'm going to go to { a/an ____ [1–9] . the ____ [10–20] .

What are some of your favorite places to go? Where are they? What do you do there?

Portuguese	#	English
ciclovia	1	bicycle path/ bike path/ bikeway
laguinho de patos	2	duck pond
área para piqueniques	3	picnic area
lixeira	4	trash can
churrasqueira	5	grill
mesa de piquenique	6	picnic table
bebedouro	7	water fountain
pista de corrida	8	jogging path

Portuguese	#	English
banco	9	bench
quadra de tênis	10	tennis court
campo de beisebol	11	ballfield
fonte	12	fountain
estacionamento de bicicletas	13	bike rack
carrossel	14	merry-go-round/ carousel
rampa para skate	15	skateboard ramp

Portuguese	#	English
playground/ parquinho	16	playground
parede para escalar	17	climbing wall
balanços	18	swings
trepa-trepa	19	climber
escorregador	20	slide
gangorra	21	seesaw
caixa de areia	22	sandbox
areia	23	sand

[1–22]
A. Excuse me. Does this park have (a) _____?
B. Yes. Right over there.

[17–23]
A. { Be careful on the ___[17–21]___ !
{ Be careful in the ___[22, 23]___ !
B. I will, Dad/Mom.

Describe a park and playground you are familiar with.

salva-vidas	**1**	lifeguard	cadeira de praia	**10**	beach chair	pedra	**20** rock
posto de observação	**2**	lifeguard stand	guarda-sol	**11**	beach umbrella	geladeira térmica	**21** cooler
do salva-vidas			castelo de areia	**12**	sand castle	chapéu de sol	**22** sun hat
bóia	**3**	life preserver	prancha de	**13**	boogie board	filtro solar/	**23** sunscreen/
lanchonete/venda	**4**	snack bar/	bodyboarding			protetor solar/	sunblock/
		refreshment	pessoa tomando	**14**	sunbather	bronzeador	suntan
		stand	banho de sol				lotion
vendedor	**5**	vendor	óculos escuros/	**15**	sunglasses	toalha grande	**24** (beach)
banhista	**6**	swimmer	óculos de sol			de praia	blanket
onda	**7**	wave	toalha de praia	**16**	(beach) towel	pá	**25** shovel
surfista	**8**	surfer	bola de praia	**17**	beach ball	balde	**26** pail
pipa	**9**	kite	prancha de surfe	**18**	surfboard		
			concha	**19**	seashell/shell		

[1–26]
A. What a nice beach!
B. It is. Look at all the _____s!

[9–11, 13, 15–18, 21–26]
A. Are you ready for the beach?
B. Almost. I just have to get my _____.

Do you like to go to the beach? Describe your favorite beach. What do you take when you go there?

campismo	**A**	**camping**
barraca	**1**	tent
saco de dormir	**2**	sleeping bag
estacas	**3**	tent stakes
lampião	**4**	lantern
machadinha	**5**	hatchet
fogão de duas bocas	**6**	camping stove
canivete suíço	**7**	Swiss army knife
repelente de insetos	**8**	insect repellent
fósforos	**9**	matches

caminhadas no campo	**B**	**hiking**
mochila	**10**	backpack
cantil	**11**	canteen
bússola	**12**	compass
mapa da trilha	**13**	trail map
aparelho de GPS	**14**	GPS device
botas de caminhada	**15**	hiking boots
escalada em rocha/ escalada técnica	**C**	**rock climbing/ technical climbing**
cinto de escalada	**16**	harness
corda	**17**	rope

mountain bike	**D**	**mountain biking**
mountain bike	**18**	mountain bike
capacete de bicicleta	**19**	(bike) helmet
piquenique	**E**	**picnic**
toalha de piquenique	**20**	(picnic) blanket
garrafa térmica	**21**	thermos
cesta de piquenique	**22**	picnic basket

A. Let's go __[A–E]__ * this weekend.
B. Good idea! We haven't gone __[A–E]__ * in a long time.

*With E, say: on a picnic.

A. Did you bring
{ the __[1–9, 11–14, 16, 17, 20–22]__ ?
{ your __[10, 15, 18, 19]__ ?
B. Yes, I did.
A. Oh, good.

Have you ever gone camping, hiking, rock climbing, or mountain biking? Tell about it: What did you do? Where? What equipment did you use?

Do you like to go on picnics? Where?
What picnic supplies and food do you take with you?

RECREAÇÃO E ESPORTES INDIVIDUAIS

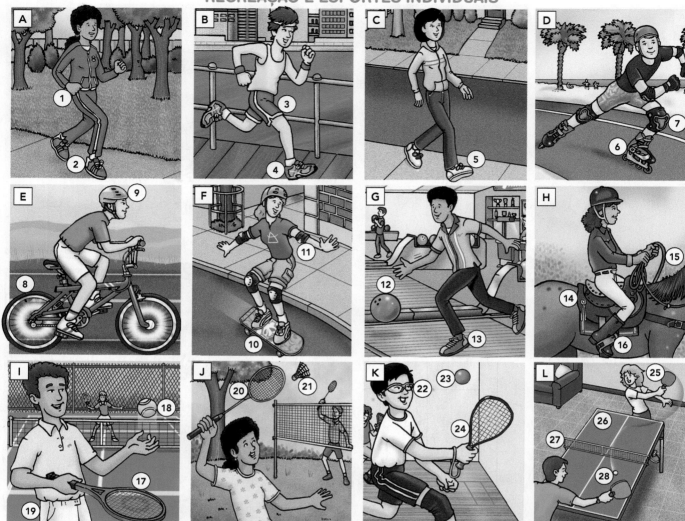

jogging	**A**	**jogging**
agasalho esportivo/jogging	**1**	jogging suit
tênis de jogging	**2**	jogging shoes
corrida	**B**	**running**
short de corrida	**3**	running shorts
tênis de corrida	**4**	running shoes
caminhada	**C**	**walking**
tênis de caminhada	**5**	walking shoes
patins inline/patins em linha	**D**	**inline skating/rollerblading**
patins inline	**6**	inline skates/rollerblades
joelheiras	**7**	knee pads
ciclismo	**E**	**cycling/biking**
bicicleta	**8**	bicycle/bike
capacete de bicicleta	**9**	(bicycle/bike) helmet
skate	**F**	**skateboarding**
skate	**10**	skateboard
cotoveleiras	**11**	elbow pads
boliche	**G**	**bowling**
bola de boliche	**12**	bowling ball
sapatos de boliche	**13**	bowling shoes

equitação	**H**	**horseback riding**
sela	**14**	saddle
rédeas	**15**	reins
estribos	**16**	stirrups
tênis	**I**	**tennis**
raquete de tênis	**17**	tennis racket
bola de tênis	**18**	tennis ball
bermuda de tênis	**19**	tennis shorts
badminton	**J**	**badminton**
raquete de badminton	**20**	badminton racket
peteca	**21**	birdie/shuttlecock
raquetebol	**K**	**racquetball**
óculos de proteção	**22**	safety goggles
bola de raquetebol	**23**	racquetball
raquete	**24**	racquet
tênis de mesa/ pingue-pongue	**L**	**table tennis/ ping pong**
raquete	**25**	paddle
mesa de pingue-pongue	**26**	ping pong table
rede	**27**	net
bola de pingue-pongue	**28**	ping pong ball

golfe	M	golf
tacos de golfe	29	golf clubs
bola de golfe	30	golf ball
Frisbee	**N**	**Frisbee**
Frisbee/ disco	31	Frisbee/ flying disc
bilhar/sinuca	**O**	**billiards/pool**
mesa de bilhar	32	pool table
taco de bilhar	33	pool stick
bolas de bilhar	34	billiard balls
artes marciais	**P**	**martial arts**
faixa preta	35	black belt

ginástica olímpica	Q	gymnastics
cavalo	36	horse
barras paralelas	37	parallel bars
esteira	38	mat
trave de equilíbrio	39	balance beam
cama elástica/ trampolim acrobático	40	trampoline
halterofilismo/ levantamento de peso	**R**	**weightlifting**
haltere	41	barbell
discos	42	weights
tiro com arco	**S**	**archery**
arco e flecha	43	bow and arrow
alvo	44	target

boxe	T	box
luvas de boxe	45	boxing gloves
calção	46	(boxing) trunks
luta	**U**	**wrestle**
uniforme de luta	47	wrestling uniform
esteira	48	(wrestling) mat
ginástica/ exercício	**V**	**work out/ exercise**
esteira ergométrica	49	treadmill
aparelho de remo seco	50	rowing machine
bicicleta ergométrica	51	exercise bike
equipamento de condicionamento físico	52	universal/ exercise equipment

[A–V]
A. What do you like to do in your free time?
B.
- I like to go ___[A–H]___.
- I like to play ___[I–O]___.
- I like to do ___[P–S]___.
- I like to ___[T–V]___.

[1–52]
A. I really like this/these new _____.
B. It's/They're very nice.

Do you do any of these activities? Which ones? Which are popular in your country?

TEAM SPORTS
ESPORTES DE EQUIPE

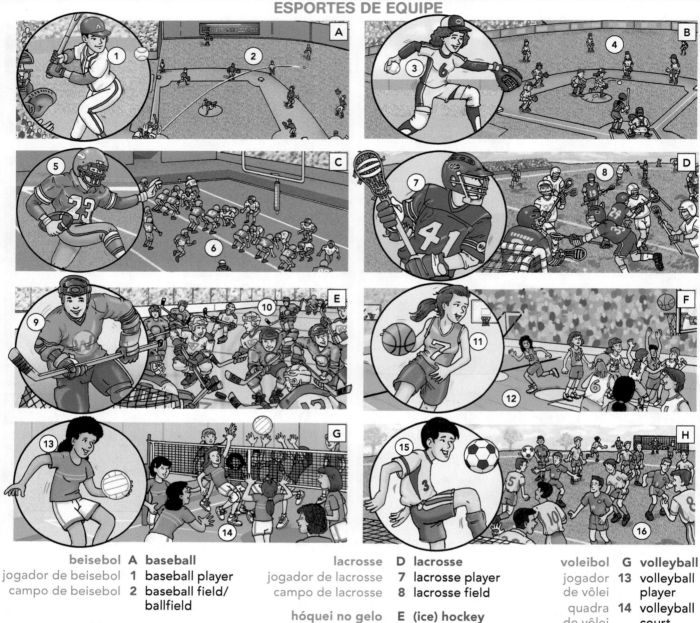

beisebol	**A**	**baseball**	lacrosse	**D**	**lacrosse**
jogador de beisebol	**1**	baseball player	jogador de lacrosse	**7**	lacrosse player
campo de beisebol	**2**	baseball field/ ballfield	campo de lacrosse	**8**	lacrosse field
softball	**B**	**softball**	hóquei no gelo	**E**	**(ice) hockey**
jogador de softball	**3**	softball player	jogador de hóquei	**9**	hockey player
campo de beisebol	**4**	ballfield	rinque de hóquei	**10**	hockey rink
futebol americano	**C**	**football**	basquetebol	**F**	**basketball**
jogador de futebol americano	**5**	football player	jogador de basquete	**11**	basketball player
campo de futebol americano	**6**	football field	quadra de basquete	**12**	basketball court

voleibol	**G**	**volleyball**
jogador de vôlei	**13**	volleyball player
quadra de vôlei	**14**	volleyball court
futebol	**H**	**soccer**
jogador de futebol	**15**	soccer player
campo de futebol	**16**	soccer field

[A–H]
A. Do you like to play **baseball**?
B. Yes. **Baseball** is one of my favorite sports.

A. .... plays __[A–H]__ very well.
B. You're right. I think he's/she's one of the best _____s* on the team.

*Use 1, 3, 5, 7, 9, 11, 13, 15.

A. Now listen, team! I want all of you to go out on that _____† and play the best game of __[A–H]__ you've ever played!
B. All right, Coach!

† Use 2, 4, 6, 8, 10, 12, 14, 16.

Which sports in this lesson do you like to play? Which do you like to watch?

What are your favorite teams?

Name some famous players of these sports.

TEAM SPORTS EQUIPMENT

EQUIPAMENTOS DE ESPORTES DE EQUIPE

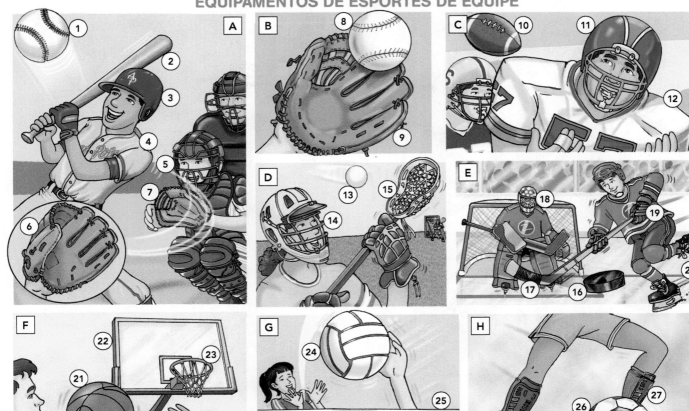

beisebol **A baseball**	futebol americano **C football**	basquetebol **F basketball**
bola de beisebol **1 baseball**	bola de futebol americano **10 football**	bola de basquete **21 basketball**
bastão **2 bat**	capacete de **11 football helmet**	tabela **22 backboard**
capacete do **3 batting**	futebol americano	cesto **23 basketball**
batedor **helmet**	protetores de ombro **12 shoulder pads**	**hoop**
uniforme de **4 (baseball)**		
beisebol **uniform**	lacrosse **D lacrosse**	voleibol **G volleyball**
máscara do **5 catcher's**	bola de lacrosse **13 lacrosse ball**	bola de vôlei **24 volleyball**
apanhador **mask**	proteção do rosto **14 face guard**	rede de vôlei **25 volleyball net**
luva de **6 (baseball)**	taco de lacrosse **15 lacrosse stick**	
beisebol **glove**		futebol **H soccer**
luva do **7 catcher's**	hóquei no gelo **E (ice) hockey**	bola de futebol **26 soccer ball**
apanhador **mitt**	disco de hóquei **16 hockey puck**	caneleiras **27 shinguards**
	taco de hóquei **17 hockey stick**	
softball **B softball**	máscara de proteção **18 hockey mask**	
bola de softball **8 softball**	de hóquei	
luva de softball **9 softball glove**	luva de hóquei **19 hockey glove**	
	patins de hóquei **20 hockey skates**	

[1–27]
A. I can't find my **baseball**!
B. Look in the closet.*

*closet, basement, garage

[In a store]
A. Excuse me. I'm looking for (a) __[1–27]__.
B. All our __[A–H]__ equipment is over there.
A. Thanks.

[At home]
A. I'm going to play __[A–H]__ after school today.
B. Don't forget your __[1–21, 24, 26, 27]__ !

Which sports in this lesson are popular in your country? Which sports do students play in high school?

esqui alpino	**A**	**(downhill) skiing**	
esquis	**1**	**skis**	
botas de esqui	**2**	**ski boots**	
fixações	**3**	**bindings**	
hastes de esqui	**4**	**(ski) poles**	
esqui de corrida de fundo/ esqui cross-country	**B**	**cross-country skiing**	
esquis de cross-country	**5**	**cross-country skis**	
patinação no gelo	**C**	**(ice) skating**	
patins de gelo	**6**	**(ice) skates**	
lâmina	**7**	**blade**	
protetor de lâmina	**8**	**skate guard**	

patinação artística	**D**	**figure skating**
patins de patinação artística/ patins de patinação no gelo	**9**	**figure skates**
snowboard	**E**	**snowboarding**
prancha de snowboard	**10**	**snowboard**
tobogã	**F**	**sledding**
tobogã	**11**	**sled**
disco de tobogã/tobogã	**12**	**sledding dish/saucer**
bobsled	**G**	**bobsledding**
trenó de bobsled	**13**	**bobsled**
snowmobile	**H**	**snowmobiling**
snowmobile	**14**	**snowmobile**

[A–H]
A. What's your favorite winter sport?
B. **Skiing.**

[A–H]
[At work or at school on Friday]
A. What are you going to do this weekend?
B. I'm going to go _____.

[1–14]
[On the telephone]
A. Hello. *Sally's* Sporting Goods.
B. Hello. Do you sell _____(s)?
A. Yes, we do. / No, we don't.

Have you ever done any of these activities? Which ones?

Have you ever watched the Winter Olympics? Which event do you think is the most exciting? the most dangerous?

RECREAÇÃO E ESPORTES AQUÁTICOS

vela	**A sailing**
barco à vela/veleiro/vela	1 sailboat
colete salva-vidas	2 life jacket/life vest
canoagem	**B canoeing**
canoa	3 canoe
remos	4 paddles
remo	**C rowing**
barco a remo	5 rowboat
remos	6 oars
caiaque	**D kayaking**
caiaque	7 kayak
remos	8 paddles
rafting por corredeiras	**E (white-water) rafting**
bote inflável	9 raft
colete salva-vidas	10 life jacket/life vest
natação	**F swimming**
maiô	11 swimsuit/ bathing suit
óculos de natação	12 goggles
touca de natação	13 bathing cap
snorkeling/snorkel	**G snorkeling**
máscara	14 mask

snorkel/tubo para respiração	15 snorkel
nadadeiras	16 fins
mergulho submarino	**H scuba diving**
roupa isotérmica/ roupa de neoprene	17 wet suit
tanque de mergulho	18 (air) tank
máscara de mergulho	19 (diving) mask
surfe	**I surfing**
prancha de surfe	20 surfboard
windsurfe	**J windsurfing**
prancha de windsurfe	21 sailboard
vela	22 sail
esqui aquático	**K waterskiing**
esquis aquáticos	23 water skis
corda	24 towrope
pesca	**L fishing**
vara de pesca	25 (fishing) rod/ pole
molinete	26 reel
fio de pesca	27 (fishing) line
rede de pesca	28 (fishing) net
isca	29 bait

[A–L]
A. Would you like to go **sailing** tomorrow?
B. Sure. I'd love to.

A. Have you ever gone __[A–L]__ ?
B. Yes, I have./ No, I haven't.

A. Do you have everything you need to go __[A–L]__ ?
B. Yes. I have my __[1–29]__ (and my __[1–29]__).
A. Have a good time!

Which sports in this lesson have you tried?
Which sports would you like to try?

Are any of these sports popular in your country? Which ones?

AÇÕES DE ESPORTE E EXERCÍCIOS

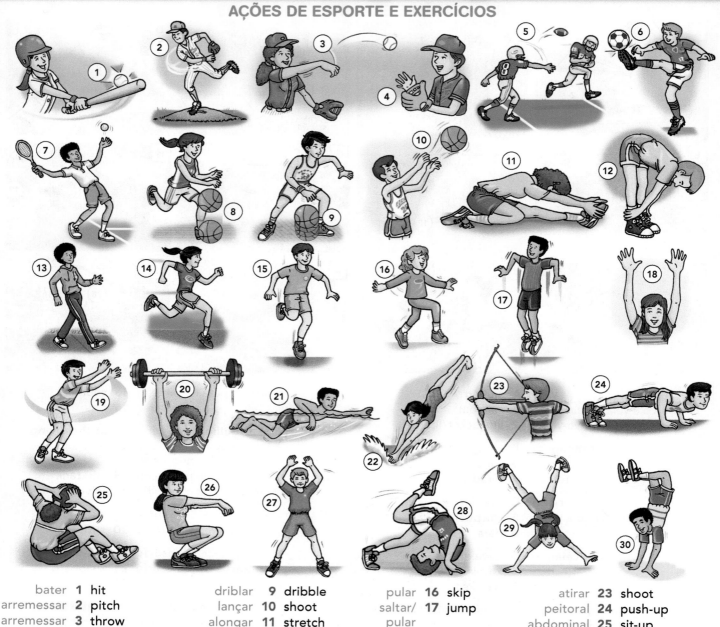

bater **1** hit	driblar **9** dribble	pular **16** skip	atirar **23** shoot
arremessar **2** pitch	lançar **10** shoot	saltar/ **17** jump	peitoral **24** push-up
arremessar **3** throw	alongar **11** stretch	pular	abdominal **25** sit-up
pegar **4** catch	curvar **12** bend	estirar/ **18** reach	flexão **26** deep knee bend
passar **5** pass	caminhar/ **13** walk	alcançar	tesoura **27** jumping jack
chutar **6** kick	andar	balançar **19** swing	cambalhota **28** somersault
dar o **7** serve	correr **14** run	levantar **20** lift	estrela **29** cartwheel
saque	pular de **15** hop	nadar **21** swim	plantar **30** handstand
bater **8** bounce	uma perna só	mergulhar **22** dive	bananeira

[1–10]
A. _____ the ball!
B. Okay, Coach!

[11–23]
A. Now _____!
B. Like this?
A. Yes.

[24–30]
A. Okay, everybody. I want you
   to do twenty _____s!
B. Twenty _____s?!
A. That's right.

Do you exercise regularly?
Which exercises do you do?

Be an exercise instructor! Lead your friends in an exercise
routine using the actions in this lesson.

ENTRETENIMENTO

peça	A	play
teatro	1	theater
ator	2	actor
atriz	3	actress

concerto	B	concert
sala de concertos	4	concert hall
orquestra	5	orchestra
músico	6	musician
maestro	7	conductor
conjunto/banda	8	band

ópera	C	opera
cantora de ópera	9	opera singer

balé	D	ballet
bailarino	10	ballet dancer
bailarina	11	ballerina

casa de show	E	music club
cantora	12	singer

cinema	F	movies
cinema/ sala de cinema	13	(movie) theater
tela de cinema	14	(movie) screen
atriz	15	actress
ator	16	actor

clube de comédia	G	comedy club
comediante	17	comedian

[A–G]
A. What are you doing this evening?
B. I'm going to { a ___ [A, B, E, G].
the ___ [C, D, F]. }

[1–17]
A. What a magnificent ___!
B. I agree.

What kinds of entertainment in this lesson do you like?
What kinds of entertainment are popular in your country?

Who are some of your favorite actors? actresses?
musicians? singers? comedians?

A

B

música	**A**	**music**
música clássica/ música erudita	**1**	classical music
música popular	**2**	popular music
música country	**3**	country music
rock	**4**	rock music
música folclórica	**5**	folk music
rap	**6**	rap music
gospel	**7**	gospel music
jazz	**8**	jazz
blues	**9**	blues
bluegrass	**10**	bluegrass
hip hop	**11**	hip hop
reggae	**12**	reggae
peças	**B**	**plays**
drama	**13**	drama
comédia	**14**	comedy
tragédia	**15**	tragedy
comédia musical	**16**	musical (comedy)

	C	movies/films
cinema/filmes		
drama	17	drama
comédia	18	comedy
faroeste/ bangue-bangue/ western	19	western
mistério	20	mystery
musical	21	musical
desenho animado	22	cartoon
documentário	23	documentary
filme de ação/ filme de aventura	24	action movie/ adventure movie
filme de guerra	25	war movie
filme de terror	26	horror movie

filme de ficção científica	27	science fiction movie
filme estrangeiro	28	foreign film
programas de TV	D	TV programs
drama	29	drama
série de comédia	30	(situation) comedy/ sitcom
programa de entrevistas	31	talk show
game-show/ programa de perguntas e respostas	32	game show/ quiz show
reality show	33	reality show

novela	34	soap opera
desenho animado	35	cartoon
programa infantil	36	children's program
noticiário	37	news program
programa esportivo	38	sports program
documentário sobre natureza	39	nature program
programa de vendas	40	shopping program

A. What kind of ___[A–D]___ do you like?

B. { I like ___[1–12]___.
{ I like ___[13–40]___s.

What's your favorite type of music?
Who is your favorite singer? musician?
musical group?

What kind of movies do you like?
Who are your favorite movie stars?
What are the titles of your favorite movies?

What kind of TV programs do you like?
What are your favorite shows?

INSTRUMENTOS MUSICAIS

Instrumentos de corda	Strings		Instrumentos de sopro	Woodwinds		Instrumentos de percussão	Percussion	
violino	1	violin	flautim	9	piccolo	bateria	20	drums
viola	2	viola	flauta/flauta transversal	10	flute	pratos	a	cymbals
violoncelo	3	cello	clarinete	11	clarinet	pandeiro	21	tambourine
contrabaixo	4	bass	oboé	12	oboe	xilofone	22	xylophone
violão acústico	5	(acoustic) guitar	flauta vertical	13	recorder			
guitarra elétrica	6	electric guitar	saxofone	14	saxophone	**Instrumentos de tecla**	**Keyboard Instruments**	
banjo	7	banjo	fagote	15	bassoon	piano	23	piano
harpa	8	harp				piano elétrico	24	electric keyboard
			Instrumentos de metal	**Brass**		órgão	25	organ
			trompete	16	trumpet			
			trombone	17	trombone	**Outros instrumentos**	**Other Instruments**	
			trompa	18	French horn	acordeão	26	accordion
			tuba	19	tuba	harmônica/gaita	27	harmonica

A. Do you play a musical instrument?
B. Yes. I play the **violin**.

A. You play the **trumpet** very well.
B. Thank you.

A. What's that noise?!
B. That's my son/daughter practicing the **drums**.

Do you play a musical instrument? Which one?

Which instruments are usually in an orchestra? a marching band? a rock group?

Name and describe typical musical instruments in your country.

casa de fazenda	**1**	**farmhouse**
fazendeiro	**2**	**farmer**
horta	**3**	**(vegetable) garden**
espantalho	**4**	**scarecrow**
feno	**5**	**hay**
empregado de fazenda	**6**	**hired hand**
celeiro	**7**	**barn**
estábulo	**8**	**stable**
cavalo	**9**	**horse**
terreiro	**10**	**barnyard**
peru	**11**	**turkey**
bode/cabra	**12**	**goat**
cordeiro	**13**	**lamb**
galo	**14**	**rooster**
chiqueiro	**15**	**pig pen**
porco	**16**	**pig**
galinheiro	**17**	**chicken coop**
frango	**18**	**chicken**
galinheiro	**19**	**hen house**
galinha	**20**	**hen**
plantação	**21**	**crop**
sistema de irrigação	**22**	**irrigation system**
trator	**23**	**tractor**
campo	**24**	**field**
pasto	**25**	**pasture**
vaca	**26**	**cow**
ovelha/carneiro	**27**	**sheep**
pomar	**28**	**orchard**
árvore frutífera	**29**	**fruit tree**
empregado de fazenda/ trabalhador rural	**30**	**farm worker**
alfafa	**31**	**alfalfa**
milho	**32**	**corn**
algodão	**33**	**cotton**
arroz	**34**	**rice**
feijão-soja	**35**	**soybeans**
trigo	**36**	**wheat**

[1–30]
A. Where's the _____?
B. In / Next to the _____.

A. The __[9, 11–14, 16, 18, 20, 26]__ s / __[27]__ are loose again!
B. Oh, no! Where are they?
A. They're in the __[1, 3, 7, 8, 10, 15, 17, 19, 24, 25, 28]__ .

[31–36]
A. Do you grow _____ on your farm?
B. No. We grow _____.

Tell about farms in your country. What crops and animals are common on these farms?

ANIMALS AND PETS

ANIMAIS SILVESTRES E DE ESTIMAÇÃO

alce	**1**	moose	coelho	**13**	rabbit	camundongo- **28** mouse-mice
chifre	**a**	antler	castor	**14**	beaver	camundongos
urso polar	**2**	polar bear	guaxinim	**15**	raccoon	rato **29** rat
cervo/veado	**3**	deer	opossum	**16**	possum/opossum	esquilo listado **30** chipmunk
casco-cascos	**a**	hoof-hooves	cavalo	**17**	horse	esquilo/serelepe **31** squirrel
lobo-lobos	**4**	wolf-wolves	rabo	**a**	tail	geômis **32** gopher
pêlo	**a**	coat/fur	pônei	**18**	pony	marmota **33** prairie dog
urso-negro	**5**	(black) bear	jumento	**19**	donkey	gato **34** cat
garra	**a**	claw	tatu	**20**	armadillo	bigode **a** whiskers
puma	**6**	mountain lion	morcego	**21**	bat	filhote de gato/gatinho **35** kitten
urso-cinzento/	**7**	(grizzly)	minhoca	**22**	worm	cachorro/cão **36** dog
urso-grizzly		bear	lesma	**23**	slug	filhote de cachorro/cachorrinho **37** puppy
búfalo/bisão	**8**	buffalo/bison	macaco	**24**	monkey	hamster **38** hamster
coiote	**9**	coyote	tamanduá	**25**	anteater	gerbilo **39** gerbil
raposa	**10**	fox	lhama	**26**	llama	cobaia **40** guinea pig
gambá	**11**	skunk	onça-pintada/jaguar	**27**	jaguar	peixinho dourado **41** goldfish
porco-espinho	**12**	porcupine	manchas	**a**	spots	canário **42** canary
espinho	**a**	quill				periquito **43** parakeet

antílope	**44**	antelope	tigre	**51**	tiger	hiena	**54**	hyena	hipopótamo	**59** hippopotamus
babuíno	**45**	baboon	pata		**a** paw	leão	**55**	lion	leopardo	**60** leopard
rinoceronte	**46**	rhinoceros	camelo	**52**	camel	juba		**a** mane	gorila	**61** gorilla
chifre		**a** horn	corcova		**a** hump	girafa	**56**	giraffe	canguru	**62** kangaroo
panda	**47**	panda	elefante	**53**	elephant	zebra	**57**	zebra	bolsa	**a** pouch
orangotango	**48**	orangutan	presa		**a** tusk	listras		**a** stripes	coala	**63** koala (bear)
pantera	**49**	panther	tromba		**b** trunk	chimpanzé	**58**	chimpanzee	ornitorrinco	**64** platypus
gibão	**50**	gibbon								

[1–33, 44–64]
A. Look at that _____!
B. Wow! That's the biggest
_____ I've ever seen!

[34–43]
A. Do you have a pet?
B. Yes. I have a _____.
A. What's your _____'s name?
B. ....

What animals are there where you live?

Is there a zoo near where you live? What animals does it have?

What are some common pets in your country?

If you could be an animal, which animal would you like to be? Why?

Does your culture have any popular folk tales or children's stories about animals? Tell a story you know.

Pássaros		Birds
tordo	**1**	robin
ninho	**a**	nest
ovo	**b**	egg
gaio	**2**	blue jay
asa	**a**	wing
cauda	**b**	tail
pena	**c**	feather
cardeal	**3**	cardinal
corvo	**4**	crow
gaivota	**5**	seagull
pica-pau	**6**	woodpecker
bico	**a**	beak
pombo	**7**	pigeon
coruja	**8**	owl
gavião	**9**	hawk
águia	**10**	eagle
garra	**a**	claw
cisne	**11**	swan

beija-flor	**12**	hummingbird
pato	**13**	duck
bico	**a**	bill
pardal	**14**	sparrow
ganso-gansos	**15**	goose-geese
pingüim	**16**	penguin
flamingo	**17**	flamingo
grou/grua	**18**	crane
cegonha	**19**	stork
pelicano	**20**	pelican
pavão	**21**	peacock
papagaio	**22**	parrot
avestruz	**23**	ostrich

Insetos		**Insects**
mosca	**24**	fly
joaninha	**25**	ladybug
vaga-lume/ pirilampo	**26**	firefly/ lightning bug

mariposa	**27**	moth
lagarta	**28**	caterpillar
casulo	**a**	cocoon
borboleta	**29**	butterfly
percevejo	**30**	tick
mosquito	**31**	mosquito
libélula	**32**	dragonfly
aranha	**33**	spider
teia	**a**	web
louva-a-deus	**34**	praying mantis
vespa	**35**	wasp
abelha	**36**	bee
colméia	**a**	beehive
gafanhoto	**37**	grasshopper
besouro	**38**	beetle
escorpião	**39**	scorpion
centopéia	**40**	centipede
grilo	**41**	cricket

[1–41]
A. Is that a/an _____?
B. No. I think it's a/an _____.

[24–41]
A. Hold still! There's a _____ on your shirt!
B. Oh! Can you get it off me?
A. There! It's gone!

What birds and insects are there where you live?

Does your culture have any popular folk tales or children's stories about birds or insects? Tell a story you know.

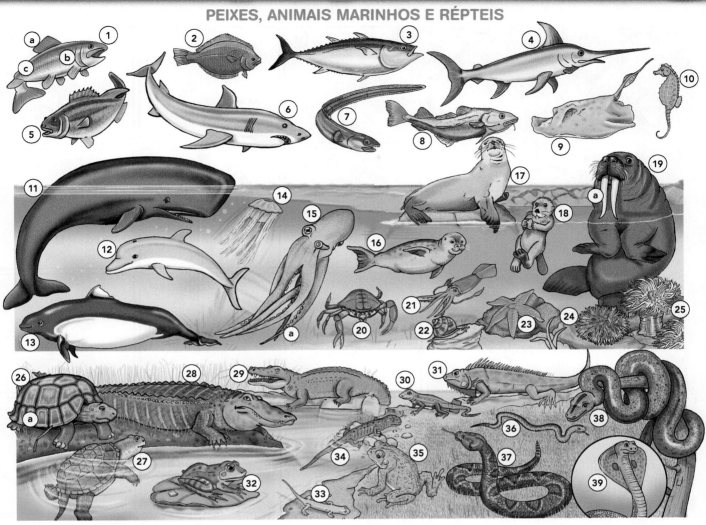

Peixes	**Fish**
truta	**1** trout
nadadeira	**a** fin
guelra	**b** gill
escamas	**c** scales
linguado	**2** flounder
atum	**3** tuna
peixe-espada	**4** swordfish
bass	**5** bass
tubarão	**6** shark
enguia	**7** eel
bacalhau	**8** cod
arraia	**9** ray/stingray
cavalo-marinho	**10** sea horse

Animais marinhos	**Sea Animals**
baleia	**11** whale

golfinho	**12** dolphin
boto	**13** porpoise
medusa/água-viva	**14** jellyfish
polvo	**15** octopus
tentáculo	**a** tentacle
foca	**16** seal
leão-marinho/lobo-marinho	**17** sea lion
lontra	**18** otter
morsa	**19** walrus
presa	**a** tusk
caranguejo	**20** crab
lula	**21** squid
caramujo	**22** snail
estrela-do-mar	**23** starfish
ouriço-do-mar	**24** sea urchin
anêmona-do-mar	**25** sea anemone

Anfíbios e répteis	**Amphibians and Reptiles**
tartaruga terrestre	**26** tortoise
casco	**a** shell
tartaruga	**27** turtle
aligátor	**28** alligator
crocodilo	**29** crocodile
lagarto	**30** lizard
iguana	**31** iguana
rã	**32** frog
salamandra-aquática	**33** newt
salamandra	**34** salamander
sapo	**35** toad
cobra	**36** snake
cascavel	**37** rattlesnake
jibóia	**38** boa constrictor
naja	**39** cobra

[1–39]
A. Is that a/an _____?
B. No. I think it's a/an _____.

[26–39]
A. Are there any _____s around here?
B. No. But there are lots of _____!

What fish, sea animals, and reptiles can be found in your country? Which ones are endangered and need to be protected? Why?

In your opinion, which ones are the most interesting? the most beautiful? the most dangerous?

TREES, PLANTS, AND FLOWERS
ÁRVORES, PLANTAS E FLORES

árvore **1** tree	agulha **9** needle	carvalho **19** oak	planta **28** plant
folha-folhas **2** leaf-leaves	pinha **10** pine cone	pinheiro **20** pine	cacto-cactos **29** cactus-cacti
raminho/ **3** twig	corniso **11** dogwood	sequóia **21** redwood	trepadeira **30** vine
galho fino	azevinho **12** holly	chorão/ **22** (weeping)	hera **31** poison
ramo/galho **4** branch	magnólia **13** magnolia	salgueiro willow	venenosa ivy
ramo principal **5** limb	olmo **14** elm	arbusto **23** bush	sumagre **32** poison sumac
tronco **6** trunk	cerejeira **15** cherry	azevinho **24** holly	venenoso
casca de árvore/ **7** bark	palmeira **16** palm	drupas **25** berries	carvalho **33** poison oak
córtex	bétula **17** birch	arbusto **26** shrub	venenoso
raiz **8** root	bordo **18** maple	samambaia **27** fern	

flor	**34**	flower	cravo-de-defunto	**43**	marigold	girassol	**52**	sunflower
pétala	**35**	petal	cravo	**44**	carnation	croco	**53**	crocus
caule	**36**	stem	gardênia	**45**	gardenia	tulipa	**54**	tulip
botão	**37**	bud	lírio	**46**	lily	gerânio	**55**	geranium
espinho	**38**	thorn	íris	**47**	iris	violeta	**56**	violet
bulbo	**39**	bulb	amor-perfeito	**48**	pansy	poinsétia	**57**	poinsettia
crisântemo	**40**	chrysanthemum	petúnia	**49**	petunia	jasmim	**58**	jasmine
narciso	**41**	daffodil	orquídea	**50**	orchid	hibisco	**59**	hibiscus
margarida	**42**	daisy	rosa	**51**	rose			

[11–22]
A. What kind of tree is that?
B. I think it's a/an _____ tree.

[31–33]
A. Watch out for the _____ over there!
B. Oh. Thanks for the warning.

[40–57]
A. Look at all the _____s!*
B. They're beautiful!

*With 58 and 59, use: Look at all the ___!

Describe your favorite tree and your favorite flower.

What kinds of trees and flowers grow where you live?

In your country, what flowers do you see at weddings? at funerals? during holidays? in hospital rooms? Tell which flowers people use for different occasions.

ENERGIA, CONSERVAÇÃO E O MEIO AMBIENTE

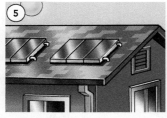

Fontes de energia	**Sources of Energy**
petróleo	**1** oil/petroleum
gás natural	**2** (natural) gas
carvão	**3** coal
energia nuclear	**4** nuclear energy
energia solar	**5** solar energy
energia hidrelétrica/ energia hidroelétrica	**6** hydroelectric power
vento	**7** wind
energia geotérmica	**8** geothermal energy

Conservação	**Conservation**
reciclar	**9** recycle
economizar energia/conservar energia	**10** save energy/conserve energy
economizar água	**11** save water/conserve water
transporte solidário	**12** carpool

Problemas ambientais	**Environmental Problems**
poluição atmosférica/poluição do ar	**13** air pollution
poluição da água	**14** water pollution
resíduos perigosos/lixo tóxico	**15** hazardous waste/toxic waste
chuva ácida	**16** acid rain
radiação	**17** radiation
aquecimento global	**18** global warming

[1–8]
A. In my opinion, _____ will be our best source of energy in the future.
B. I disagree. I think our best source of energy will be _____.

[9–12]
A. Do you _____?
B. Yes. I'm very concerned about the environment.

[13–18]
A. Do you worry about the environment?
B. Yes. I'm very concerned about _____.

What kind of energy do you use to heat your home? to cook? In your opinion, which will be the best source of energy in the future?

Do you practice conservation? What do you do to help the environment?

In your opinion, what is the most serious environmental problem in the world today? Why?

DESASTRES NATURAIS

terremoto	**1**	**earthquake**	ciclone/tornado	**5**	**tornado**	fogo selvagem	**10**	**wildfire**
furacão	**2**	**hurricane**	alagamento	**6**	**flood**	deslizamento de terra	**11**	**landslide**
tufão	**3**	**typhoon**	tsunami	**7**	**tsunami**	deslizamento de lama	**12**	**mudslide**
nevasca/	**4**	**blizzard**	seca	**8**	**drought**	avalanche	**13**	**avalanche**
tempestade de neve			incêndio florestal	**9**	**forest fire**	erupção vulcânica	**14**	**volcanic eruption**

A. Did you hear about the _____ in ......(country)......?
B. Yes, I did. I saw it on the news.

Have you or someone you know ever experienced a natural disaster? Tell about it.

Which natural disasters sometimes happen where you live? How do people prepare for them?

FORMAS DE IDENTIFICAÇÃO

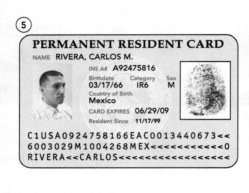

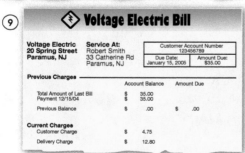

carteira de motorista/carteira de habilitação/carta de motorista	**1**	driver's license
cartão de seguridade social	**2**	social security card
carteira de estudante	**3**	student I.D. card
crachá de identificação de funcionários	**4**	employee I.D. badge
carteira de residente permanente	**5**	permanent resident card
passaporte	**6**	passport
visto	**7**	visa
visto de trabalho	**8**	work permit
comprovante de residência	**9**	proof of residence
certidão de nascimento	**10**	birth certificate

A. May I see your _____?
B. Yes. Here you are.

A. Oh, no! I can't find my _____!
B. I'll help you look for it.
A. Thanks.

Which forms of identification do you have? When do you need to show them?

GOVERNO AMERICANO

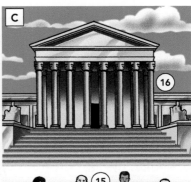

Poder legislativo	**A**	**legislative branch**
legisla/faz leis	1	makes the laws
representantes/ deputados/deputadas	2	representatives/ congressmen and congresswomen
câmara dos deputados	3	house of representatives
senadores	4	senators
senado	5	senate
Edifício do Capitólio	6	Capitol Building
Poder executivo	**B**	**executive branch**
executa as leis	7	enforces thelaws
presidente	8	president
vice-presidente	9	vice-president
gabinete	10	cabinet
Casa Branca	11	White House
Poder judiciário	**C**	**judicial branch**
explica as leis	12	explains the laws
ministros da Suprema Corte	13	Supreme Court justices
presidente do plenário da Suprema Corte	14	chief justice
Suprema Corte	15	Supreme Court
edifício da Suprema Corte	16	Supreme Court Building

A. Which branch of government __[1, 7, 12]__ ?
B. The __[A, B, C]__ .

A. Who works in the __[A, B, C]__ of the government?
B. The __[2, 4, 8–10, 13, 14]__ .

A. Where do/does the __[2, 4, 8–10, 13, 14]__ work?
B. In the __[6, 11, 16]__ .

A. In which branch of the government is the __[3, 5, 10, 15]__ ?
B. In the __[A, B, C]__ .

Compare the governments of different countries you are familiar with. What are the branches of government?
Who works there? What do they do?

A CONSTITUIÇÃO E A CARTA DE DIREITOS

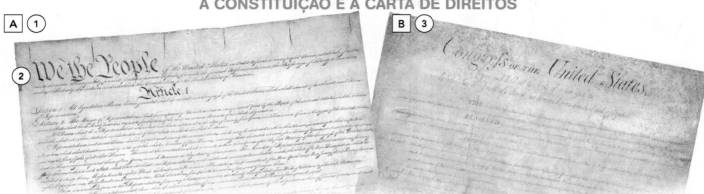

13th

15th

16th

19th

26th

Constituição (a)	A The Constitution	Outras emendas	D Other Amendments
"lei suprema do país (a)"	1 "the supreme law of the land"	acabaram com a escravidão	8 ended slavery
Preâmbulo (o)	2 the Preamble	deram aos afro-americanos o direito ao voto	9 gave African-Americans the right to vote
Carta de Direitos (a)	B The Bill of Rights	estabeleceram impostos de renda	10 established income taxes
primeiras 10 emendas da Constituição (as)	3 the first 10 amendments to the Constitution	deram às mulheres o direito ao voto	11 gave women the right to vote
Primeira Emenda (a)	C The 1st Amendment	deram aos cidadãos maiores de dezoito anos o direito ao voto.	12 gave citizens eighteen years and older the right to vote
liberdade de expressão	4 freedom of speech		
liberdade de imprensa	5 freedom of the press		
liberdade religiosa	6 freedom of religion		
liberdade de reunião	7 freedom of assembly		

A. What is ____[A ,B]____ ?
B. ____[1 ,3]____ .

A. Which amendment guarantees people ____[4–7]____?
B. The 1st Amendment.

A. Which amendment ____[8–12]____?
B. The _____ Amendment.

A. What did the _____ Amendment do?
B. It ____[8–12]____ .

Describe how people in your community exercise their 1st Amendment rights. What are some examples of freedom of speech? the press? religion? assembly?

Do you have an idea for a new amendment? Tell about it and why you think it's important.

EVENTOS DA HISTÓRIA DOS ESTADOS UNIDOS

TIMELINE

1607	Colonists come to Jamestown, Virginia. Colonizadores chegam em Jamestown, na Virgínia.
1620	Pilgrims come to the Plymouth Colony. Peregrinos chegam à Colônia de Plymouth.
1775	The Revolutionary War begins. Começa a Guerra Revolucionária.
1776	The colonies declare their independence. As colônias declaram sua independência.
1783	The Revolutionary War ends. Termina a Guerra Revolucionária.
1787	Representatives write the United States Constitution. Os deputados escrevem a Constituição dos Estados Unidos.
1789	George Washington becomes the first president. George Washington se torna o primeiro presidente.
1791	The Bill of Rights is added to the Constitution. A Carta de Direitos é adicionada à Constituição.
1861	The Civil War begins. Começa a Guerra Civil.
1863	President Lincoln signs the Emancipation Proclamation. O presidente Lincoln assina a Proclamação da Independência.
1865	The Civil War ends. Termina a Guerra Civil.
1876	Alexander Graham Bell invents the telephone. Alexander Graham Bell inventa o telefone.
1879	Thomas Edison invents the lightbulb. Thomas Edison inventa a lâmpada.
1914	World War I (One) begins. Começa a Primeira Guerra Mundial.
1918	World War I (One) ends. Termina a Primeira Guerra Mundial.
1920	Women get the right to vote. As mulheres ganham o direito ao voto.
1929	The stock market crashes, and the Great Depression begins. A bolsa de valores despenca e começa a Grande Depressão.
1939	World War II (Two) begins. Começa a Segunda Guerra Mundial.
1945	World War II (Two) ends. Termina a Segunda Guerra Mundial.
1950	The Korean War begins. Começa a Guerra da Coréia.
1953	The Korean War ends. Termina a Guerra da Coréia.
1954	The civil rights movement begins. Começa o movimento pelos direitos civis.
1963	The March on Washington takes place. A Passeata em Washington é realizada.
1964	The Vietnam War begins. Começa a Guerra do Vietnã.
1969	Astronaut Neil Armstrong lands on the moon. O astronauta Neil Armstrong aterrissa na lua.
1973	The Vietnam War ends. Termina a Guerra do Vietnã.
1991	The Persian Gulf War occurs. Acontece a Guerra do Golfo.
2001	The United States is attacked by terrorists. Os Estados Unidos são atacados por terroristas.

A. What happened in .....(year).....?
B. .....(Event).....ed.

A. When did .....(event).....?
B. In .....(year)......

In your opinion, which event in this lesson is the most important? Why?

Tell about important events in the history of your country.

Ano Novo	**1**	New Year's Day
Dia de Martin Luther King, Jr.*	**2**	Martin Luther King, Jr.* Day
Dia de São Valentim	**3**	Valentine's Day
Dia do Soldado	**4**	Memorial Day
Dia da Independência/ Quatro de Julho (o)	**5**	Independence Day/ the Fourth of July
Halloween/Dia das Bruxas	**6**	Halloween

Dia dos Veteranos	**7**	Veterans Day
Dia de Ação de Graças	**8**	Thanksgiving
Natal	**9**	Christmas
Ramadã	**10**	Ramadan
Kwanzaa	**11**	Kwanzaa
Chanucá	**12**	Hanukkah

* Jr. = Junior

A. When is _____[1, 3, 5, 6, 7, 9]_____ ?
B. It's on ....(date)........

A. When is __[2, 4, 8]__ ?
B. It's in ....(month).......

A. When does _____[10–12]_____ begin this year?
B. It begins on ....(date)........

Which of these holidays do you celebrate? How?

What holidays do people celebrate in your country?

O SISTEMA JURÍDICO

ser detido	**A**	be arrested	algemas	**3**	handcuffs	prova	**16** evidence
ser autuado na delegacia de polícia	**B**	be booked at the police station	direitos de Miranda	**4**	Miranda rights	oficial de justiça	**17** bailiff
contratar um advogado	**C**	hire a lawyer/ hire an attorney	impressões digitais	**5**	fingerprints	júri	**18** jury
			fotografia de ficha policial	**6**	mug shot/ police photo	veredito	**19** verdict
comparecer em juízo	**D**	appear in court	advogado	**7**	lawyer/attorney	inocente/ não culpado	**20** innocent/ not guilty
ser julgado	**E**	stand* trial	juiz	**8**	judge	culpado	**21** guilty
ser absolvido	**F**	be acquitted	réu	**9**	defendant	sentença	**22** sentence
ser condenado	**G**	be convicted	fiança criminal	**10**	bail	multa	**23** fine
ser sentenciado	**H**	be sentenced	sala do juizado	**11**	courtroom	guarda do presídio	**24** prison guard
ir para a cadeia/prisão	**I**	go to jail/prison	promotor público	**12**	prosecuting attorney	réu convicto/ prisioneiro/ presidiário	**25** convict/ prisoner/ inmate
ser liberado	**J**	be released	testemunha	**13**	witness		
suspeito	**1**	suspect	escrevente	**14**	court reporter		
policial	**2**	police officer	advogado de defesa	**15**	defense attorney		

*stand-stood

[A–J]
A. Did you hear about ......(name).....?
B. No, I didn't.
A. He/She _____ed.
B. Really? I didn't know that.

[A–J]
A. What happened in the last episode?
B. ......(name of character).......... _____ed.

[1, 2, 7–9, 12–15, 17, 24, 25]
A. Are you the _____?
B. No. I'm the _____.

Tell about the legal system in your country.
Describe what happens after a person is arrested.

Do you watch any crime shows on TV? Which ones?
Tell about an episode you remember.

CIDADANIA

Direitos e responsabilidades dos cidadãos	Citizens' Rights and Responsibilities
votar	1 vote
obedecer às leis	2 obey laws
pagar impostos	3 pay taxes
servir num júri	4 serve on a jury
participar da vida da comunidade	5 be part of community life
acompanhar as notícias para se manter informado sobre eventos atuais	6 follow the news to know about current events
inscrever-se no Sistema de Serviço Seletivo*	7 register with the Selective Service System

O caminho para se adquirir cidadania	The Path to Citizenship
pedir cidadania	8 apply for citizenship
aprender sobre o governo e a história dos EUA	9 learn about U.S. government and history
fazer um teste de cidadania	10 take a citizenship test
comparecer à entrevista de naturalização	11 have a naturalization interview
participar de uma cerimônia de naturalização	12 attend a naturalization ceremony
declamar o Juramento de Fidelidade	13 recite the Oath of Allegiance

* Todas as pessoas do sexo masculino nos Estados Unidos, entre 18 e 26 anos de idade, devem inscrever-se no Serviço Militar.

A. Can you name one responsibility of United States citizens?
B. Yes. Citizens should ____[1–7]____.

A. How is your citizenship application coming along?
B. Very well. I ____[8–11]____ed, and now I'm preparing to ____[9–13]____.
A. Good luck!

In your opinion, what are the most important rights and responsibilities of all people in their communities?

In your opinion, should non-citizens have all the same rights as citizens? Why or why not?

ESTADOS UNIDOS E CANADÁ

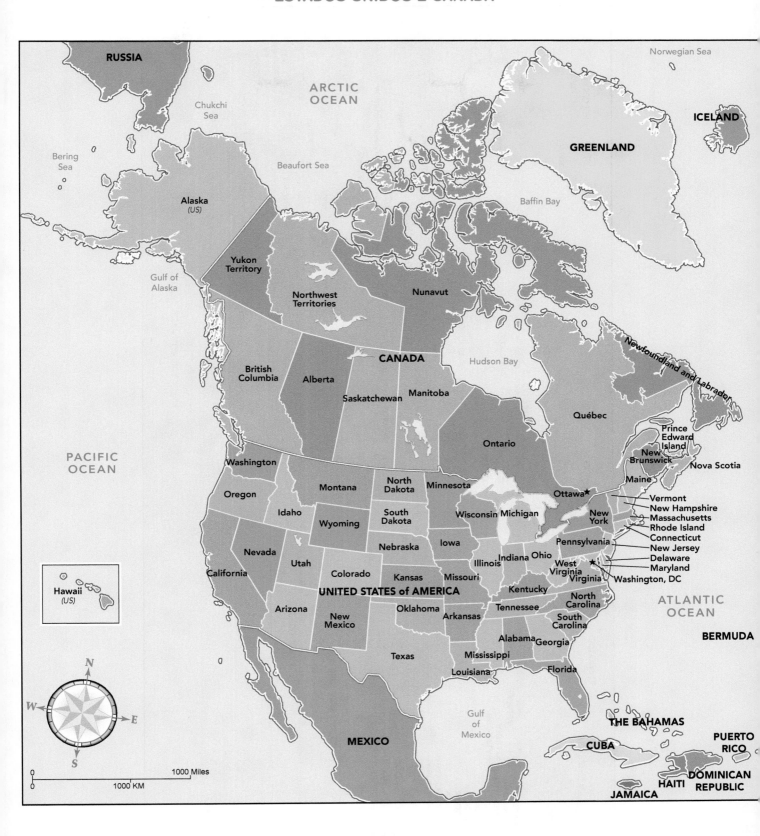

RUSSIA

ARCTIC
OCEAN

Chukchi
Sea

Norwegian Sea

ICELAND

Bering
Sea

Beaufort Sea

GREENLAND

Alaska
(US)

Baffin Bay

Gulf of
Alaska

Yukon
Territory

Northwest
Territories

Nunavut

PACIFIC
OCEAN

British
Columbia

Alberta

CANADA

Hudson Bay

Newfoundland and Labrador

Saskatchewan

Manitoba

Québec

Prince
Edward
Island

New
Brunswick

Nova Scotia

Ontario

Maine

Washington

Montana

North
Dakota

Minnesota

Ottawa★

Vermont
New Hampshire
Massachusetts
Rhode Island
Connecticut
New Jersey
Delaware
Maryland
Washington, DC

Oregon

Idaho

Wyoming

South
Dakota

Wisconsin Michigan

New
York

Pennsylvania

Nebraska

Iowa

Indiana Ohio

West
Virginia

Hawaii
(US)

Nevada

Utah

Colorado

Kansas

Missouri

Illinois

Virginia

California

UNITED STATES of AMERICA

Kentucky

North
Carolina

ATLANTIC
OCEAN

Arizona

New
Mexico

Oklahoma

Arkansas

Tennessee

South
Carolina

BERMUDA

Alabama

Georgia

N

Texas

Mississippi

Louisiana

Florida

W   E

Gulf
of
Mexico

THE BAHAMAS

PUERTO
RICO

S

MEXICO

CUBA

DOMINICAN
REPUBLIC

1000 Miles

HAITI

1000 KM

JAMAICA

MÉXICO, AMÉRICA CENTRAL E CARIBE

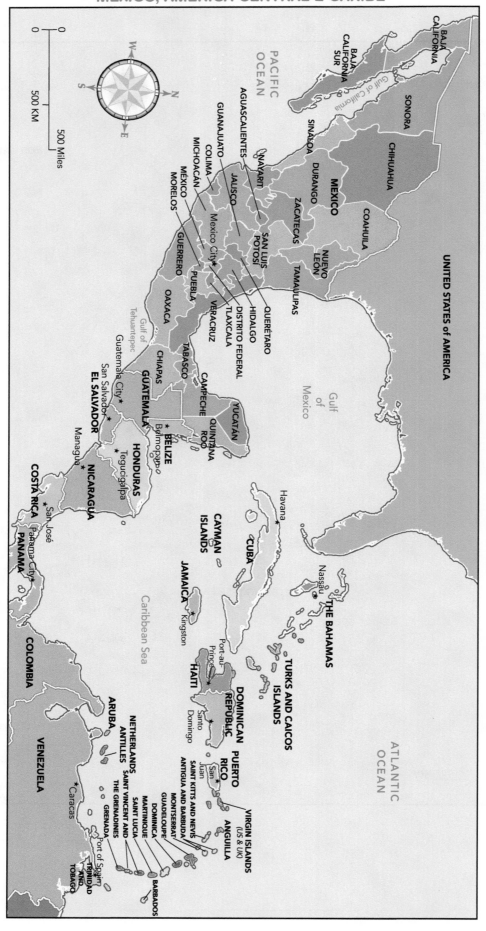

AMÉRICA DO SUL

Caribbean Sea

Barranquilla
Cartagena
Maracaibo
Valencia
Barquisimeto
Caracas

ATLANTIC
OCEAN

VENEZUELA

Medellín

Georgetown
Paramaribo

GUYANA

Cayenne

COLOMBIA

Bogotá

Cali

SURINAME **FRENCH GUIANA**

Equator

Quito

Equator

ECUADOR

Belém

Guayaquil

Gulf of
Guayaquil

Manaus

Fortaleza

Teresina

PERU

BRAZIL

Recife

Lima

Salvador

La Paz

Brasília

BOLIVIA

Goiânia

Sucre

Belo Horizonte

Rio de Janeiro

Campinas

CHILE

PARAGUAY

São Paulo

Asuncion

Curitiba

PACIFIC
OCEAN

ARGENTINA

Pôrto Alegre

Córdoba

Rosario

URUGUAY

Santiago

Buenos Aires

Montevideo

Gulf of San Matías

ATLANTIC
OCEAN

Gulf of
San Jorge

N
W E
S

**FALKLAND
ISLANDS**

Strait of Magellan

Port Stanley

**SOUTH GEORGIA
ISLAND**

0   500 Miles

0   500 KM

ARCTIC OCEAN

Baffin Bay

GREENLAND

ICELAND

Bering Sea

Hudson Bay

CANADA

ALEUTIAN ISLANDS

NORTH AMERICA

UNITED STATES OF AMERICA

ATLANTIC OCEAN

AZORES (Portugal)

MOROCCO

BERMUDA

CANARY ISLANDS (Spain)

WESTERN SAHARA

HAWAIIAN ISLANDS (US)

MEXICO

Gulf of Mexico

CUBA

THE BAHAMAS

DOMINICAN REPUBLIC

MAURITANIA

SENEGAL

CAPE VERDE

PACIFIC OCEAN

JAMAICA

BELIZE

PUERTO RICO

HAITI

GAMBIA

GUINEA-BISSAU

GUINEA

GUATEMALA

HONDURAS

EL SALVADOR

NICARAGUA

SIERRA LEONE

D'IV

COSTA RICA

VENEZUELA

GUYANA

SURINAME

LIBERIA

GHA

LINE ISLANDS

PANAMA

COLOMBIA

FRENCH GUIANA

PHOENIX ISLANDS

Equator

GALÁPAGOS ISLANDS

SOUTH AMERICA

EQUATO GUINE

KIRIBATI

ECUADOR

AMERICAN SAMOA

MARQUESAS ISLANDS

PERU

BRAZIL

COOK ISLANDS

WESTERN SAMOA

FRENCH POLYNESIA

BOLIVIA

TAHITI

TONGA

SOCIETY ISLANDS

PARAGUAY

AUSTRAL ISLANDS

CHILE

N

ARGENTINA

URUGUAY

W E

FALKLAND/MALVINAS ISLANDS

S

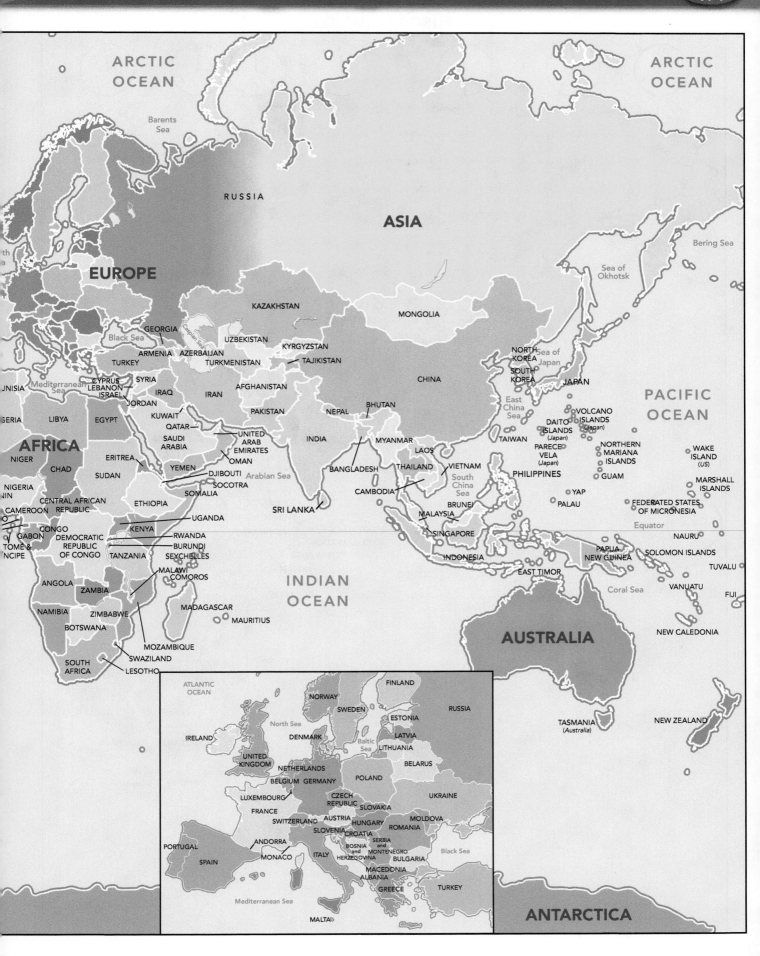

ARCTIC OCEAN

ARCTIC OCEAN

Barents Sea

RUSSIA

ASIA

Bering Sea

Sea of Okhotsk

EUROPE

KAZAKHSTAN

MONGOLIA

GEORGIA

Black Sea

UZBEKISTAN

KYRGYZSTAN

NORTH KOREA

Sea of Japan

ARMENIA   AZERBAIJAN

TURKMENISTAN

TAJIKISTAN

SOUTH KOREA

JAPAN

TURKEY

CYPRUS

SYRIA

AFGHANISTAN

CHINA

PACIFIC OCEAN

Mediterranean Sea

LEBANON
ISRAEL

IRAQ

IRAN

East China Sea

DAITO ISLANDS (Japan)

VOLCANO ISLANDS (Japan)

TUNISIA

JORDAN

PAKISTAN

NEPAL

BHUTAN

TAIWAN

NORTHERN MARIANA ISLANDS

WAKE ISLAND (US)

GERIA

LIBYA

EGYPT

KUWAIT

QATAR

PARECE VELA (Japan)

AFRICA

SAUDI ARABIA

UNITED ARAB EMIRATES

INDIA

MYANMAR

LAOS

PHILIPPINES

GUAM

MARSHALL ISLANDS

NIGER

CHAD

ERITREA

OMAN

YEMEN

DJIBOUTI

BANGLADESH

THAILAND

VIETNAM

South China Sea

YAP

FEDERATED STATES OF MICRONESIA

NIGERIA

SUDAN

SOCOTRA

SOMALIA

Arabian Sea

SRI LANKA

CAMBODIA

MALAYSIA

BRUNEI

PALAU

NIN

CENTRAL AFRICAN REPUBLIC

ETHIOPIA

UGANDA

SINGAPORE

Equator

NAURU

CAMEROON

CONGO

DEMOCRATIC REPUBLIC OF CONGO

KENYA

RWANDA

BURUNDI

SEYCHELLES

INDONESIA

PAPUA NEW GUINEA

SOLOMON ISLANDS

TUVALU

GABON

TOME & NCIPE

TANZANIA

EAST TIMOR

Coral Sea

VANUATU

FIJI

ANGOLA

ZAMBIA

MALAWI

COMOROS

INDIAN OCEAN

MOZAMBIQUE

MADAGASCAR

MAURITIUS

AUSTRALIA

NEW CALEDONIA

NAMIBIA

ZIMBABWE

BOTSWANA

SWAZILAND

SOUTH AFRICA

LESOTHO

TASMANIA (Australia)

NEW ZEALAND

ATLANTIC OCEAN

FINLAND

NORWAY

SWEDEN

RUSSIA

IRELAND

North Sea

DENMARK

Baltic Sea

ESTONIA

LATVIA

LITHUANIA

UNITED KINGDOM

NETHERLANDS

BELGIUM   GERMANY

POLAND

BELARUS

LUXEMBOURG

CZECH REPUBLIC

SLOVAKIA

UKRAINE

FRANCE

SWITZERLAND

AUSTRIA

HUNGARY

MOLDOVA

SLOVENIA

CROATIA

ROMANIA

PORTUGAL

ANDORRA

ITALY

BOSNIA and HERZEGOVINA

SERBIA and MONTENEGRO

Black Sea

MONACO

SPAIN

BULGARIA

MACEDONIA

ALBANIA

GREECE

TURKEY

Mediterranean Sea

MALTA

ANTARCTICA

FUSOS HORÁRIOS

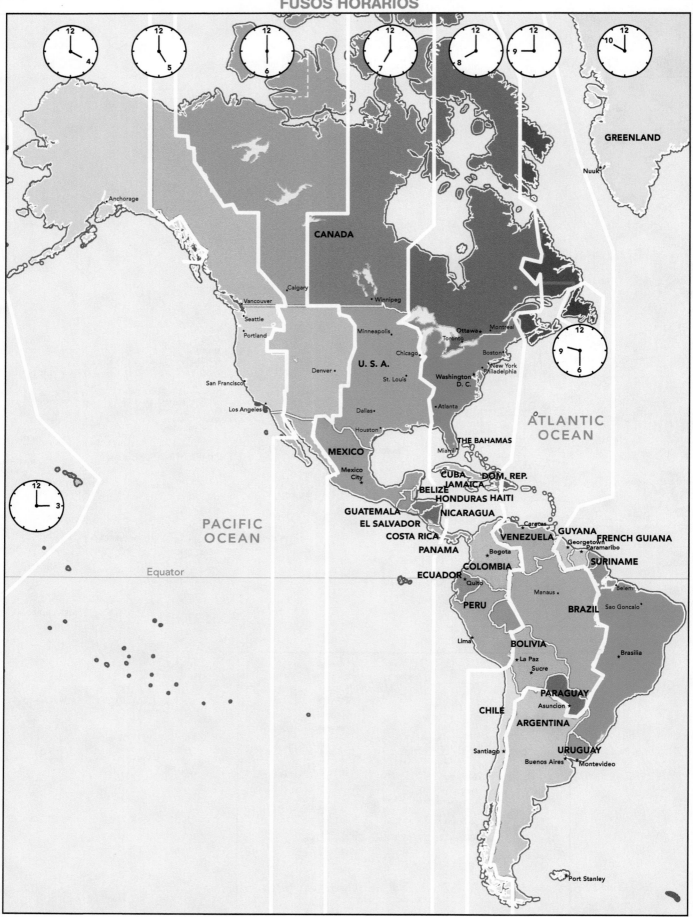

PAÍSES, NACIONALIDADES E IDIOMAS

Country	Nationality	Language
Afghanistan	Afghan	Afghan
Argentina	Argentine	Spanish
Australia	Australian	English
Bolivia	Bolivian	Spanish
Brazil	Brazilian	Portuguese
Bulgaria	Bulgarian	Bulgarian
Cambodia	Cambodian	Cambodian
Canada	Canadian	English/French
Chile	Chilean	Spanish
China	Chinese	Chinese
Colombia	Colombian	Spanish
Costa Rica	Costa Rican	Spanish
Cuba	Cuban	Spanish
(The) Czech Republic	Czech	Czech
Denmark	Danish	Danish
(The) Dominican Republic	Dominican	Spanish
Ecuador	Ecuadorian	Spanish
Egypt	Egyptian	Arabic
El Salvador	Salvadorean	Spanish
England	English	English
Estonia	Estonian	Estonian
Ethiopia	Ethiopian	Amharic
Finland	Finnish	Finnish
France	French	French
Germany	German	German
Greece	Greek	Greek
Guatemala	Guatemalan	Spanish
Haiti	Haitian	Haitian Kreyol
Honduras	Honduran	Spanish
Hungary	Hungarian	Hungarian
India	Indian	Hindi
Indonesia	Indonesian	Indonesian
Israel	Israeli	Hebrew

Country	Nationality	Language
Italy	Italian	Italian
Japan	Japanese	Japanese
Jordan	Jordanian	Arabic
Korea	Korean	Korean
Laos	Laotian	Laotian
Latvia	Latvian	Latvian
Lebanon	Lebanese	Arabic
Lithuania	Lithuanian	Lithuanian
Malaysia	Malaysian	Malay
Mexico	Mexican	Spanish
New Zealand	New Zealander	English
Nicaragua	Nicaraguan	Spanish
Norway	Norwegian	Norwegian
Pakistan	Pakistani	Urdu
Panama	Panamanian	Spanish
Peru	Peruvian	Spanish
(The) Philippines	Filipino	Tagalog
Poland	Polish	Polish
Portugal	Portuguese	Portuguese
Puerto Rico	Puerto Rican	Spanish
Romania	Romanian	Romanian
Russia	Russian	Russian
Saudi Arabia	Saudi	Arabic
Slovakia	Slovak	Slovak
Spain	Spanish	Spanish
Sweden	Swedish	Swedish
Switzerland	Swiss	German/French/Italian
Taiwan	Taiwanese	Chinese
Thailand	Thai	Thai
Turkey	Turkish	Turkish
Ukraine	Ukrainian	Ukrainian
(The) United States	American	English
Venezuela	Venezuelan	Spanish
Vietnam	Vietnamese	Vietnamese

A. Where are you from?
B. I'm from **Mexico**.

A. What's your nationality?
B. I'm **Mexican**.

A. What language do you speak?
B. I speak **Spanish**.

Tell about yourself: Where are you from? What's your nationality? What languages do you speak?

Now interview and tell about a friend.

VERB LISTS

LISTAS DE VERBO

Verbos regulares

Os verbos regulares têm quatro padrões diferentes de terminação para os tempos passado e particípio passado.

1 Adicionar **–ed** ao final do verbo. Por exemplo:

act → act**ed**

act	cook	grill	pass	simmer
add	correct	guard	peel	sort
answer	cough	hand (in)	plant	spell
appear	cover	help	play	sprain
ask	crash	insert	polish	steam
assist	cross (out)	invent	pour	stow
attack	deliver	iron	print	stretch
attend	deposit	kick	reach	surf
bank	design	land	record	swallow
board	discuss	leak	register	talk
boil	dress	learn	relax	turn
box	drill	lengthen	repair	twist
brainstorm	dust	lift	repeat	unload
broil	edit	listen	request	vacuum
brush	end	load	respond	vomit
burn	enter	look	rest	walk
burp	establish	lower	return	wash
carpool	explain	mark	roast	watch
cash	faint	match	rock	wax
check	fasten	mix	saute	weed
clean	fix	mow	scratch	whiten
clear	floss	obey	seat	work
collect	fold	open	select	
comb	follow	paint	shorten	
construct	form	park	sign	

2 Adicionar **–d** a verbos que terminam em **–e**. Por exemplo:

assemble → assemble**d**

assemble	declare	grate	pronounce	shave
bake	describe	hire	prune	slice
balance	dislocate	manage	raise	sneeze
barbecue	dive	measure	rake	state
bathe	dribble	microwave	recite	style
bounce	enforce	move	recycle	supervise
browse	erase	nurse	remove	translate
bruise	examine	operate	revise	type
bubble	exchange	organize	rinse	underline
change	exercise	overdose	save	unscramble
circle	experience	practice	scrape	use
close	file	prepare	serve	vote
combine	gargle	produce	share	wheeze

3 Dobrar a consoante final e adicionar **–ed** ao final do verbo. Por exemplo:

chop → chop**ped**

chop	mop	skip	transfer
hop	plan	stir	trim
knit	occur	stop	

4 Tirar o -y final e adicionar **–ied** ao final do verbo. Por exemplo:

apply → appl**ied**

apply	dry	fry	study
copy	empty	stir-fry	try

Verbos irregulares

Os verbos a seguir têm formas irregulares no passado e/ou particípio passado.

be	was/were	been		know	knew	known
beat	beat	beaten		leave	left	left
become	became	become		let	let	let
bend	bent	bent		make	made	made
begin	began	begun		meet	met	met
bleed	bled	bled		pay	paid	paid
break	broke	broken		put	put	put
bring	brought	brought		read	read	read
build	built	built		rewrite	rewrote	rewritten
buy	bought	bought		run	ran	run
catch	caught	caught		ring	rang	rung
choose	chose	chosen		say	said	said
come	came	come		see	saw	seen
cut	cut	cut		sell	sold	sold
do	did	done		set	set	set
draw	drew	drawn		shoot	shot	shot
drink	drank	drunk		sing	sang	sung
drive	drove	driven		sit	sat	sat
eat	ate	eaten		sleep	slept	slept
fall	fell	fallen		speak	spoke	spoken
feed	fed	fed		stand	stood	stood
fly	flew	flown		sweep	swept	swept
get	got	gotten		swim	swam	swum
give	gave	given		swing	swung	swung
go	went	gone		take	took	taken
grow	grew	grown		teach	taught	taught
hang	hung	hung		throw	threw	thrown
have	had	had		understand	understood	understood
hit	hit	hit		withdraw	withdrew	withdrawn
hold	held	held		write	wrote	written
hurt	hurt	hurt				

O número em negrito indica a página (ou páginas) em que a palavra aparece. O número ao lado indica a localização da palavra na ilustração e na lista de palavras da página. Por exemplo, "endereço **1**-5" indica que a palavra *endereço* está na página 1 e é o item número 5.

à direita de **8**-9
à esquerda de **8**-8
à procura de um apartamento **28**
abacate **48**-14
abacaxi **48**-18
abafado **14**-8
abafador de ruídos **123**-8
abaixar as persianas **7**-41
abaixo **8**-2
abajur **21**-25, **23**-16
abajur de parede **25**-11
abastado **45**-49
abdome **86**-25
abdômen **86**-25
abdominal **146**-25
abelha **154**-36
abelhas **30**-11d
aberta **45**-57
abóbora butternut **49**-14
abóbora mogango **49**-13
abobrinha **49**-12
aborrecido **47**-28
abotoaduras **70**-13
abrir o seu livro **6**-11
abreviações de classificados de emprego **118**
abricó **48**-7
abridor de garrafas **59**-3
abridor de latas **24**-18, **59**-2
abridor de latas elétrico **24**-18
abrigo **20**-9
abril **18**-16
abrir **31**-19
abrir uma conta **80**-E
absolver **165**-F
academia de ginástica **38**-3
acelerador **127**-73
acelga japonesa **49**-11
acender **31**-13
acessórios do aspirador **32**-6
acidente de carro **85**-1
acima **8**-1
acolchoado **23**-11
acompanhamentos **64**
acompanhar as notícias para se manter informado sobre eventos atuais **166**-6
aconselhamento **94**-19
acordeão **150**-26
acostamento **128**-16
açougueiro **112**-13
acrescentar **58**-10
açúcar **53**-36
açucareiro **22**-7
acupunturista **96**-15
adesivos **79**-31
adjetivo **107**-5
adolescente **42**-6
adulto **42**-7
advérbio **107**-7
advogada **114**-2, **165**-C,7
advogado de defesa **165**-15
aerograma **82**-3
afiada **45**-67
afirmativa **107**-A

afro-americano **162**-9
agasalho esportivo **69**-4, **140**-1
agência de viagens **39**-27
agenda **120**-6
agenda pessoal **120**-12
agente de passagens **131**-3
agente de proteção da aviação civil **131**-8
agente de viagens **115**-33
agosto **18**-20
água **62**-B, **158**-11
água mineral **51**-25
água oxigenada **90**-6
água-viva **155**-14
águia **154**-10
agulha **92**-4, **134**-5, **156**-9
agulha de costura **134**-5
agulha de crochê **134**-10
agulha de tricô **134**-8
AIDS **91**-25
aipo **49**-1
air bag **127**-49
airbag **127**-49
ajudar **116**-3
ajudar-se um ao outro **6**-28
alagamento **159**-6
alargar **72**-24
alarme de incêndio **29**-39
alavanca de mudança de marcha **127**-75
alavanca de mudança de marcha manual **127**-77
álbum de colorir **79**-27
álbum de selos **135**-25
alcachofra **49**-27
alcançar **146**-18
alce **152**-1
álcool **93**-10
além **129**-8
alergista **96**-5
alface **49**-9
alfafa **151**-31
alfaiate **115**-29
alfândega **131**-22
alfândega e imigração **131**-E
alfinete **134**-2
alfinete de fralda **100**-9
alfinete de segurança **134**-7
álgebra **105**
algemas **165**-3
algodão **71**-17, **151**-33
alho **49**-15
aliança **70**-3
alicate **34**-16
alicate descascador de fios **34**-13
aligátor **155**-28
alimentar **100**-A
alimentar o bebê **10**-5
alimentar o gato **10**-6
alimento para cães **54**-21
alimento para gatos **54**-20
alimentos congelados **52**
alimentos embalados **53**
alimentos para animais **54**

almoçar **9**-19
almoço **9**-16,19
almofada **21**-19
almofada de alfinetes **134**-3
almofada para carimbo **120**-28
almofada térmica **94**-9
almoxarifado **119**-G,24
alojamento estudantil **20**-6
alojamento universitário **20**-6
alongar **146**-11
alternador **126**-38
alto **42**-14, **44**-5,27,45, **72**-7
alto-falante **4**-14, **21**-16, **29**-29
alto-falantes **76**-27
altura **42**, **92**-A, **106**-1
altura dos ombros **43**-25
altura média **42**-15
aluguel **81**-6
aluno **4**-3
alvejante **73**-9
alvo **141**-44
amaciante **73**-8
amamentar **100**-E
amanhã **19**-3
amanhã à noite **19**-18,19
amanhã à tarde **19**-17
amanhã de manhã **19**-16
amarelo **65**-4
ambulância **84**-8
ambulante **41**-40
amedrontado **47**-27
ameixa **48**-6
ameixas secas **48**-26
amônia **32**-14
amor-perfeito **157**-48
anágua **68**-17
analgésico sem aspirina **90**-14, **95**-5
andador **25**-18, **94**-13
andaime **122**-12
andar **146**-13
anel **70**-1
anel de casamento **70**-3
anel de noivado **70**-2
anêmona-do-mar **155**-25
anestesia **93**-F
anestésico **93**-F
anestesista **97**-17
anfíbios **155**
ângulo agudo **106**-20a
ângulo obtuso **106**-20b
ângulo reto **106**-19b
animação da torcida **104**-6
animais marinhos **155**
aniversário **18**-26,27
ano **18**-1
Ano Novo **164**-1
anoitecer **19**-6
anotações **7**-44
anotar os pedidos **62**-C
antena **126**-14
antena de satélite **27**-28
antena de TV **27**-29
antepasto **64**-10
anterior **118**-10

antílope **153**-44
anúncio **118**-A
anúncio classificado **28**-1, **118**-3
anúncio de emprego **118**-2
anúncios de emprego **118**
anúncios imobiliários **28**-1
ao lado **8**-5
ao redor **129**-4
apagador **5**-33
apagão **85**-13
apagar a lousa **6**-9
aparador **22**-3
aparador de grama **35**-3
aparar a cerca viva **35**-F
aparar os arbustos **35**-G
aparelho **94**-20
aparelho de barbear **99**-21
aparelho de CD **76**-23, **127**-65
aparelho de DVD **21**-7, **76**-8
aparelho de GPS **139**-14
aparelho de MP3 **76**-32
aparelho de raio X **92**-9, **131**-9
aparelho de remo seco **141**-50
aparelho de som portátil **76**-28
aperitivo de cascas de batata **64**-6
apertado **44**-30
apertar o cinto de segurança **132**-K
aplicar uma injeção de anestesia **93**-F
aplicar uma injeção de anestésico **93**-F
aplicar uma injeção de procaína (Novocaine™) **93**-F
apoio de cabeça **127**-83
apoio do braço **127**-82
apontador de lápis **5**-23
apontador elétrico **120**-9
apóstrofe **107**-12
aprender sobre o governo e a história dos EUA **166**-9
aquarela **134**-14b
aquário **136**-14
aquecedor **127**-66
aquecedor de água **30**-3
aquecimento global **158**-18
ar **88**-25, **126**-48
ar condicionado **28**-28, **31**-21, **127**-67
aranha **154**-33
arbusto **35**-G, **156**-23,26
arco e flecha **141**-43
área de carregamento dos clientes **74**-7
área de embarque **131**-14
área de recebimento de bagagem **131**-15
área de risco **123**-19
área de trabalho **119**-D
área para piqueniques **137**-3
areia **137**-23
argila **134**-23
aritmética **105**

bigode **43**-37, **152**-34a
bilhar **141**-O
bilhete **108**-15, **124**-22
bilhete de agradecimento **108**-17, **118**-L
bilhete para transferência **124**-5
binóculos **135**-32
biografia **108**-6
biologia **103**-7
biorrisco **123**-20
biquíni **68**-13
bisão **152**-8
biscoitos **53**-2
biscoitos salgados **53**-3
blazer **66**-10,22
blecaute **85**-13
bloco auto-adesivo Post-It **120**-11
bloco de papel **120**-18
blocos **79**-4
blocos de construção **79**-4
bluegrass **148**-10
blues **148**-9
blusa **66**-1
blusão **67**-11
blusão de moletom **69**-7
blush **99**-39
bobsled **144**-G
boca **86**-16
bochecha **86**-14
bode **151**-12
bóia **138**-3
bola de basquete **143**-21
bola de beisebol **143**-1
bola de boliche **140**-12
bola de borracha **79**-5
bola de futebol **143**-26
bola de futebol americano **143**-10
bola de golfe **141**-30
bola de lacrosse **143**-13
bola de pingue-pongue **140**-28
bola de praia **79**-6, **138**-17
bola de raquetebol **140**-23
bola de softball **143**-8
bola de tênis **140**-18
bola de vôlei **143**-24
bolas de bilhar **141**-34
bolha **88**-18
boliche **140**-G
bolinha de sabão **79**-23
bolinhas **71**-28
bolinho tipo muffin **61**-2
bolo **53**-34
bolo de carne **64**-12
bolo de chocolate **64**-24
bolsa **70**-21, **153**-62a
bolsa de valores **163**
bolsa tiracolo **70**-22
bolsinha de maquiagem **70**-26
bolso **72**-18, **132**-B
bom **44**-31
bomba de ar **126**-41
bomba de gasolina **126**-42
bombeiro **84**-5, **113**-28
bombeiro hidráulico **30**-A
boné **67**-8,10
boneca **25**-14, **79**-8
boneco **79**-12

bonequinho **79**-12
bonito **45**-51,53
borboleta **154**-29
bordado **134**-F,18
bordar **134**-F
bordo **156**-18
borracha **5**-22
bosque **109**-1
botão **72**-20, **157**-37
botão para chamar enfermeira **97**-5
botão para chamar o comissário de bordo **132**-13
botas **69**-23
botas de caminhada **69**-25, **139**-15
botas de caubói **69**-26
botas de chuva **67**-18
botas de esqui **144**-2
botas de segurança **123**-5
botas de trabalho **69**-24
bote inflável **145**-9
boto **155**-13
box **23**-24
boxe **141**-T
bracelete **70**-11
braço **86**-28
branco **65**-15
branqueador de dentes **98**-5
branquear meus dentes **98**-D
brilhante **45**-65
brim **71**-18
brincar **11**-6
brincar com **100**-I
brincos **70**-4
brincos de orelha furada **71**-12
brincos de pressão **71**-13
brinquedos **100**-23
britadeira **122**-5
broca **34**-20, **93**-26
broche **70**-9
brócolis **49**-3
bronzeador **138**-23
bueiro **40**-10
búfalo **152**-8
bufê de saladas **62**-13
bulbo **157**-39
buldôzer **122**-17
bule de café **22**-6
bule de chá **22**-5
burrito **60**-10
bússola **139**-12
buzina **127**-60
cabeça **86**-1
cabeceira **23**-2
cabeleireiro **38**-1, **113**-34
cabelo **43**
cabelo **86**-2, **98**-G,K
cabide **73**-23
cabide de casacos **119**-1
cabina de comando **132**-1
cabina de pilotagem **132**-1
cabo **78**-18
cabo de bateria para chupeta **126**-30
cabra **151**-12
cachecol **67**-5
cacho **56**-4
cachoeira **109**-23
cachorrinho **152**-37
cachorro **152**-36

cachorro-quente **60**-3
cachumba **91**-16
cacto **156**-29
cadarços **99**-49
cadeia **40**-12, **165**-I
cadeira **4**-5, **22**-2
cadeira de balanço **100**-21
cadeira de cozinha **24**-33
cadeira de criança **62**-6
cadeira de jardim **27**-17
cadeira de praia **138**-10
cadeira de rodas **94**-14
cadeira para automóvel **25**-22
cadeira para mesa de jantar **22**-2
cadeirão **25**-27, **62**-6
caderno **5**-27
caderno de anotações **120**-8
caderno de esboços **134**-15
caderno espiral **5**-26
café **51**-26, **61**-15
café da manhã **9**-15,18
café descafeinado **51**-27, **61**-16
café solúvel **51**-28
cafeteira **22**-6
cafeteira elétrica **24**-28
caiaque **145**-D,7
cair granizo **14**-12
cais de carga **121**-20
caixa **55**-12, **56**-3,6, **80**-10, **112**-15
caixa automático **80**-12
caixa de alarme de incêndio **40**-8
caixa de areia **137**-22
caixa de correio **27**-2, **29**-31, **40**-9, **82**-30
caixa de ferramentas **34**-17
caixa de material reciclável **32**-24
caixa de sugestões **121**-16
caixa eletrônico **80**-12
caixa postal **119**-9
caixa rápido **55**-15
caixa registradora **55**-7
caixa-forte **80**-8
caixa-forte do banco **80**-8
caixinhas de suco **51**-21
calafrio **88**-21
calça **66**-4
calça de moleton **69**-8
calça jeans **66**-6
calçada **40**-13
calcanhar **87**-49
calção **69**-11, **141**-46
calção de banho **69**-11
calcinha **68**-13,14
calculadora **5**-31, **77**-10,11, **119**-13
calculadora de bolso **77**-10
cálculo **105**
calendário de mesa **120**-10
calha **27**-26
calorento **46**-5
calota **126**-7
calvo **43**-35
cama **9**-10
cama **23**-1
cama de hospital **97**-3
cama elástica **141**-40

câmara **135**-42
câmara de vídeo **76**-11
câmara dos deputados **161**-3
camarão **50**-29
camareira **113**-38, **133**-23
cambalhota **146**-28
câmbio automático **127**-74
câmbio de moeda **80**-G
câmbio manual **127**-76
camelo **153**-52
camelô **41**-40
câmera **77**-14
câmera de 35 milímetros **77**-14
câmera digital **77**-18
caminhada **140**-C
caminhadas no campo **139**-B
caminhão **125**-16
caminhão basculante **122**-13
caminhão com cesta aérea **122**-16
caminhão de bombeiro **84**-4
caminhão de brinquedo **79**-15
caminhão de lixo **40**-19
caminhão de mudança **28**-8, **125**-15
caminhão de sorvete **41**-28
caminhão do correio **82**-29
caminhão reboque **125**-17
caminhão-betoneira **122**-19
caminhar **146**-13
caminho da entrada da casa **27**-3
caminho do ônibus **124**-2
caminhoneiro **115**-34
caminhonete **122**-20, **125**-11
caminhonete de mudança **28**-8
camisa **66**-3
camisa com gola olímpica **71**-4
camisa com gola rulê **71**-4
camisa de manga comprida **71**-1
camisa de manga curta **71**-2
camisa esporte **66**-5
camisa pólo **66**-7
camisa sem manga **71**-3
camiseta **66**-16, **68**-7, **69**-5
camiseta regata **69**-1
camisola curta **68**-3
camisola de hospital **97**-2
camisola longa **68**-2
campainha **27**-8, **29**-30, **31**-14
camper **125**-14
campina **109**-8
campismo **139**-A
campo **20**-15, **102**-J, **151**-24
campo de beisebol **137**-11, **142**-2, **142**-4
campo de futebol **142**-16
campo de futebol americano **142**-6
campo de lacrosse **142**-8
camundongo **152**-28
camundongos **30**-11g
canário **152**-42
câncer **91**-19
caneca **22**-30
canela **86**-37
caneleiras **143**-27
caneta **5**-20

cinturão de ferramentas **122**-9
cinza **65**-16
círculo **106**-21
circunferência **106**-21d
cirurgia **94**-18
cirurgião **97**-15
cisne **154**-11
clarinete **150**-11
claro **44**-26, **72**-14
classe **7**-40
classes gramaticais **107**
classificado de emprego **118**-3
cliente **55**-2, **62**-A,3
clima **14**
clínica **36**-11
clipe **120**-14
clube de comédia **147**-G
clube de computação **104**-14
clube de debates **104**-13
clube de xadrez **104**-16
clube internacional **104**-15
coala **153**-63
cobaia **152**-40
cobertor **23**-7
cobertor elétrico **23**-8
cobra **155**-36
coceira (com) **89**-50
côco **48**-13
código de área **1**-12
código de endereçamento postal **1**-11
código de endereçamento postal **82**-21
coelho **152**-13
cofre **80**-9
cogumelo **49**-26
coiote **152**-9
cola **33**-16, **120**-30, **135**-30
cola branca **120**-30
cola de borracha **120**-31
colar **70**-5
colar de contas **70**-8
colar de pérolas **70**-6
colarinho **72**-17
colcha **23**-10
colchão **23**-23
colchonete de trocador **25**-9
coleção de moedas **135**-28
colecionar moedas **135**-L
colecionar selos **135**-K
colega **7**-37
coletar sangue **92**-D
colete **66**-20
colete acolchoado **67**-28
colete de segurança **123**-4
colete salva-vidas **132**-19, **145**-2, **145**-10
coletor de lixo **115**-21
colher **22**-28
colher de chá **57**, **63**-35, **95**-18
colher de pau **59**-35
colher de pedreiro **35**-7, **122**-10
colher de sopa **57**, **63**-36, **95**-19
colher medidora **59**-33
cólica **88**-22
colina **109**-2
colírio **95**-10
collant **67**-7, **68**-21

college **101**-8
colméia **154**-36a
colocar **58**-13
colocar a mala na esteira transportadora **132**-C
colocar a maquiagem **9**-7, **99**-O
colocar curativo no ferimento **93**-C
colocar na lavadora **73**-B
colocar na secadora **73**-D
colocar o cartão do banco **81**-22
colocar o computador na bandeja **132**-D
colônia **99**-37
colonizadores **163**
colocar as palavras em ordem **7**-59
coluna vertebral **87**-72
calor (com) **46**-5
fome (com) **46**-7
frio (com) **46**-6
medo (com) **47**-27
saudade da família (com) **47**-24
saudade de casa (com) **47**-24
sede (com) **46**-8
vergonha (com) **47**-30
comadre **97**-9
combinação **68**-18
comédia **148**-14, **149**-18,30
comédia musical **148**-16
comediante **147**-17
comércio **103**-16
cometa **111**-10
comissário de bordo **132**-5
cômoda **23**-13,22, **25**-3
compactador de lixo **24**-29
comparecer à entrevista de naturalização **166**-11
comparecer a uma entrevista **118**-G
comparecer em juízo **165**-D
compartimento de bagagem **132**-6
compensado **122**-24
comprar **75**-A
comprar cheques de viagem **80**-D
compressa para curativo estéril **90**-5
comprido **43**-24, **44**-7, **72**-1
comprimento **106**-4,18a
comprimido **95**-15
comprimidos contra gripe **95**-2
comprimidos de antiácido **95**-8
comprovante **81**-29
comprovante de residência **160**-9
computador **4**-7, **11**-14, **78**-1, **110**-2, **132**-D
computador de mesa **78**-1
computador notebook **78**-11
concerto **136**-3, **147**-B
concha **59**-11, **138**-19
concha para sorvete **59**-1
conclusões **110**-F
concreto **122**-19a

condenado **165**-G
condicionador **98**-10
condimentos **53**, **53**-22
condomínio **20**-5
condutor **124**-18
cone **106**-26
conectar-se **135**-Q
conectar-se na rede **135**-Q
conferir o saldo **81**-16
conferir as respostas **6**-23
conferir as suas respostas **7**-49
confluência **130**-12
confortável **45**-69
confuso **47**-32
congelador **24**-2
congelando **14**-26
congestão nasal (com) **89**-31
conjunto **147**-8
conjunto de balanço **79**-36
conjunto de ciência **79**-19
conjunto de construção **79**-3
conjunto de lápis de cor **134**-16
conjunto de trem **79**-17
conjunto jogging **69**-4
conselheiro **96**-11
consertar **72**-25, **117**-22
conservação **158**
conservar energia **158**-10
console de lareira **21**-4
constelação **111**-3
Constituição **162**-A
constituição **163**
construir **116**-5
construir modelos **135**-M
consultar um especialista **94**-7
consultar o dicionário **7**-31
conta **63**-F,21, **80**-E
conta da TV a cabo **81**-13
conta de água **81**-12
conta de aquecimento **81**-11
conta de gás **81**-10
conta de luz **81**-8
conta de telefone **81**-9
conta do cartão de crédito **81**-15
conta do óleo de aquecimento **81**-11
contador **112**-1
conta-gotas **110**-15
contas domésticas **81**
conto **108**-3
contrabaixo **150**-4
contratar um advogado **165**-C
contrato de aluguel **28**-6
contravento **27**-12
controladora de parquímetros **40**-17
controlar estoque **117**-30
controle da cama **97**-4
controle remoto **76**-6
conversão de 3 pontos **130**-25
conversível **125**-3
convite **108**-16
copa **63**-17
copas **135**-34c
copiadora **83**-6, **119**-14
copiar a palavra **7**-35
co-piloto **132**-3
copo **22**-31, **26**-10
copo de água **63**-27

copo de vinho **63**-28
copos de papel **54**-2, **60**-19
coquetel de camarão **64**-3
coração **87**-56, **92**-G
coral **104**-3
corcova **153**-52a
corda **139**-17, **145**-24
corda de pular **79**-22
cordeiro **151**-13
cordilheira **109**-3
coriza **88**-15
córnea **86**-11
corniso **156**-11
coro **104**-3
corpete **68**-16
correções **107**-19
corredor **29**
corredor **55**-1, **102**-F, **132**-7, **133**-20
córrego **109**-9
correia da ventoinha **126**-37
correio **39**-19
corrente **29**-35, **70**-7
corrente de segurança **29**-35
correr **146**-14
correspondência **119**-c
correto **7**-51,52
corretivo líquido **120**-32
corrida **140**-B
corrigir os seus erros **6**-24
corrosivo **123**-16
cortador de biscoitos **59**-29
cortador de grama **27**-18, **35**-1
cortador de unha **99**-28
cortar **58**-1, **89**-45, **116**-17
cortar a grama **35**-A
córtex **156**-7
cortina de chuveiro **26**-30
cortinas **21**-12, **23**-15
coruja **154**-8
corvo **154**-4
costa **109**-16
costas **86**-27
costela **50**-5
costelas **87**-70
costeleta de vitela **64**-17
costeletas de cordeiro **50**-7
costeletas de porco **50**-11
costura **72**-25
costurar **117**-25, **134**-A
cotonete **100**-15
cotoveleiras **140**-11
cotovelo **86**-29
couro **71**-15
couve-de-bruxelas **49**-21
couve-flor **49**-4
coxa **86**-34
coxas **50**-17
coxas de frango **50**-17
cozinha **30**-11, **62**-15
cozinhar **58**-14, **116**-7
cozinhar em fogo baixo **58**-21
cozinhar no vapor **58**-18
cozinheiro **112**-16
CPU **78**-2
crachá de identificação de funcionários **160**-4
crânio **87**-69
cravo **157**-44
cravo-de-defunto **157**-43
cream cheese **51**-10

creche **36**-9, **84**-G, **100**-19
creme **95**-12
creme anti-histamínico **90**-11
creme azedo **51**-9
creme de barbear **99**-20
creme rinse **98**-10
cremeira **22**-8
crespo **43**-29, **44**-20
criado-mudo **23**-19
criança **42**-1
criança pequena **42**-3
criança perdida **85**-8
crisântemo **157**-40
croco **157**-53
crocodilo **155**-29
croissant **61**-7
cruzamento **41**-24, **128**-26
cubículo de trabalho **119**-10
cubo **106**-23
cueca **68**-8
cueca samba-canção **68**-9
cuidador domiciliar **113**-36
cuidar de **117**-29
culpado **165**-21
cultivar **116**-14
cunhada **3**-11
cunhado **3**-10
cupins **30**-11a
cupons **55**-11
curativo **90**-3
curativo adesivo **90**-3
curativo estéril **90**-5
currículo **118**-D
curso de direção **103**-18
curto **43**-26, **44**-8, **72**-2
curvar **146**-12
dados **135**-38a
damas **135**-36
dar banho **100**-C
dar o saque **146**-7
data de nascimento **1**-18
datilografar **117**-33
dar a preferência **130**-13
de segunda a sexta-feira **118**-8
decifrar a palavra **7**-58
declamar o Juramento de Fidelidade **166**-13
dedal **134**-6
dedetizador **30**-F
dedo **87**-41
dedo do pé **87**-50
deficiente auditivo **42**-23
deficiente físico **42**-21
deficiente visual **42**-22
definição **7**-34
definir o problema **110**-A
degraus **31**-18
degraus da frente **27**-4
deixar uma gorjeta **63**-G
delegacia de polícia **40**-11, **84**-A, **165**-B
delicatessen **37**-17
delineador **99**-43
dente **9**-3, **86**-18, **93**-H, **98**-A,D
dentista **93**-24
dentro **8**-10, **129**-9
departamento de expedição **121**-17

departamento de folha de pagamento **121**-21
departamento de radiologia **97**-G
departamento pessoal **121**-22
depósito **29**-43, **80**-A, **81**-25, **121**-11
depósito-caução **28**-7
depressão **91**-20
deputadas **161**-2
deputados **161**-2
deque **27**-23
derramamento de produto químico **85**-17
derramar **58**-9
desapontado **46**-14
descansar **11**-16
descarrilhamento de trem **85**-18
descascador **59**-4
descascador de legumes **59**-4
descascando **30**-6
descascar **58**-5
desconfortável **45**-70
desconsolado **46**-12
descontar um cheque **80**-C
desconto **75**-5
descrever **43**
desembaçador **127**-68
desembaçador traseiro **126**-16
desenhar **116**-10, **134**-E
desenho animado **149**-22,35
desenho de cachemira **71**-31
desentupidor **26**-22, **33**-3
deserto **109**-14
desfibrilador **123**-24
desligar as luzes **7**-42
deslizamento de lama **159**-12
deslizamento de terra **159**-11
deslocar **89**-47
desmaio **89**-27
desodorante **99**-33
desonesto **45**-72
despertador **23**-17
desvio **130**-14
detector de fumaça **29**-37
detector de metais **131**-7, **132**-E
deter **165**-A
detergente líquido **24**-10
detergente para máquina de lavar louça **24**-9
devagar **44**-12
devolver **75**-B
dezembro **18**-24
dia **18**-4
Dia da Independência **164**-5
Dia das Bruxas **164**-6
Dia de Ação de Graças **164**-8
Dia de Martin Luther King, Jr. **164**-2
Dia de São Valentim **164**-3
Dia do Soldado **164**-4
Dia dos Veteranos **164**-7
diabetes **91**-21
diagonal **106**-18c
diâmetro **106**-21c
diante de **8**-3
diarréia **88**-23
dicionário **7**-31, **83**-26
dieta **94**-4

difícil **44**-42
dizer o seu nome **6**-1
digitador de dados **112**-22
digitar **117**-33
digitar a senha **81**-23
digitar uma carta **119**-f
dinheiro **17**, **81**-1,26,27
direitos **165**-4
direitos **166**
direitos civis **163**
direitos de Miranda **165**-4
diretor **102**-2
diretor de atividades **84**-12
diretoria **102**-B
diretório **74**-1
diretório acadêmico estudantil **104**-7
diretório da loja **74**-1
dirigir **116**-11
dirigir embriagado **85**-21
disco **76**-20, **141**-31
disco de hóquei **143**-16
disco de memória **77**-19
disco de tobogã **144**-12
disco voador **111**-31
discos **141**-42
discutir sobre a questão **6**-27
dispnéia **88**-25
disponível **118**-6
disquete **78**-7
distância **106**-10
distensão abdominal (com) **89**-30
distribuir os testes **7**-47
distribuir a correspondência **119**-c
dividir um livro **6**-26
dividir-se em grupos pequenos **7**-38
divisão **105**
divisória **128**-7
dobradinha **50**-8
dobrar as roupas **73**-G
documentário **149**-23
documentário sobre natureza **149**-39
doença cardíaca **91**-22
doente **46**-4
dois pontos **107**-14
domingo **18**-6
dono de loja **115**-27
dono-de-casa **113**-37
donut **61**-1
dor de barriga **88**-4
dor de cabeça **88**-1
dor de dente **88**-3
dor de garganta **88**-6
dor de ouvido **88**-2
dor nas costas **88**-5
dor no peito **88**-24
dor torácica **88**-24
dormir **9**-14
dourado **65**-18
drama **148**-13, **149**-17,29
driblar **146**-9
drive-thru **41**-41
drogaria **37**-21
drupas **156**-25
duas vezes por semana **19**-24
duna **109**-13
duna de areia **109**-13

duro **44**-40
duto da lixeira **29**-42
duto de lixo **29**-42
dúzia **56**-8
DVD **21**-7, **76**-7, **83**-20
eclipse lunar **111**-8
eclipse solar **111**-7
economia doméstica **103**-14
economizar água **158**-11
economizar energia **158**-10
edifício da Suprema Corte **161**-16
edifício de escritórios **41**-35
Edifício do Capitólio **161**-6
edifício do terminal **132**-21
editorial **108**-12
edredon **23**-11
educação física **103**-17
elástico **120**-13
elefante **153**-53
eletricidade **31**-15
eletricista **31**-H
elevador **29**-32, **74**-5, **133**-18
elevador de carga **121**-14
elipse **106**-22
em **8**-6
em choque **91**-2
em conta **45**-62
em direção a **129**-13
em ordem **7**-59
e-mail **108**-19
embalador **121**-12
embalagem **56**-12
embalar **100**-G
embaraçado **47**-30
embarcar no avião **132**-H
embreagem **127**-78
emenda **162**-C,D,3
empacotador **55**-14, **121**-12
empilhadeira **121**-13
empolgado **46**-13
empregado de fazenda **151**-6,30
empresa de TV a cabo **30**-D
empréstimo **80**-F
encanador **30**-A
encarregado do balcão de informações **133**-12
encerar o chão **32**-F
enciclopédia **83**-27
encomenda postal **82**-8
encompridar **72**-22
encontrar seu assento **132**-J
encorpado **44**-13
encurtar **72**-21
endereço **1**-5
endereço de e-mail **1**-15
endereço de internet **135**-41
endereço do destinatário **82**-20
endereço do remetente **82**-19
energia **158**
energia geotérmica **158**-8
energia hidrelétrica **158**-6
energia hidroelétrica **158**-6
energia nuclear **158**-4
energia solar **158**-5
enfermo **46**-4
enfermaria **102**-C
enfermeira **93**-8, **102**-3
enfermeira cirúrgica **97**-16

rinoceronte **153**-46
rinque de hóquei **142**-10
rins **87**-65
rio **109**-22
risco de choque elétrico
123-21
riscar a palavra **7**-57
robe **68**-4
rock **148**-4
rodo absorvente **32**-10
rodo de esponja **32**-10
rodovia **128**-5
rodoviária **36**-5, **124**-7
rolo **56**-14
rolo de pintura **33**-25
rolo de selos **82**-12
romance **108**-2
rosa **65**-2, **157**-51
rosbife **52**-1, **64**-13
rosto **9**-6, **86**-4
rota do ônibus **124**-2
roubo **85**-4
roubo de automóvel **85**-9
roupa de neoprene **145**-17
roupa isotérmica **145**-17
roupão **68**-4
roupas **71**, **73**-G,H
roupas amassadas **73**-18
roupas claras **73**-2
roupas de boneca **79**-9
roupas escuras **73**-3
roupas limpas **73**-21
roupas molhadas **73**-10
roupas para lavar **73**-A
roupas passadas **73**-19
roxo **65**-13
rua **1**-7, **40**-14, **128**-22
rua de mão única **128**-23
rua sem saída **130**-8
ruge **99**-39
ruim **44**-32
ruivo **43**-33
sábado **18**-12
sabão em pó **73**-7
sabonete **26**-3, **54**-10, **98**-6
sabonete líquido **54**-11
saboneteira **26**-4
saco **56**-1
saco de dormir **139**-2
saco de lixo de jardim **35**-16
saco de papel **55**-13
saco do aspirador **32**-7
sacola **70**-23
sacola de roupas **73**-5
sacola plástica **55**-19
sacos para lixo **54**-9
sacos plásticos para sanduíche
54-8
sagüão **29**, **133**-7
saia **66**-2
saia para cama **23**-9
saída **128**-20
saída de emergência **29**-38,
123-25, **132**-15
saída de incêndio **28**-19
saída de praia **69**-9
sair do trabalho **10**-14
sal **53**-20
sala cirúrgica **97**-C
sala de aula **102**-E
sala de brinquedos **84**-19

sala de cinema **147**-13
sala de concertos **147**-4
sala de correspondência
119-C
sala de espera **93**-1, **97**-D
sala de estar **31**-15
sala de estoque **119**-F
sala de exame **92**-5, **93**-5
sala de ginástica **133**-17
sala de jogos **84**-13
sala de orientação pedagógica
102-D
sala de parto **97**-E
sala de reuniões **84**-10, **119**-B,
133-14
sala do juizado **165**-11
sala dos funcionários **119**-H
salada **60**-13
salada César **64**-11
salada de batata **52**-13
salada de espinafre **64**-9
salada de frutas **64**-1
salada de frutos do mar **52**-17
salada de macarrão **52**-15,16
salada de repolho **52**-14
salada grega **64**-8
salada mista **64**-7
saladas **64**
saladeira **22**-13
salamandra **155**-34
salamandra-aquática **155**-33
salame **52**-3
salão de beleza **38**-1
salão de manicure **38**-14
salão do restaurante **62**-14
salário **118**-J
balcão de atendimento a
clientes **74**-14
balcão de serviço a clientes
74-14
saleiro **22**-21
salgadinhos **52**
salgadinhos de tortilla **52**-24
salgueiro **156**-22
salmão **50**-22
salsão **49**-1
salsichão **52**-2
salsinha **49**-6
saltar **146**-17
saltear **58**-24
salto alto **69**-14
salva-vidas **138**-1
samambaia **156**-27
sandálias **69**-21
sandálias de dedo **69**-22
sandálias estilo havaianas
69-22
sanduíche de atum **61**-22
sanduíche de bacon, alface e
tomate **61**-27
sanduíche de carne em
conserva **61**-26
sanduíche de frango **60**-5
sanduíche de ovos com
maionese **61**-23
sanduíche de peixe **60**-4
sanduíche de presunto e
queijo **61**-25
sanduíche de rosbife **61**-28
sanduíche de salada de frango
61-24

sangramento **90**-19e
sangramento nasal **88**-16
sangrando **90**-19e
sangrar **89**-38
sangue **92**-D
sapataria **39**-22
sapatos **69**-13, **99**-P, **132**-A
sapatos de boliche **140**-13
sapatos de salto alto **69**-14
sapatos de salto baixo **69**-15
sapo **155**-35
saponáceo em pó **32**-19
saquinho para enjôo **132**-18
sarampo **91**-15
satélite **111**-28
satisfeito **46**-9
Saturno **111**-17
saúde **103**-10
saxofone **150**-14
scanner **55**-18, **78**-17
seca **159**-8
secador **98**-11
secador de cabelo **26**-14,
98-11
secadora **73**-D,11
secadora de roupas **73**-D,11
seção de aparelhos
domésticos **74**-12
seção de aparelhos eletrônicos
74-13
seção de fitas, cds e dvds
83-14
seção de línguas estrangeiras
83-21
seção de livros de referência
83-23
seção de mobiliário **74**-11
seção de móveis **74**-11
seção de periódicos **83**-10
seção de roupas femininas
74-8
seção de roupas infantis **74**-9
seção de roupas masculinas
74-6
seção de utensílios domésticos
74-10
seção infantil **83**-8
secar meu cabelo **98**-H
seco **45**-56
secretaria **102**-A,1, **119**-19
secretária da escola **102**-1
secretária eletrônica **77**-6
secretário **115**-22
seda **71**-22
sedã **125**-1
sedento **46**-8
Segunda Guerra Mundial **163**
segunda-feira **18**-7
segundo andar **28**-15
segurança **131**-B
segurar no colo **100**-D
seio **86**-26
sela **140**-14
selo **82**-10,23
selva **109**-15
sem **31**-15
sem fio **45**-68
sem pulso **90**-15a
sem respiração **90**-16b
sem saída **130**-8
semáforo **41**-23, **128**-27

semana **18**-3
semana passada **19**-20
semana que vem **19**-22
sementes de legumes **35**-5
senado **161**-5
senadores **161**-4
senha **81**-23
sentar-se **6**-10
sentença **165**-22
sentenciado **165**-H
sentar-se **6**-10
sentido único **130**-7
separador central **128**-7
separar as roupas para lavar
73-A
seqüestro **85**-7
sequóia **156**-21
ser contratado **118**-M
ser julgado **165**-E
serelepe **152**-31
série de comédia **149**-30
seringa **92**-4
serra circular **34**-21
serra elétrica **34**-21
serra para metais **34**-5
serrote **34**-4
serviço comunitário **104**-8
serviço de aquecimento e ar
condicionado **31**-L
serviço de entrega até a
manhã seguinte **82**-7
serviço de entrega expressa
82-7
serviço de entrega prioritária
82-6
serviço de quarto **133**-25
servir **117**-24
servir a refeição **62**-D
servir água **62**-B
servir num júri **166**-4
servir os pratos **62**-D
setembro **18**-21
sexo **1**-17
sexta-feira **18**-11
shampoo **98**-9
shampoo de bebê **100**-14
shopping **39**-23
shopping center **39**-23
short **66**-17
short de corrida **69**-2, **140**-3
silenciador **126**-23
simples **45**-64, **72**-10
sinagoga **84**-J
sinais de mão **130**-26
sinais de pontuação **107**
sinais de trânsito **130**
sinal de trânsito **41**-23
sinal rodoviário **128**-4
sintonizador **76**-24
sinuca **141**-O
sistema de aquecimento **31**-20
sistema de injeção de
combustível **126**-34
sistema de irrigação **151**-22
sistema de navegação **127**-63
Sistema de Serviço Seletivo
166-7
sistema de som **76**-19
sistema de videogame **76**-33
sistema estéreo **21**-17, **76**-19
sistema solar **111**

GLOSSÁRIO (INGLÊS)

The bold number indicates the page(s) on which the word appears. The number that follows indicates the word's location in the illustration and in the word list on the page. For example, "address 1-5" indicates that the word *address* is on page 1 and is item number 5.